ENTERPRISE *and* ADVENTURE

The Genoese in Seville and the
Opening of the New World

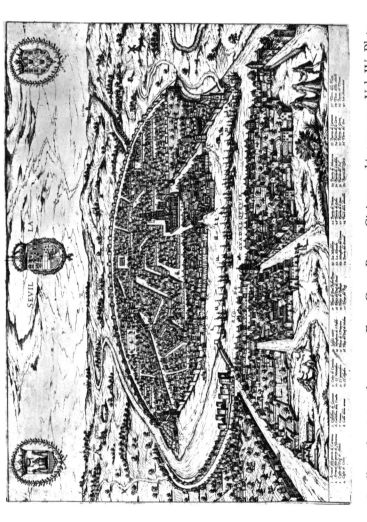

Seville in the sixteenth century. From Georg Braun, *Civitates orbis terrarum*, Vol. IV, Plate II (courtesy of The New York Public Library, Rare Books Division).

ENTERPRISE *and* ADVENTURE

The Genoese in Seville and the

Opening of the New World

By RUTH PIKE

Hunter College of the
City University of New York

Cornell University Press

ITHACA, NEW YORK

Copyright © 1966 by Cornell University

CORNELL UNIVERSITY PRESS

First published 1966

Library of Congress Catalog Card Number: 66–23777

PRINTED AND BOUND IN THE UNITED STATES OF AMERICA
BY KINGSPORT PRESS, INC.

Preface

THE sixteenth century, like our own age, directed its attention to the exploration of the unknown. Today we are exploring space in the hope of reaching other planets; men of the sixteenth century crossed what the early chroniclers called the Ocean Sea and discovered new continents. The countries of the Iberian Peninsula, favorably located for oceanic exploration, initiated the outward expansion. The Portuguese moved south along the African coast until they rounded the Cape of Good Hope and reached India. The Spaniards went westward and found a New World. Columbus, a Genoese sailing under the Spanish flag, led the way, and a host of Spanish explorers and conquerors followed him. It was not a coincidence that the discoverer of America was a Genoese or that his compatriots, particularly those resident in the city of Seville—after 1503 the emporium of the Indies—were among the most active participants in the opening of the New World. Ever since the twelfth century, when the Genoese galleys moved out into the Mediterranean to trade along the coasts of North Africa and southern Europe, the Genoese had been responding to the call of new lands farther west.

The following chapters represent an attempt to describe the commercial and financial role of the compatriots of Columbus—the Genoese merchant colony of Seville—in the Spanish overseas expansion of the sixteenth century. In such a study, based upon a reconstruction from scattered and fragmentary records, completeness is an elusive goal. But an effort has been made to give some account of all the most important entrepreneurial activities of the Sevillian Genoese, ranging from their investments in exploratory voyages to their monetary operations with the Spanish monarchs. Since the prime reason for their existence in Seville, and the basis for their wealth and prominence, was the transatlantic trade, particular emphasis has been placed on their participation in it—the methods they used, their shipments, and their degree of investment. But although the Genoese were first of all merchants and therefore primarily concerned with day-to-day business activities, they also occupied a strategic position in Sevillian society. I have tried, wherever possible, to relate their business lives with their political and social concerns, and to see them as a part of the changing scene in the Seville of the sixteenth century.

The principal source material for this study has been the Sevillian Protocols, since the private papers of the Genoese merchants of Seville are no longer in existence. This is the first time that these documents have been used to describe the lives of the Genoese residents of Seville. In addition to the Sevillian Protocols, I found a number of valuable sources at the Archivo de Indias and the Municipal Archives of Seville. The Archivo Histórico Nacional in Madrid provided me with some important material on the Sevillian Inquisition, and the Biblioteca Nacional (Madrid) with an interesting manuscript dealing with economic conditions and the position of foreign merchants in Seville at the end of the sixteenth century.

My sincere appreciation goes to Professor Charles Verlinden, Director of the Belgian Academy in Rome, who first introduced me to the role of the Genoese in Spain and suggested it as a possible field of research, and to the late Professor Garrett Mattingly, whose work has always been a source of inspiration to me from the time that I was a member of his doctoral seminar at Columbia University. I should also like to thank Professor Shepard Clough and Professor Robert Lopez for their kind interest in my work. I am grateful to all those who gave so freely of their time to assist me in Spain, especially Señor José de la Peña, Director of the Archivo de Indias, and Señor Francisco Collantes de Terán, Director of the Municipal Archives of Seville.

I wish to thank the American Council of Learned Societies for a grant-in-aid, 1963–1964, and Hunter College for granting me released time from teaching during the spring semester of 1965 to complete this study. Sections of Chapters I and III have appeared in the *Journal of Economic History* and in *Hispania*. Most of Chapter II has been published in the *Hispanic American Historical Review*. One final remark: throughout this work the names of the Sevillian Genoese have been given in their hispanized form as they appear in the documents; the Italian spelling in parentheses follows the first mention of each name.

R. P.

New York
March 1966

Contents

Tables

Abbreviations

Unpublished Sources

AGI: Archivo General de Indias (General Archives of the Indies), Seville.

AMS: Archivo Municipal (Municipal Archives), Seville.

APS: Archivo de Protocolos (Notarial Archives), Seville.

Published Sources

CDI, 1st ser.: *Colección de documentos inéditos, relativos al descubrimiento, conquista y organización de las antiguas posesiones españolas de América y Oceanía.* Madrid, 1864–1884. 42 vols.

CDI, 2d ser.: *Colección de documentos inéditos relativos al descubrimiento, conquista y organización de las antiguas posesiones españolas de ultramar.* Madrid, 1885–1932. 25 vols.

CPI, *Catálogo de pasajeros a Indias durante los siglos XVI, XVII y XVIII.* Seville, 1940–1946. 3 vols.

ENTERPRISE *and* ADVENTURE

The Genoese in Seville and the Opening of the New World

CHAPTER I

The Genoese Colony
in Seville

THE turning point in the history of the Genoese merchants in Spain was the discovery of America and the subsequent opening of trading relations with the new continent.[1] From then on, their ascent to economic predominance in Spain paralleled that nation's emergence as the dominant power of the sixteenth-century world. Fortune gave Spain two empires simultaneously, one in the Old World, the other in the New. Spain's unpreparedness for imperial responsibilities, particularly in the economic sphere, was the springboard for Genoese advancement. Strengthening and enlarging their colony in Seville—after 1503 the "door and port of the Indies" [2]—the Genoese prepared to move across the Atlantic in the wake of Columbus.

At the opening of the sixteenth century the Genoese residents of Seville formed a colony that had become the largest of its kind in Spain. The Ligurian population of Seville had been small during the fourteenth and early fifteenth centuries, but in the second half of the fifteenth it experienced steady growth.[3] Civil strife within the Ligurian Republic, the gradual loss of her eastern colonies to the Turks, and the opening of Africa by the Portuguese attracted numerous representatives of the great commercial families of Genoa to Seville. Between 1450 and 1500 the Genoese population of that city almost doubled; [4] in the course of the sixteenth century it was augmented by compatriots who felt uneasy in their native city after the

1

triumph of the Doria and the failure of the Fieschi conspiracy.[5]

If political reasons motivated the Genoese to leave their native city, economic considerations drew them to Seville. After 1503, through control of the American trade, it became the most important commercial and financial center in Spain. It is not surprising, then, that the greatest increase in the resident Genoese population during the sixteenth century occurred between 1503 and 1530. The opportunities for profit that Seville offered provided an important stimulus for the Genoese migration.[6]

Not only did the "emporium of the Indies" draw Genoese from their native city, but those who had resided in neighboring Andalusian cities moved to Seville. Many who had established themselves in Cordova at the end of the fifteenth century because of the presence of the Spanish court during the Granada campaign now returned to Seville; others, who retained permanent residence in Cadiz, Jerez, Granada, or Malaga, spent several months a year in Seville.[7]

Of the twenty-eight noble Genoese houses established by the law of 1528, twenty-one were represented in Seville during the sixteenth century.[8] Among the eight whose names do not appear in the Sevillian Protocols of the period, three—the Cicala, De Franchi, and Usodimare—had been in Seville during the Middle Ages, but had either returned to Genoa or disappeared through assimilation.[9] The largest family among the Genoese merchants of Seville was that of the Spínola (Spinola).[10] The names of twenty-one members appear in the notary books in the course of the century. The Pinelo (Pinelli) and Cataño (Cattaneo) establishments followed with thirteen and eleven respectively. Both the Grimaldo (Grimaldi) and Centurión (Centurione) counted nine representatives. Among the smaller houses were the Forne (Fornari), Justinián (Giustiniani), Gentil (Gentile), Salvago, Castellón (Castello), and Vivaldo (Vivaldi). Not all of the Genoese merchants of Seville belonged to the ancient nobility; the Adorno, Riberol (Rivarolo), and Sopranis represented the large "popular group" or *popolari*.[11]

2

The Sevillian Genoese colony was divided into denizens (*vecinos*), residents (*residentes*), and transients (*estantes*)—the last two categories being the most numerous. The relatively small number of denizens is not surprising, for the Genoese still wanted to preserve the mobility that had characterized their medieval commercial activities.[12] With naturalization came stability and assimilation, which in sixteenth-century Spanish society could only lead to the abandonment of trade by their descendants. That the Genoese were correct in such assumptions is demonstrated by the experience of those who became denizens and intermarried with the Sevillian nobility. With few exceptions, their children turned away from trade and entered the service of Church or state. By the third generation the commercial background of the family was forgotten, and the family can be considered as completely hispanized.

The Pinelo family is one of the best examples of what might be called "rapid hispanization," accomplished in only two generations. Francisco Pinelo, paterfamilias of this branch of the family, was a denizen of Seville and one of the wealthiest Genoese merchants in the city during the last decades of the fifteenth century.[13] His economic position soon brought him to the attention of Ferdinand and Isabella, who needed funds to sponsor the first Columbian voyage. In collaboration with Luis de Santángel, Treasurer of Aragon, Pinelo loaned 1,400,000 maravedís to the government to cover the cost of outfitting the ships.[14] He also provided funds for the second voyage. Pinelo's experience as a backer of these two voyages resulted in his appointment in 1503 as factor of the newly created Casa de Contratación (House of Trade), overseer of trade with the New World, a post he held until his death in 1509.[15]

Pinelo's wealth and prominence in Sevillian society had early enabled him to make an advantageous marriage: María de la Torre belonged to one of the noble families. Neither this marriage, his consequent close association with the Sevillian aristocracy, nor even his government post led Pinelo to abandon his commercial activities. He remained a merchant until his

3

death.[16] His two sons, Pedro and Jerónimo, however, were not educated for trade, and both entered the Church. Jerónimo held a canonry in the Seville cathedral and was a well-known professor of theology. According to the Sevillian humanist Argote de Molina, Padre Jerónimo Pinelo was one of the city's outstanding intellectuals of Genoese descent during the century.[17] Pedro Pinelo was also a canon of the cathedral, but never equaled the renown of his brother.[18]

In contrast to the Pinelo, the Negrón family underwent much slower assimilation and more gradual hispanization. Born in Seville in 1507, Carlos de Negrón was the son of a naturalized Genoese merchant who had settled in the city early in the sixteenth century. He received the usual commercial training, but was then sent on to the University where he obtained a law degree. Although for many years he practiced his chosen profession as a legal advisor to the Sevillian Inquisition, Licentiate Negrón carried on the family tradition by engaging in business as well. He was particularly active in the slave trade; at mid-century he owned two galleons which ran slaves between Africa and Vera Cruz in Mexico.[19] By 1572 his legal knowledge and skill brought him to the attention of Phillip II, who named him prosecuting attorney for both the Council of the Indies and the Council of the Treasury. Seven years later he was named prosecuting attorney of the Council of Castile, the highest governmental body in the kingdom.[20]

Like Francisco Pinelo, Carlos de Negrón married into the Sevillian nobility. Through his wife, Ana de la Cueva, he allied himself with the powerful regional aristocracy that controlled the government of Seville. This alliance not only strengthened his social position, but tended to erase the stigma of his commercial background.[21] Of his seven children, none entered trade. Julio, the eldest son, inherited the entailed estate and lived the life of a great lord; through his marriage to Leonora Zapata Osorio he joined the Negrón to one of the noblest families in all Andalusia. Doña Leonora was the first cousin of Francisco Zapata de Cisneros, the Count of Barajas, chief justice of

Seville, and later president of the Council of Castile. The second son, Camilo, received properties of sufficient number and wealth to support him in noble style. The three remaining sons entered the Church, and all reached positions of importance within the ecclesiastical hierarchy.[22] Ambrosio and Jerónimo were members of the Dominican Order; Ambrosio was rector of the Colegio de Santo Tomás in Seville.[23] Luciano, inquisitor and later vicar-general, was by far the best known of the three: A graduate of the University of Salamanca, he achieved fame in Seville as preacher, humanist, and poet.[24] Against the background of an impressive collection of rare manuscripts, books, and *objets d'art,* which his fellow humanist Argote de Molina called the "museum of Dr. Negrón," [25] this descendant of Genoese merchants played host to the important figures of Sevillian literary society. The poet Francisco Medrano wrote a sonnet in his honor; the artist Francisco Pacheco painted his portrait and included a spirited eulogy of him in his famous *Libro de retratos de ilustres y memorables varones.*[26]

Although very few of the Sevillian Genoese achieved the political and intellectual prominence of Carlos de Negrón or his son Luciano, those who became denizens and intermarried with the inhabitants were quickly integrated into Sevillian society. It is not surprising to find their descendants holding high positions in the government and the Church. In striking contrast to the hispanized Genoese, those who remained transients lived on the margin of Sevillian life, concentrating their energies on commercial and financial transactions. In general, they preferred to marry among themselves in order to preserve the commercial tradition. As foreigners and transients, they left little evidence of their sojourn in Seville. Today only the Protocols preserved in the Sevillian archives testify to their presence there in the sixteenth century.

The assimilation of the Genoese and their entrance into the ranks of the native nobility was undoubtedly facilitated by the rapidly changing character of Sevillian life during this period. In the sixteenth century Sevillian society underwent profound changes: new sets of values were being created and old ones discarded, the result of the city's new economic position. Medieval concepts that stressed virtue and valor as the essence of nobility fell into decline; an acquisitive society and the spirit of profit making embraced the whole city.[27] The position and ideas of the local nobility in particular changed. The respectable activities of the Sevillian nobility (as of their counterparts in the rest of Spain) had for centuries been warfare, politics, religion, and traditional farming. Trade, which carried with it a social stigma, was left to outsiders and foreigners. In the sixteenth century the opening of the New World and the subsequent conversion of their city into a thriving commercial emporium forced the Sevillian nobility to revise both their concepts and pattern of life.[28] Fray Tomás de Mercado, keen analyst of Sevillian life, carefully noted this phenomenon. According to him, "the discovery of the Western Indies seventy years ago, presented a magnificent opportunity to acquire great wealth which lured the nobility to be merchants since they saw in it [trade] great profits." [29] *Don Dinero,* in the words of Quevedo, subdued the nobility as he had triumphed over the rest of the population of Seville.[30]

The conversion of the nobility to commerce automatically opened what had heretofore been a closed society. Marriages between the scions of the oldest noble families of Seville and the daughters of wealthy merchants became a normal procedure in the city.[31] In fact, even the nobility who did not engage in commerce were forced by necessity, or at times cupidity, "to marry the daughters of merchants," and the "power of gold made *hidalgos* and nobles out of merchants and commoners." The desire for nobility was particularly strong. Once a merchant had accumulated sufficient capital he "developed a taste for nobility and *hidalguía* and tried to raise himself by creating an entailed estate for his son." [32] A large part of the wealth obtained by Seville merchants from the American trade went into the purchase of landed estates in Aljarafe and Sierra Morena, out of which they created rich *mayorazgos* for their heirs.[33] The

ennobled merchants, or new nobility, then took their places
beside the old nobility, and through continuous intermarriage
the century, a compact social class—the city's new ruling elite.
and bonds of interest, both groups merged to form, by the end of
The coming together of the ennobled merchants and the old
nobility stimulated still further the development of capitalistic
attitudes on the part of the Sevillian aristocracy.[34] It has been
generally believed that members of the nobility went into trade
to maintain their standard of living in face of the price
revolution of the sixteenth century and to engage in the
conspicuous consumption characteristic of the period, and thus,
since trade was then only a means to an end, the basic attitudes
of the nobles remained the same. In Seville nothing could be
more incorrect. The desire for profits as an end in itself, and the
shrewd pragmatic calculation of gains and losses became just as
much a part of the nobles' mentality as that of the merchant-
commoner class.

The commercialization of the nobility and the ennoblement
of wealthy merchants were two parallel currents that operated in
Seville during the sixteenth century. Both of these trends aided
the Genoese to stabilize their position within Sevillian society,
that is, to be accepted socially by the ruling class. While it is true
that the Genoese owed their importance in Sevillian life to their
economic power—to their capital and capitalistic technique—
these factors alone could not bring about their acceptance by the
native nobility. For centuries they had played a vital economic
role in the city, but had remained on the fringes of society.
Clearly their assimilation into the Sevillian nobility in the
sixteenth century was assisted by the changing social scene. It
was an indication of the final acceptance by the Seville nobles of
a new pattern of values, and the triumph of materialism in the
city.[35]

Genoese alignment with the local nobility increased their
control over the municipal government. Since at least the
fifteenth century their economic power had enabled them to
exert subtle pressure over the municipality,[36] but in the sixteenth

7

century their incorporation into the ruling elite allowed them to intervene directly in city affairs. In 1563 one of Simón Ruiz's factors in Seville correctly appraised the situation when he reported that "everything here goes as the Genoese desire and order it." [37] No better example of Genoese influence can be given than their role in the events surrounding the failure of the bank of Domingo de Lizarrazas in 1553. As secret partners of the banker, they conspired with the members of the city council to prevent the case from being settled. The royal officials charged with investigating this bankruptcy finally complained to the King that they were powerless to move against the Genoese because of the latter's control over the municipality.

Even during the last years of the century when popular opinion in Seville, as in the rest of Spain, was moving against them, the Genoese maintained their influential position in Sevillian affairs. Surely we can perceive their hand behind a memorial written at this time by an anonymous Sevillian author extolling the virtues of foreign merchants resident in his city. The writer's use of statistics and his informed comments indicate that he was a government functionary of some sort, even perhaps a member of the city council. Using a variety of arguments ranging from the economic to the religious and demographic, his work attempted to refute the anti-Genoese feelings abroad in the city and country as a whole. [38] It was in essence, a defense of the Genoese position: their economic usefulness was cleverly combined with the reality of what their spokesman claimed was their complete identification with Sevillian society and the best interests of the city. According to the author, the high degree of assimilation manifested by the Genoese and many other foreign residents of Seville was the result of long years of residence in the city, intermarriage, and naturalization. [39] The majority of them had children who were born in Seville and owned considerable property both in the city and surrounding countryside—all of which gave them a firm and binding interest in the welfare of the city and nation as a whole. Moreover, their devotion to the faith and their willingness to aid the Church was well-known. This made them an asset from the religious point of view, "considering the large number of souls in the world today who have espoused heretical views." [40]

As for the economic contribution of the Genoese, the author expressed doubt, given the conditions of trading with the New World—long delays, risks, large capital investment—that the Sevillians could undertake it without Genoese financial aid. This argument, based on the need for Genoese capital, while valid in the first half of the sixteenth century, was no longer true at the time that the author was writing, for by then the Sevillian nobility and merchant class, enriched by years of participation in the transatlantic trade, were well able to carry on their trade without the financial aid of the Genoese. Indeed, the Geneose themselves had recognized the gradual decline of their role as pure capitalists by turning to other aspects of the American trade such as the traffic in African slaves and New World products. Their increased participation in royal finance during the second part of the century was also related to this fact. Nevertheless, if there was less need for Genoese capital, the Seville traders still depended on the foreign goods that the Genoese and other non-native merchants brought into their city from other parts of Europe. By the last quarter of the century, the fleets bound for the New World carried almost nothing else but foreign manufactured products. Without the textiles and manufactured wares of Flanders, France, and England, brought into Seville by foreign merchants such as the Genoese, it would have been very difficult for the Sevillians to maintain the transatlantic trade. Goods, therefore, rather than capital, became a more important Genoese contribution to the American trade during the last years of the century, and enabled the Genoese to maintain their influential position in the Sevillian market throughout the next one hundred years. It was not until the closing years of the seventeenth century that the French moved ahead of the Genoese. The growing economic power of the former was closely related to political conditions, that is, the increased strength and prestige of the French monarchy and the decline of the Habsburg line in Spain.[41]

As one of the most important pressure groups in Seville, the Genoese used their influence to protect and further the interests of their city. It is not unlikely that the establishment of the Casa de Contratación in Seville was due to the intervention of the Genoese through the Councilman Francisco Pinelo. An anonymous document discovered in the Simancas Archives in 1934 by Ernst Schäfer, containing a detailed plan for the creation of such an institution, is believed to have been written by Pinelo in 1502. This work served as a model for the actual Casa founded a year later by the Catholic kings.[42] Pinelo's plan called for the establishment of a royal trading house, corresponding with royal "factories" in the New World—possibly in imitation of the Casa da India set up by the Portuguese in Lisbon for the control of the spice trade with the Orient. In suggesting that all trade with America be channeled through one central agency and restricted to a single port, Seville, Pinelo was speaking not only as a Genoese, but also as a Sevillian. It is quite possible that Pinelo's colleagues on the city council played some part in urging him to draw up this plan for they knew that his role in the preparations for the Columbian voyages had won him the respect and confidence of the Catholic kings. Who else was better prepared to inform the Spanish rulers as to the best way to organize the trade with the New World and to influence them to make Seville the center of that trade.

The establishment of the Casa de Contratación in their native city represented a triumph for the Sevillians, while the appointment of Pinelo as its first factor gave the Genoese a double victory. And for two centuries, in spite of the claims of other cities, in spite of the protests from the colonies, Seville retained her high distinction.[43] In the sixteenth century there was only one real serious attempt to break the monopoly of Seville. Charles V, in an effort to encourage emigration and trade, issued a decree in January 1529 permitting ships to sail directly to

America from other specified ports on the Peninsula. On the return voyage, however, the cargoes had to be landed at Seville and reported to the Casa de Contratación.[44] The well-intentioned efforts of the Emperor were soon doomed to failure through the combined efforts of the Seville merchants and the Genoese. While the former protested, the latter exerted financial pressure on Charles until he gave in to their joint demands that the Sevillian monopoly be re-established.[45] The Genoese, holding the power of the purse over the Emperor, had once again used it to protect the interests of Seville.

Although the position and influence of the Genoese in Sevillian political and economic affairs clearly emerges from the official documents preserved in the various Sevillian archives, we have no way of penetrating into the daily routine of their lives because their private papers have been lost. To know anything at all about them—their ideas and way of life—we must depend on scattered bits of information drawn from many sources, one of the most important of them being contemporary Spanish literature. References to the Genoese appear in many of the works of the writers of the Golden Age, and through them we can obtain some idea of the concepts and manner of life of the Genoese in Seville, and elsewhere in Spain during the period.

Among the characteristics that the Spaniards considered to be typically Genoese were cupidity and parsimony; in fact, the stereotype that we find in the literature of the period was based on this concept. The Genoese reputation for parsimony, however, was not born in Spain in the Golden Age. Centuries before, Boccaccio had selected Erminio Grimaldi as an excellent example of an avaricious and niggardly individual. In the sixteenth century Bandello noted that the wealthy and prominent Ansaldo Grimaldi was so stingy that he counted everything he posessed including each piece of paper and string. Even Ansaldo's contemporary countryman and eulogist, Jacobo Bonfadio, described him as "a man of friendly and serene countenance, sparing in words, proud, very rich, but extremely frugal in his conduct of life." A century later, Castillo Solórzano's Genoese merchant of Cordova still reflected similar tendencies: "He was a man of more than forty years of age, good appearance, and simple dress . . . [but] he was incredibly avaricious . . . [although] he had more than 20,000 escudos in cash and more than 50,000 in credits." [46] One particular manifestation of Genoese frugality was their reluctance to spend their money on conspicuous consumption—the large entourages of servants, coaches, and banquets so characteristic of the wealthier classes of the period. In *La gitanilla* Cervantes ridiculed the Genoese for their stinginess when he had a page say: "I am neither rich nor poor; and without lamenting it or discounting it, as the Genoese do when they invite a guest to dinner, I can give a florin, and even two, to whomever I like." [47]

Even though the Genoese cultivated frugality as a way of life, they were not averse to spending large sums of money on the embellishment of their homes. There was general agreement among all those who visited Genoa during the Middle Ages and Early Modern Era that it was a city which contained an extraordinary number of beautiful homes. Villalón, for example, did not believe that there was "another city in Italy that had within so short a distance so many fine homes." Outside of the city, the *ribera* was covered with "so many magnificent palaces, called *vilas* by the Genoese that it seems like another city." [48] The Genoese, according to Villalón, vied with each other in constructing these *vilas*, and cost was no obstacle. In Seville the majority of the Genoese lived in the fashionable Santa Maria quarter, which was a veritable beehive of construction activity during the century.[49] Like the rest of the prosperous Sevillian traders, the Genoese remodeled and embellished their homes as visible symbols of their good fortune.

Wealth, above all, was the cornerstone of Genoese life. In the sixteenth century as in the previous period, the Genoese measured the worth of an individual in economic terms.[50] The growth of Genoese materialism was largely due to the geographic position of their city. Genoa, situated at the bottom of a gulf open to the sea, was isolated from the hinterland by a mountain wall; as a landless city facing the open sea she was predestined to a maritime career.[51] Her entire population was either actively engaged in commerce, or dependent upon it for a living. In this type society a spirit of initiative, a sense of adventure, and a disdain for risk were all essential characteristics necessary for survival. From very early times commercial profits had created a class of rich traders whose social status was based upon continued enrichment. In the thirteenth century the famous admiral and merchant Benedetto Zaccaria expressed the true spirit of Genoese civilization when he named his ship *Divizia* (Wealth).[52]

Since success was measured in material terms, no other considerations were permitted to interfere with the pursuit of gain.[53] The end justified the means, and the end was that which allowed the individual to enjoy all the things of this world. In business each went his own way without worrying about his neighbor, who was almost always a competitor. Reserved and taciturn, the Genoese guarded their business secrets so jealously that, in the contracts drawn up in Genoa before the public notaries, they often refused to mention the final destination of their merchandise.[54] Egotism seemed to rule supreme in their commercial life. Not even the possibility of injury to compatriots, friends, or collaborators appeared to stir the Genoese from a course leading to a profitable conclusion. In fact, the Genoese attitude toward life can be summed up in two words: "Enrichissez-vous." [55]

Although the Genoese cultivated materialism, it should not be assumed that they lacked religious feelings; nevertheless, no matter how profound and sincere their religion, it was adapted to their commercial policy—their role in the Crusades was a clear indication of this.[56] The attitude of Christopher Columbus, for example, was typically Genoese. Although at times the Great Admiral manifested mystic tendencies such as his belief that he was personally sent by God to carry Christ to the pagans— "Christum Ferens," as he called himself—nothing could be further from reality.[57] Columbus was trained as a merchant and worked many years as an agent for the Centurione firm.[58] He thought in terms of profits and losses; the First Voyage was essentially a business venture for him. This explains his actions when, "instead of allowing himself to be carried away by enthusiasm for his enterprise, he kept postponing it while he negotiated interminably, and refused to risk the venture until he had secured for himself a dazzling series of rewards and profits." Again it was Columbus who "suggested to the Catholic kings the enslavement of the Indians—an economic proposition at so much a head." [59] No clearer expression of this combination of economic calculation and religious piety, so typical of the Genoese, can be found than Columbus' statements in his last will and testament. In this document he entreats his son, Diego, to "establish a fund in the Bank of Saint George in Genoa which gives interest of six per cent and is secure money" and to devote this money to charitable and pious acts since "it becomes every man of rank and property to serve God either personally, or by means of his wealth, and all moneys deposited with Saint George are quite safe." [60] Even in matters of faith, Columbus, like his compatriots in Seville, wanted to make sure his investment was safe. To the Genoese, religious duties and pious acts were important, but so was economic interest.[61]

The calculated attitude of the Genoese toward every aspect of life including religion, reveals itself in their relations with the Church in Seville. Like other wealthy Sevillians, they gave generously to religious and pious foundations, and it was not unusual for children of assimilated and hispanized families to enter the priesthood and religious orders. Moreover, the Sevillian Genoese had a reputation for orthodoxy at a time when the religious loyalties of many Sevillians were being tested. In the first half of the sixteenth century the influx of foreigners, particularly those from northern Europe, brought heresy in the form of Lutheranism.[62] The new beliefs won numerous adherents among all social classes, but seemed to have some special appeal for the Sevillian nobility, especially those families active in the American trade. Among the aristocrats attracted to

Lutheranism were the Councilman Diego de Virués, who was forced to abjure his beliefs in the *auto de fe* of 1560, and several members of the Ponce de León family. Juan Ponce de León, son of the Count of Bailén, was executed and his remains burnt in the auto of 1559; Catalina Sarmiento, widow of Fernando Ponce de León, was condemned in the auto of 1560 and forced to do penance.[63] The Genoese, on the other hand, remained indifferent toward Lutheranism, and no members of their community were ever accused or brought up before the Inquisition for heresy during the sixteenth century.[64] Nor for that matter were they denounced to the Holy Office for immoral actions, which, besides heresy, was then a common charge. Many of those who were condemned by the Inquisition and forced to appear in the *autos de fe* had been convicted of moral offences—bigamy and concubinage being the most usual.[65]

In the Genoese scheme of values there were only two lives, the temporal and the eternal. That third life so vital to the Spaniards of the Golden Age—the life of fame—was not important. Neither valiant deeds nor self-sacrifice for a higher cause, or even the desire to perpetuate their names through personal distinction, mattered to the Genoese merchants. They lived to the fullest extent, tried to insure their salvation, and when they died they left to their heirs their account books, personal belongings, property, and cash. Even if funds were left for charitable purposes, this was not done to perpetuate their names, but to comply with the requisites of religion and society.[66]

The businesslike spirit of the Genoese to a great degree accounts for their limited role in Sevillian cultural life. With the exception of the Negrón and Pinelo families, the Genoese merchants and their descendants showed little aptitude for the more aesthetic fields of endeavor.[67] Nor do we find the names of wealthy Genoese residents among the patrons of Seville writers or artists during the sixteenth century.[68] Robert Lopez' thesis that investment in culture was inversely proportional to the intensity of business spirit in Renaissance Italy also seems to apply to Seville. The sixteenth century represented an era of economic expansion for the city—a boom period—in which the Genoese were too busy making money to consider lyric poetry or artistic creations. When they did invest their money, it went into practical works of art such as home decoration.[69]

Besides investing in practical culture, the Genoese found many other outlets for their capital in Seville. Undoubtedly, some of it went into urban real estate, then a popular form of investment. The increase of rents under the stimulus of the price revolution, and the rise of land values due to the building boom, encouraged all members of the Seville business community to invest in urban property. Rural land provided another investment opportunity. Although a large portion of the wealth of the rising native merchant class was invested in country estates, very little Genoese money went in that direction. The purchase of an estate by newly ennobled merchants was a status symbol for those parvenus—a manifestation of having arrived—rather than a sound investment. Although it is true that the impact of American demands for products of the Andalusian countryside during the first decades of the century caused the market value of land to rise, this rise in value proved to be ephemeral.[70] By the second half of the century capital that went into land did so at an economic disadvantage, one which the Genoese were not willing to risk for symbolic importance bearing no relationship to market value.[71]

Like country property, *juros,* or annuities, another form of investment that appealed to most Sevillians, won little enthusiasm among the Genoese. If numerous Genoese merchants of Seville held *juros,* this was due to the government's fiscal policies rather than any special desire on their part to invest their money in annuities. As the needs of the royal treasury increased from the 1520's on, the government adopted the policy of confiscating American gold and silver destined for private individuals as a means of supplementing the deficit. Dispossessed persons were recompensed with annuities, either perpetual or redeemable, paying 3 to 6 per cent on the capital seized. The Genoese became annuity holders, then, not through choice but circumstance.[72]

Although most Sevillians, in line with the contemporary belief that "living off rents was a sign of nobility," [73] considered *juros* and real estate to be the best kind of investments, the Genoese still preferred to place the bulk of their money in trade, both of goods and money. Large sums still went into the trade of Sevillian agricultural products—fruits, oil, and wine—which they had for centuries exported to the rest of Europe.[74] To these traditional items of trade, they now added various American products like sugar, hides, drugs, and cochineal, most of which they sent to the great European emporium of Antwerp, which served as a distribution center for the rest of Europe.[75] Thus the Genoese and other Sevillian merchants developed a profitable re-export trade in New World commodities from Seville to Antwerp. All of these American products brought good prices on the Antwerp market, and it was possible for the Genoese and others to manipulate prices to their own advantage in Antwerp by holding up shipments from Seville. Again prices in both cities were subject to wide fluctuations, since they were completely dependent on the arrival of the American fleets. Delay or loss of a fleet caused scarcity, high prices, tightness in the money market, and bankruptcies in both Seville and Antwerp.

With the proceeds from the sale of American and Andalusian products, the Genoese purchased all kinds of northern European textiles and manufactured items which they brought back to Seville. Some of this foreign merchandise was sold locally— foreign clothes enjoyed quite a vogue in Seville—but most of it was re-exported to America. In this way, the Genoese and other foreign merchants developed, in the shadow of inflation, a profitable trade based upon the importation of foreign goods to fill the gap created by declining Spanish production.

The grain trade was another of the traditional Genoese activities in Seville.[76] Although the Andalusian countryside was one of the richest agricultural regions in Spain, comparatively little grain was grown, and such natural catastrophes as drought, floods, and locusts were common.[77] Hardly a year passed in which there was not a serious shortage of wheat in Seville, caused either by these natural phenomena or by the manipulations of speculators. This situation was made more critical by the demographic increase that the city experienced during the course of the sixteenth century. The lack of bread caused several large-scale riots: one of the most famous of these mass uprisings occurred in 1521 when the residents of the impoverished Feria district seized a quantity of arms from the palace of the Duke of Medina Sidonia, and taking as their standard a green Moorish banner that had been preserved in their parish church of Omnium Sanctorum, ran riot through the city. After three days of continuous pillage, violence, and disorder, they were finally put down by the armed nobility.[78]

The irregularity of local grain crops made it possible for the Genoese and others to realize large profits on the sale of wheat. Whenever there was the possibility of high prices during a severe winter, or in the spring following bad crops, the Genoese made sure to bring large supplies into the city, which they stored until they could set their own price. In 1523, for example, the Mayor of Seville, Count of Osorno, tried to purchase 25,000 *fanegas* of wheat and 45,000 *fanegas* of barley from Esteban Centurión and Adán de Vivaldo who, according to the Mayor, "had so much wheat that they could not possibly sell it all at once." He offered them 3½ reals per *fanega* for the wheat and 1½ for the barley, prices that the two businessmen felt were too low. Besides, the Genoese had a license to ship 15,000 *fanegas* of this wheat to San Sebastian where, due to a critical shortage, they stood to double their profit. When it became apparent that the Genoese would not negotiate with him, Osorno wrote the King asking him to intervene in the deadlocked transaction and to force Centurión and Vivaldo to sell their wheat to city officials. Furthermore, the Mayor entreated His Majesty to prevent the two Genoese from shipping any wheat outside the city, for "in the previous year 3,000 persons had died here, the majority of them from starvation due to lack of bread." Osorno also warned the King that the "Genoese are using all kinds of tricks and subtleties to blur the real issues in this affair," and he readily admitted that he was simply "not unscrupulous enough to deal with them." [79]

At the same time that the Sevillian Genoese engaged in the trade of goods, they also dealt in money. Public banking, moneylending, and royal finance all provided profitable investment opportunities for Genoese capital. Their loans to the government, although sporadic in the first half of the century, grew in importance by the second half, when several members of the Seville colony began to devote a large part of their time and money to supporting the Spanish monarchy. Royal finance, however, never became the main outlet for their capital, nor was it their principal economic activity. The Sevillian Genoese invested the greater part of their capital in the American trade, which was their prime interest and the *raison d'etre* for their existence in Seville.

CHAPTER II

Seville in the
Sixteenth Century

THE wealth and power of the members of the Genoese colony
of Seville were closely related to the profound transformation
that their city experienced during the course of the sixteenth
century. In that period Seville became the most famous and
important city in Spain. Although one of the busiest mercantile
towns in Andalusia during the Middle Ages, Seville was not its
chief port. Seville lay fifty-four miles from the sea; the sand bar
at San Lucar was dangerous to cross, and the channel narrow
and tortuous. Cadiz, on the other hand, was located directly on
the sea and offered superior maritime facilities against which
Seville could not compete. Genoese ships and galleys en route to
Flanders and England stopped regularly at Cadiz, and only
infrequently made the difficult trip up the Guadalquivir River to
Seville.[1] In the sixteenth century, however, Cadiz lost out to her
rival, and Seville became "not a city but a world," as her native
son Francisco de Herrera described her in his *Soneto a Sevilla*.[2]
The fabulous riches that arrived from the Indies attracted to her
banks individuals from all parts of Spain and from the rest of
Europe. She soon became a "new Babylonia."[3] Seville's population, which had grown very slowly during the Middle Ages,
increased from 49,395 in 1530 to 90,000 in 1594, making her
the largest city in Spain.[4]

There exists sufficient documentation, of both a literary and historical character, to enable us to reconstruct a picture of the city of Seville during the sixteenth century. The two most useful historical sources are Luis de Peraza's *Historia de la imperial ciudad de Sevilla,* written in the first half of the century, and the *Historia de Sevilla* of Alonso de Morgado, published in 1589.[5] Both present detailed but orderly eulogized accounts of the city and her development. Moreover, it should be noted that the countenance of the Andalusian port emerges with as much clarity from the pages of Cervantes, Mateo Alemán, Lope de Vega, and the other great writers who used her as the setting for many of their literary creations, as from the descriptions of the city's historians.

At the opening of the century the structure of Seville had scarcely varied from the medieval form. Surrounded by strong walls and towers, she preserved the outline of former centuries. Narrow and winding streets, many joined by arches and covered crossings, constituted the shell of the city. Everywhere there could be found—even in the most congested places—palaces, churches, and monasteries with large orchards and gardens, such as the Monastery of San Francisco and the palace of the Duke of Medina Sidonia.[6]

The plan of the river port had been drawn up by King Ferdinand III of Castile shortly after his reconquest of the city from the Moslems in 1248. According to Peraza, "the King divided the various parts of Seville—the districts and streets—among the knights and others who had fought in the conquest of the city. He further commanded that the several trades and professions should be settled in specific areas and the streets upon which they were to be established should bear their names."[7] As early as the fourteenth century, nevertheless, modifications in the original plan appeared. Although the designated districts (*barrios*) and the streets continued, on the whole, to carry their assigned names, they began to reflect a more diversified population.[8] By the sixteenth century few of the existent descendants of the two hundred knights who had received property in the Andalusian metropolis lived in the *barrios* that had been granted to them. Members of the craft and professional guilds were scattered throughout the city.

One of the most densely populated and important *barrios* of Seville was Triana. It lay across the Guadalquivir River and outside the walls of the city, and it was joined to the metropolis by a wooden pontoon bridge. Triana's proximity to the river made it the favored residential quarter of the seafaring population of Seville, most of whom were engaged in the *carrera de Indias*. They were organized in confraternities through which they patronized and managed several hospitals in the quarter.[9] Among these was the important Hospital of Santa Ana, located in the Calle Larga, Triana's principal thoroughfare. The *barrio* also contained some of the most important industrial establishments of Seville; all contemporary accounts agree that it was, in fact, the undisputed industrial center of the city. Some fifty establishments alone were engaged in producing pottery, particularly the kind known as Málaga ware.[10] The famous glazed tile of Seville and sculptured pieces of all types originated in the Triana workshops. Soap and gunpowder were also produced on a large scale.

The pontoon bridge that connected Triana with Seville was, in the opinion of contemporaries, one of the most impressive sights in the river port. The sandy condition of the land on both sides of the Guadalquivir had, for centuries, made it impossible to construct a more permanent type of bridge. According to Morgado, the Triana bridge measured 240 varas wide and 12 long and was constructed over seventeen barges. "It would be difficult to imagine," exclaimed the clergyman, "any bridge more frequented, or containing greater numbers of people, carts, coaches, and beasts of burden." [11] All day long wagons loaded with the industrial products of Triana and the fruits and vegetables of the surrounding countryside rumbled across the bridge into Seville. Traffic soon became so heavy and conditions so congested that a loud demand arose for the construction of a new bridge; the task was undertaken by the municipality as part of its plan of general urban improvement during the last decades of the century.

Although the old and new Triana bridges were able to accommodate the heavy traffic between Seville and Triana, many Sevillians preferred to cross the river by boat. Small craft, steered by a special group of river boatmen, transported people from one side of the Guadalquivir to the other. The two principal characters of Vélez de Guevara's *Diablo cojuelo,* for example, chose to cross over to Triana by boat. The author relates that "after having arrived at the river bank and at what is called the Passage [el Pasaje], where one crosses over from Seville to Triana and from Triana to Seville, they engaged a boat and spent the night in the Calle de Altozano in Triana."[12]

The Guadalquivir was the mainspring of Seville's economic life. It brought the fabulous riches of the Indies to her shores and despatched her products to those distant and newly-opened lands. Lope de Vega did not exaggerate when he said that the city was founded on the river.[13] The Guadalquivir was the nerve center of the metropolis: What excitement, noise, and confusion there was along its banks! Sailors, merchants, royal and munici-pal officials, tradesmen—Sevillians of all walks of life—mingled in the crowds that assembled along the wharves. The arrival of an Indies fleet shook the whole city. All hastened to the banks of the river to see the wondrous treasure being unloaded near the Golden Tower (Torre de Oro) by the "huge two-wheeled crane that since time immemorial had served the port."[14]

Here, in sight of the incessant movement and turmoil of the port, could be found one of the major focal points in the Andalusian metropolis, the Arenal, a public promenade built outside the city's walls along the riverside. The Arenal was the favored meeting place for all elements of the city's population, but in particular for the picaros and beggars who abounded in Seville. It also served as a secondhand market where cheating and fraud were the order of the day. It was from the Arenal that the characters of Lope de Vega's play of that name observed the magnificence of Seville and her grandiose commerce.[15]

Let us obtain a bird's-eye view of this throbbing port city from a convenient location near the city walls. Don Cleofás and his friend the Limping Devil of Vélez de Guevara's *Diablo cojuelo* give an excellent description of Seville from the roof of an inn on the Calle del Agua: "Now that tower over there," begins the Limping Devil, "tells us that the beautiful edifice near it is the Cathedral. I do not want to spend too much time describing its grandeur; it is sufficient to say that its pashal candle weighs 76 arrobas and its bronze tenebrae candlestick is of such workmanship that it could not have cost more if it was of gold." In close proximity to the Cathedral, can be found the Lonja (Exchange). To its right is the Alcázar, former residence of the Castilian monarchs. Further on we see the pulse of Sevillian economic life, the Casa de Contratación, and close to the Jerez gate, the Casa de Moneda (Mint) where "gold and silver are stored like wheat." Nearby is the Aduana (Customhouse), with its two principal doors, one opening to the city, the other to the river.[16] In that same locality we find the Golden Tower and the wharves along the Guadalquivir. To the right is the Triana bridge, and further along, on the other side of the river, is the Carthusian monastery of Las Cuevas with its beautiful gardens. On the Seville side we can see the famous Huerta del Rey (King's Garden), which belonged to the Marquis of Tarifa. It was here that the Venetian traveler, Andrea Navajero, saw orange trees as large as the walnut trees of his native Venice.[17]

It was during the sixteenth century that the Andalusian river port experienced her greatest period of urban expansion. The magnificent Cathedral, begun in the fifteenth century, was completed during the first years of the sixteenth century, and the twin symbols of Seville's ascendancy and prosperity, the new Mint and the Exchange, by the end of the century. The new Customhouse, the Hospital de la Sangre, the house of Pilatos, and the Audiencia of Gradas, all rose above the medieval structure of the river port and accentuated her new glory.[18] Numerous churches, convents, and palaces completed the transformation of the city.

Not only did Seville experience a building boom, but there was an attempt to improve the outward appearance of the city. One aspect of this urban redevelopment was the gradual paving of the important streets and thoroughfares; here the initiative came from the city government with only infrequent interventions by the monarchs. A notable example of such intervention did occur in 1501 when the Catholic kings, in response to a series of complaints, ordered the members of the *cabildo* "to see that the said Calle de las Armas be paved as promptly as possible according to the manner in which the other streets of the said city of Seville have been paved."[19] Once a street was paved, precise regulations governed its maintenance and repair. The City Ordinances provided for a *visitador* (inspector) of paved streets who had the authority to compel residents to repair at their own cost, within a period of five days, any damage to the pavement occurring within their property limits.[20] Unfortunately, these stipulations had fallen into disuse by the last decades of the century and the municipal government proved unable to provide for the necessary maintenance.

The widening of streets and the filling in and utilization of swamp and waste lands were but logical consequences of the urban expansion. The erection of the Exchange caused the disappearance of the narrow lanes and alleys around the Cathedral and the Alcázar; wide plazas and thoroughfares took their place.[21] The new Customhouse and the new Mint were built adjoining the city walls on land that for centuries had been used for dung heaps. The construction of the Hospital de la Sangre on similar terrain in the Macarena parish changed the whole complexion of that *barrio*. Finally, the pestilential Laguna at the end of the Calle del Puerco was converted into a magnificent park.

Nor were the walls and gates of the city allowed to retain their medieval form. The gradual growth of effective government and general security created less need for the strong walls and towers characteristic of the previous period. New districts grew up outside of the walls, secure in the relative peace and tranquility of the surrounding countryside. Throughout the century alterations and repairs continued to modify the appearance of the city's walls. Important changes were also made in the form and structure of her fifteen gates.[22] The Triana Gate was remodeled and the Royal, Meatmarket, and Arenal gates were completely rebuilt in order to enlarge them. Moreover, the increased economic activity that Seville was experiencing made it necessary to construct additional postern gates. By the last decade of the century travelers desiring to enter the river port found it most convenient to do so by way of the Puerta del Carbón, renamed de la Aduana (Customhouse Gate) because of its location near the new Customhouse.[23] It was here that all baggage had to be inspected and duties paid.

Once within the city the newcomer could not fail to be impressed, as was Don Cleofás in *El diablo cojuelo,* with what he called "a veritable army of houses built one against the other." [24] Nevertheless, a closer scrutiny of the houses would most probably disappoint the visitor. Sevillian dwellings were quite unprepossessing, since they contained no exterior decoration of any type. Sevillians, after the reconquest of their city from the Moslems, had continued to follow the latter's conception of house design—concentration on the interior parts to the neglect of the exterior. It was only under the impact of the city's new economic position in the sixteenth century that there occurred what can be considered a revolution in house design. The new opulence of this "Golden Age" caused the newly-rich merchant class to make a conspicuous display of worldly wealth in the outward decoration of their homes. Pedro Mexía in his *Coloquios y Diálogos,* published in 1547, gives an interesting commentary on these architectural changes. One of Mexía's interlocutors admires the beautiful façade that a merchant had constructed on his house and remarks that "all of Seville seems to be following the same pattern since more windows and gratings have been built in the last ten years than in the previous thirty." [25] In 1587 Alonso de Morgado noted that "the citizens of Seville in building their homes now place special attention on the exterior in contrast to what was done in the past when all decoration was concentrated within the house according to Moorish tradition. Moreover all desire ostentation which means many windows with iron gratings and lattices, that open to the street."[26]

In general, Sevillian houses were built very low as compared with those of Castile, observed Padre Morgado, "since the inhabitants believe that in this way they will secure a greater amount of air circulation in their warm and humid city." Also, tall buildings shut out the sun from the streets, making the city damper and cooler in the winter and warmer in the summer. A typical Sevillian house contained two stories, a flat roof which served as a terrace from which its inhabitants could catch a breath of fresh air at night, open corridors, and central patio.[27] The whole structure was built around the patio, which was protected from the sun during the day by awnings. Cervantes gives us a vivid glimpse into a Sevillian patio in his *Rinconete y Cortadillo*. Although its proprietor was the infamous Monipodio, it was representative of the greater number of homes in the Andalusian metropolis. The two young thieves, Rinconete and Cortadillo, entered and were asked to wait in

a small brick-paved courtyard so clean and well scrubbed that it appeared to be covered with the finest carmine. On one side was a three-legged stool and on the other a pitcher with a broken spout on top of which stood a small jug that was in equally bad shape. On the third side was a reed mat and in the middle of it a flower pot, or, as they are called in Seville, a sweet basil jar.[28]

Patios, in the homes of the wealthier and more respectable Sevillians, contained large central fountains. These fountains ejected streams of cool water which refreshed the whole courtyard. In addition there were usually several water basins, surrounded by sweet-scented flowers. Jasmine and rosebushes, orange trees, and flower pots containing "a thousand different kinds of fragrant flowers and plants" completed the scene. "What a pleasure for both the sight and sound is a Sevillian patio!" remarked the usually unappreciative Padre Morgado.[29]

The residents of Seville seemed extravagant with their water supply, utilizing large amounts of it to cool their patios, but they could afford this luxury as their city had abundant reserves. Seville was supplied not only from her river, but water was piped into the town from the surrounding countryside. The largest amounts came from the Caños de Carmona. Pedro de Medina gives the following description of it:

There flows into this city from the east a large supply of sweet water that travels underground for more than four leagues through deep conduits. At a little more than a league from Seville, the water appears above the ground and runs along toward the city. At a quarter of a league from her, it flows into an aqueduct and from there enters the city near the Carmona Gate, and is distributed to the churches, monasteries, plazas, streets, and houses that contain fountains and water spouts.[30]

The streets and plazas of the Andalusian port abounded with fountains. The principal one, located in the Plaza de San Francisco, was a masterly creation of white marble, adorned with a bronze figure sculptured by Diego de Pesquera. Second in importance was the Pila del Hierro, situated in Gradas opposite the Calle de la Mar, but it disappeared by the end of the century as a result of the construction of the Exchange.[31] Exceedingly abundant in sweet water was the fountain located in the Plaza de la Feria, redone at mid-century in marble and decorated with two bronze lions. Other fountains particularly frequented by Sevillians were those of Salvador, San Vicente, and Pila del Tesoro. After the construction of the Alameda park, its two main fountains, one with a statue of Bacchus by Pesquera and the other with a group representing Neptune with some nymphs by Bautista Vázquez, became popular drinking spots.

The abundance of water permitted the existence and continuation of one of Seville's oldest institutions, the public baths. Morgado, a true son of the century, marveled that "no one conceals the fact that he frequents the baths; not even the women are criticized since it is a custom among them since time immemorial." There were two principal baths in the Andalusian metropolis, one located in San Ildefonso parish, and the other in San Juan de la Palma. Both dated from the Moslem period. Although these baths did not offer any private accommodations, they were strictly reserved for women during the daytime and men in the evening. Both hot and cold running water were available, in addition to special ointments and perfumes which were utilized by the Sevillian ladies after their baths.[32]

While the ladies of Seville passed their leisure time at the public baths, the business-minded men spent their days in the Gradas of the Cathedral, center of the city's economic life. In 1526 the Venetian ambassador, Andrea Navajero, described this site as follows:

Around the whole building [the Cathedral] there is a long marble terrace, enclosed by chains, from which one descends by steps to the street below. Throughout the day merchants and hidalgos congregate in this place . . . which is called las Gradas. In the neighboring street and plaza, which is a type of public market, there are always great numbers of people and it is here that frauds of all kinds are committed.[33]

Here in the shadow of the Cathedral were located the famous Sevillian banks where "an infinity of silver coin was handled"; this locality was the site of the silversmiths' establishments, and of the great public auctions. According to Morgado, "jewelry, gold and silver objects, rich tapestries, arms and slaves are sold in the continuous auctions that take place here throughout the day."[34] It was only at the very end of the century that Sevillian commercial and financial life ceased to radiate outward from the terrace, steps, and plaza of the Cathedral. The plea of Archbishop Cristóbal de Rojas to Philip II in 1572 to end the desecration of the Cathedral by the merchants and bankers resulted in the construction of the Exchange, which had by the opening of the seventeenth century replaced the former center.

The business area of the city extended outward from Gradas through the Calle de Génova, famous for its bookshops, through the tortuous lanes of the Alcaicería and finally terminated in the Calle de la Sierpe. "It is a marvelous thing," exclaimed Morgado, "to see in this district all the rich and exotic merchandise from Flanders, Greece, Genoa, England, France, Italy, Brittany and more Northern parts, and from the Indies." [35] Moreover, the Alcaicería was itself "so full of shops containing all kinds of precious goods" that it was locked at night and vigilantly guarded by selected personnel.

In the middle of the Alcaicería stood the Plaza de San Francisco, which began to acquire prominence as an important public square only at the end of the century. As late as the year 1579 Francisco de Sigüenza maintained that "what Seville lacks is a good central plaza." [36] The future importance of the site had nevertheless been recognized as early as 1545 by the construction there of the Casa de Ayuntamiento (City Hall). On the opposite side of the square, the Audiencia and the city jail took their places by the end of the century, thereby converting the Plaza de San Francisco into the administrative center of the metropolis.

Here in the economic heart of the city was the Casa de Contratación, overseer of the Indies trade and creator of Sevillian prosperity. What a spectacle the Casa presented at the arrival of a fleet from the New World, when multitudes of businessmen, officials, and seamen roamed through its wide corridors and spacious chambers. In the diary of Francisco de Ariño, the activities of the year 1595 were noted when, according to his account, the largest treasure shipment thus far brought from America was placed in the Casa. He wrote:

On March 22 the silver fleet from the Indies arrived at the wharf and they unloaded and placed in the Casa de Contratación 332 cart loads of silver, gold, and precious pearls. On May 8 they took 103 cart loads of gold and silver from the *Capitana* [Flagship] and on May 8, 583 loads of silver from the *Almiranta* [Rear-admiral's ship] arrived over-land from Lisbon where she had been forced to put in because of storms. For six days cargoes from the Almiranta continued to cross the Triana Bridge. . . . All this treasure in addition to what was taken from the two other fleets that arrived here this year was placed in the Casa de Contratación and detained there by the king for four months. As a result the chambers of the Casa could not accommodate it all and it overflowed on to the patio.[37]

A short distance from the Casa was the Royal Mint, where the American treasure was eventually taken to be coined. According to Padre Morgado, more than two hundred men labored within the establishment to convert the precious metals into coins. He marveled at "the mountains of money that can be seen in it and the large amounts that depart from it on the backs of mules as if it was a type of common merchandise." [38] During the last years of the century, when the American bullion imports reached a high point, the old mint proved unable to process so much silver and gold, and so construction on a new one was begun.

In violent contrast to Seville's grandeur and richness was the unsanitary condition of the river port; during her whole "golden period," the greater part of the outskirts of Seville was a formless rubbish heap. Even in the principal public walk, the Arenal, there existed the Monte del Malbaratillo, formed by refuse deposited there by generations of Sevillians.[39] In 1574 the Count of Barajas, chief justice of Seville, succeeded in converting one of the city's foul lagoons and dumping areas into a beautiful park which came to be called the Alameda de Hércules.[40] Thirteen years later Morgado wrote that "the fountains provided irrigation for 1700 trees, among which were alders, white poplars, cypresses, and orange trees, which had been planted in this lagoon." [41]

Within the city proper, street cleaning was left to the property owners who were not inclined to exert themselves to any great degree. In 1598 one of the assistants to the Chief Justice stated in a *cabildo* meeting that "conditions in the city are shameful; garbage and mountains of rubbish can be found in all the streets and plazas which have become nothing more than dung heaps." [42] The City Ordinances were nevertheless strict in regard to public hygiene and sanitation. There existed an inspector of sanitation who was given sufficient power to force property owners to maintain the portions of the street bordering their own property. In the dry season every resident was required to sweep his sector of the street every fifteen days.[43] In practice, however, the inhabitants paid the inspector twelve maravedís plus a 3 per cent commission for which sum he and his assistants performed the task. As might be imagined, this system fostered graft and neglect.

The ordinances also stipulated the penalties for willfully littering the streets. A sum of twelve maravedís could be exacted from anyone who threw "human excrement, garbage, or any other kind of waste on the street." If the culprit could not be found, the twelve residents living nearest the spot would be assessed at one maravedí apiece. Regardless of the regulations, the stroller in Seville found the majority of the streets carpeted with filth, and the central gutters were a succession of stagnant pools choked with dung, entrails, and litter of all kinds.[44] The vile odors abounding throughout the town were relieved only by the happy presence of fragrant flowers and trees. It is not difficult then to understand the frequency with which the plague ravaged Seville during the century.

More than anything else, the transformation of Seville from a provincial Andalusian port city into a thriving international metropolis—a "new Babylonia" as she was called by contemporaries—was the discovery of the New World. "Was not Seville and all Andalusia before this event the utmost point and end of all land, and now it is the middle to which come the best and most esteemed of the Old World . . . to be carried to the New." [45] The whole city lived under the spell of the fabulous American treasure that "at the arrival of the fleet was carried in carts pulled by four oxen along the streets from the Guadalquivir to the Casa de Contratación." [46] Even Guzmán de Alfarache found that in Seville "riches are not highly esteemed since silver runs as freely here as does copper in other parts." [47] The chief desire of all inhabitants of the port was to acquire money to spend on luxuries, vices, novelties, and fancies. Both Europe and the New World supplied the means to gratify their desires for food, dress, and equipage. Among the most highly prized novelties were exotic food products from the New World. Even the Venetian Navajero was curious enough to sample some of them. "I saw in Seville," he noted, "many products from the Indies and sampled and ate the roots which they call batatas [potatoes] that taste like chestnuts. I also tried a beautiful fruit that tastes like something between a melon and a peach." [48]

Sevillians—the nobility, the middle class, and all others who could—indulged themselves in fine and expensive clothes. The historian Peraza wrote that "since the commerce of Seville is so extensive and prosperous, Sevillians clad themselves in cloth that regularly costs two to three ducats a vara and use silk, velvet, taffeta, camlet, fustian, and serge in their doublets, coats, breeches, and shoes, and have breeches that cost 40 and 50 ducats." [49] As for the women, "there is not one that covers herself with a woolen mantle; everything is silk, taffeta, chiffon, or at least serge. Dresses are all of silk or fine cloth with elaborate embroidery and quilting." [50] The attire of the wealthy classes contrasted sharply with that of the less fortunate residents of the river port, who were reduced to using coarse woolen cloth, particularly baize, in the dark colors universally worn by the poorer classes in Spain.

By the last years of the century the coach also had become a sign of wealth and prestige. Owning a costly and elaborate coach was not only a requisite for members of the upper classes, but a means by which those recently arrived could enter into their ranks. Noble and merchant families competed in the size and luxury of their equipage. Coaches began to be utilized to such an extent that streets had to be widened to allow the larger ones to pass. [51] All types and sizes of coaches rumbled through the streets of the Andalusian city, carrying their owners to spend "one afternoon in the Alameda and the other in the Arenal." [52]

Not all the wealth that flowed into Seville from the New World went into conspicuous consumption, nor was it reinvested in the American trade—large amounts were spent for religious and charitable purposes. The nobility, merchants, guilds, confraternities, and the municipality vied with each other in constructing hospitals, schools, asylums, monasteries, and convents. The

33

municipal government was particularly interested in the patronage of schools; in 1580 the Jesuits founded their Academy of San Hermenegildo with the aid of funds donated by the city. The nobility, on the other hand, was the most active contributor toward the establishment and expansion in Seville of the several religious orders. Large and continued contributions by old and illustrious Sevillian families enabled the Dominicans to maintain as many as three houses in the city.[53]

Although Seville could rightly be called the city of charity, her streets were overrun with all kinds of poor, sick, and maimed individuals who tried to make a living from their misfortunes. The most disconcerting spectacle was presented by abandoned children, who, hungry and almost naked, found no other solution than to become apprenticed to the brotherhood of thieves that existed in the city.[54] During the last years of the century an attempt was made to alleviate their sufferings by the creation of the Confraternity of the Vagrant Child. A short time after its foundation, the director, Andrés de la Losa, reported to the *cabildo* that "more than 600 boys who did not serve in this city in any other capacity than petty thieves and rogues have been rescued from the streets and placed in respectable positions." [55] In 1582 the municipality donated substantial sums for the establishment of a home and hospital for orphan girls who "in the majority have come into Seville from the outside and become vagrants." [56]

Such a city, overflowing with wealth, vice, and poverty, presented the most favorable conditions for the shelter and protection of criminals and lawbreakers of every sort. Seville was, in the words of Cervantes, "the refuge of the outcast." [57] With a large population and an exceedingly lax and corrupt municipal government, the town was filled to capacity with all types of disreputable elements: Disorder and confusion reigned. By simply moving from one *barrio* to another criminals were able to escape the law, and there was always the possibility of fleeing to the Indies. Law officials and thieves often worked together while *espías dobles* lent their services to both sides. Even small boys imitated their elders, carrying small swords (*espadicas*) at their sides, and thieves' jargon (*germanía*) was used in common speech throughout the city.[58] One of the city's most representative types was the bully or ruffian. Castillo Solórzano, the author of *La garduña de Sevilla y anzuelo de las bolsas,* noted that the majority of Sevillians liked to boast of being bravados. Particularly well known were those of the San Román parish and La Feria quarter. Cervantes, who was well acquainted with these famous Sevillian ruffians, gave the following description of them: "Among the latest arrivals were a couple of swaggering young ruffians with large mustaches, broad-brimmed hats, walloon ruffs, colored stockings, and large showy garters. Their swords exceeded the length allowed by law, each carried a brace of pistols in place of daggers, and their bucklers were suspended from their girdles." [59]

The material prosperity that the Andalusian metropolis experienced during this period led to a rapid decline in both public and private morals: All contemporary accounts agree that Seville was a center of corruption and fraud.[60] Mateo Alemán, keen observer of human nature and particularly that of his fellow Sevillians, remarked that "what you know is not respected, but what you have; not your virtue but your purse and not really your purse but what you spend." [61]

Although money was the prime mover of men, presents of jewelry, clothes, and even things to eat were highly solicited. "The two poles around which this orb revolves are women and gifts," wrote Licentiate Porras de la Cámara in an informative letter to the future Cardinal of Seville, Fernando Niño de Guevara.[62] As for the administration of justice, there was, according to Luque Fajardo, "no law, statute or decree that is obeyed, followed, or worth as much as a real, doubloon, or escudo; the real subdues enemies, the escudo defends, and the doubloon influences justice." [63] Alemán, who was thoroughly acquainted with Sevillian justice, gave the following advice to those who desired a favorable decision in a Sevillian court: "Gild the judges books and present the notary with a silver pen so that he may sleep and take no further notice of the matter and in this way you will not need a Doctor or Proctor to plead or solicit your case." [64]

Along with the corrupt judges and notaries there were many false witnesses who for six maravedís would swear innumerable falsehoods and destroy anyone's reputation. They frequented the public squares and streets and could even be found in the courts and notary offices. They freely offered their services to whoever desired them "as do workers and journeymen who sell their daily labor." [65]

Although there was little justice in Seville, there were many to administer, corrupt, and sell it. The city's principal law enforcement officer was the chief constable (Alguacil Mayor). Four assistants, one of whom was specifically assigned to Triana, aided him in carrying out his manifold duties. To facilitate the work of policing the city, the Chief Constable could name twenty constables on horseback (*alguaciles a caballo* or *de los viente*) who were chosen from among the non-taxpaying residents (*hidalgos*) of the parishes.[66] The latter were required to provide themselves with horses at their own expense and to reside in the parish from which they had been selected. Unfortunately for the cause of justice, too many of the constables were like Cervantes's "constable in charge of vagabonds" who, according to Monipodio, the thieves' chieftain, "is a friend and never comes to do us harm." [67]

The municipal constables, however, were not the only law enforcement officers in the river port. There was an infinity of others representing royal, ecclesiastical, and seignioral courts who traveled about the town, proudly exhibiting their emblems of authority and attempting to serve writs.[68] Alemán described these traveling constables in vehement terms:

The constable is no more than a common catchpole who has neither soul nor shame . . . who either bought that *vara* which he bears, to find meat to put into his mouth; or else he hired it from another, as a man does a mule . . . and under the pretence that he is the King's officer and carrying the King's white wand [*vara*] in his hand . . .

he will offer you a hundred excesses, a hundred indignities, both in words and deeds . . . that he may make you resist justice (which is the trap he sets for you) and pretend that your offense is criminal and persuade others (all he can) to believe it.[69]

In addition to the authentic constables there also existed false ones. On March 30, 1599, one of the members of the *cabildo* reported that "many of the 'constables of the twenty' carried rented emblems with signatures that were counterfeit."[70] Lope de Vega was not exaggerating when, in the *Arenal de Sevilla*, he caused one of his characters to appear with the emblem of a constable, saying that he had bought it that day and since there were so many constables in Seville he knew that he could carry it a year without being discovered.[71] In view of this welter of conflicting jurisdictions and corruption, effective policing of Seville was impossible.

If Sevillian life was characterized by materialism and covetousness, this was only natural in a city that was, in all respects, a house of trade. From the highest nobility to the lowest picaro, all attempted to share in the fruits of the American commerce. We have already seen how the spirit of gain changed the traditional concepts of the Sevillian aristocrats and made them into traders, while the newly-rich merchants—in an attempt to gain social prestige—used their wealth to purchase titles of nobility. Another factor that contributed to the ennoblement of wealthy merchants in Seville, as elsewhere in Spain during this period, was the penury of the royal treasury. The government found in the sale of rights of *hidalguía* a profitable source of income at a time when royal financial demands were great. Repeatedly the Seville city council complained to the King about this practice, and finally in 1582, in return for a loan of 50,000 ducats, secured his promise not to sell any more patents of nobility in Seville or in the area under her jurisdiction.[72]

With the sale of *hidalguías* went the distribution of municipal offices traditionally reserved to the nobility. The positions of *veinticuatro* (alderman) and *jurado* (common councilman were placed on the market, and opened to the highest bidder.[73]

Merchants solicited these posts not only for the social prestige inherent in them, but also for the economic advantages and exemptions they brought. The minutes of a city council meeting of April 8, 1598 clearly describe the situation:

"The people who try to purchase *hidalguías* and *veinticuatrías* are merchants, and businessmen who do so in order to further their own interests, and to facilitate the shipment of their merchandise, and the activities of their agents. . . . They pay excessive prices for the said patents [of nobility] and councilmanships in order to use these positions to avoid paying the customs duties [*almojarifazgo*] and to pressure the officials of the latter to pass their shipments without inspect-inspecting them." [74]

Although the special circumstances in Seville undoubtedly facilitated the rise of wealthier members of the middle class into the nobility, this phenomenon was not limited to Seville, for all over western Europe during the sixteenth and seventeenth centuries there was a strong tendency toward the ennoblement of the middle class.[75] It was the reality of nobles' trading in a country where commerce was frowned upon and considered dishonorable that especially marks Seville. Spanish traditional thought held that nobility and trade were incompatible, and that a noble would lose his status if he entered such a profession. As Suárez de Figueroa points out in his *El pasajero,* "I am sure that the only thing that prevents many from entering trade, although it is the way to become wealthy quickly, is the stigma of dishonor that it brings." [76]

Regardless of contemporary opinion as represented by the author of *El pasajero,* there is no evidence that the Sevillian nobility felt dishonored because of their mercantile activities. On the contrary, they believed that trade and nobility were compatible, and that they could engage in commerce without any loss of status or prestige. In the well-known commentary by Veitia on the Spanish trade with America, for example, we read: "Trading with the Indies by purchasing and shipping cargoes for wholesale disposal or exchange for native products is not detrimental to nobility. There is no objection thereto according to the prevailing customs and systems of sanctions. In fact, it is usual for very respected *caballeros* and even magnates to ship goods to the Indies." [77] This decisive change in attitude on the part of the Sevillian nobility during this period is also reflected in the contemporary plays and novels whose scene is set in Seville. In Castillo Solórzano's picaresque novel *La garduña de Sevilla,* one of the characters, Feliciano, is the son of a wealthy hidalgo who had increased his fortune through the American trade. [78] And in Lope de Vega's *El premio del bien hablar,* the main character, Leonarda, tells her suitor Don Juan—a typical unoccupied and impoverished Castilian hidalgo of the period, who has come to Seville on his way to America where he intends to seek his fortune—that she is the daughter of an *hidalgo* who trades with the New World, and that this does not dishonor her father in any manner. Lope expresses the same opinion in *La esclava de su galán* when Doña Elena describes herself as the daughter of a businessman who is a "well-born *hidalgo*." [79]

As all classes of Sevillian society clamored to share in the trade of the city, the river port became one of the most unique and attractive markets in Europe. Sevillian industry in itself, however, was never able to reach the production necessary to provision that famous market. Even the clothing industry, which was the most highly developed, could not meet the demands of both the city and the overseas trade. There was, moreover, a definite concentration upon the production of luxury goods. The largest guilds were those of the embroiderers, silversmiths, engravers, painters of religious images, and glaziers. [80] With the exception of agricultural products, Seville traded in foreign goods brought from other regions of Spain or from abroad; the city consumed this merchandise or sent it to the Indies. "What is unloaded in Seville comes from Flanders, England, Italy, and Venice," wrote Padre Tomás de Mercado in 1569. [81]

In contrast with Seville's limited industrial development was the abundant agricultural production of the city and surrounding areas. The districts between Seville and Alcalá and the region of Aljarafe were the richest olive and grape growing areas

39

in the peninsula. Seville olive oil, long an important item in international commerce, was furnished during the sixteenth century to "all the Kingdom, to the Indies and to so many other parts of the world." According to Morgado there were days during a year of good harvest when from 6,000 to 8,000 arrobas were registered in the Customhouse, and in the space of three or four hours it was all sold even before it had been unloaded. The olive was also an important export item. "It was highly solicited," wrote Morgado, "to eat alone or among the ingredients of salad or dressing." [82] Among the various olives grown, the best were those of manzanilla, and the finest of these was the *gordal*, which grew only in the proximity of the city. Even Navajero confessed that he had not seen their equal in any part.[83] Those of secondary class, called *moradas* from their purple color, were consumed locally or converted into an inferior oil.

The abundance of oil had, as early as the Moslem period, fostered the development of soap manufacturing. Two factories were in operation in the sixteenth century, one located in San Salvador parish and the other in Triana. The Triana establishment belonged to the Dukes of Alcalá, who leased it for periods of ten years at 20,000 ducats a year. This sum did not include the taxes and the "greater cost of the oil, lime, ashes, candles, and other materials, in addition to the many slaves and other workers that are neded in this manufacture." The scale of production of both factories was large: Morgado reports that in the Triana factory, which made only white soap, there were twelve cauldrons "which held 400 arrobas of oil, plus lime and ashes." [84] The dark soap of San Salvador manufacture was used locally, while the white soap of Triana was exported to the Indies, Flanders, and England.

In Seville and the region under her jurisdiction wine was as plentiful as olive oil.[85] Morgado believed that the wine produced in the city was as good as that brought into the river port from Cazalla and Guadalcanal. Contemporary literature, however, did not reflect his opinion; the wines of Alanís, Cazalla, Guadalcanal, and Membrilla were mentioned continuously, and it is apparent that even Sevillians considered them to be the best.[86] Nevertheless, the city government attempted to protect Sevillian production from competition: wines originating in areas outside her control were permitted entrance only on the payment of a duty. The largest market for both native and imported wine was the Indies, but Seville also exported to England and Flanders. In fact, the majority of the Spanish wines received in Antwerp during the sixteenth century arrived from southern ports, particularly Seville.[87]

Honey, sugar, and fruits of all kinds were abundant in the city and surrounding area, and made up a good part of Seville's exports abroad. Sugar, although not grown in Seville, was easily accessible at neighboring Las Cabezas de San Juan. As for fruits, all of the Sevillian region was an orchard, according to Andrea Navajero. The Venetian was especially impressed by the "infinitive groves of orange trees which in the month of May and all summer long, give off an odor so sweet that there is nothing like it in all the world." [88] Along the banks of the Guadalquivir he noted the extensive cultivation of citrus and other trees that produced all kinds of delicate fruits.

If everything that was bought and sold in Seville, except for agricultural products, arrived from the outside, then foreign vessels must have been continuously present in the river port. Nevertheless, very little is known about this trade because of the insufficiency of documentation.[89] We know, for example, that in the beginning of October, ships loaded with linens and other merchandise arrived at Seville and other Andalusian ports. The availability of these goods gave rise to a yearly fair called La Vendeja, and the linens sold there were known as "*vendeja* linens." [90] At the termination of the fair, the ships, their cargoes now composed of olive oil, wine, and the diverse fruits of the fertile Sevillian countryside, continued their voyages into the Mediterranean or turned northward to their home ports. Lope de Vega, in his *Arenal de Sevilla*, gives us a glimpse into this trade. "The French," observes Doña Laura, "bring cutlery, mercery and Roven cloth, and load oil [while] the Germans exchange their linen and fustian for Alanís wine." [91] Padre Mercado supplies us with a few more details; according to him, "The Sevillian merchants send wool, oil, and leather goods to Flanders, and receive mercery, tapestries, linen, and books. Florence, on the other hand, ships them spun gold, brocades, and silks in return for cochineal and leather." [92]

It was the American trade, however, which occupied most Sevillians and brought their city the largest profits. This trade has been described for us by the Dominican Friar, Tomás de Mercado, in his *Summa de tratos y contratos*, first published in 1569. [93] Mercado, a native Sevillian, compiled the *Summa* as a handbook for merchants engaged in the India trade. In it he pointed out the various pitfalls they would encounter that might endanger their salvation. In addition to his theological aims, the author presented a faithful image of the mechanics of the trade between Seville and the Indies. At times a caustic critic but always an attentive observer, Padre Mercado describes a vast chain of economic activity from the Andalusian metropolis to America.

Like most of his contemporaries, Mercado was deeply concerned with the inflation prevalent in both his native city and the New World. According to him, the price levels in the Indies were determined by the value of merchandise in Seville. If this was the impetus for the rise of prices in America, what, then, caused the high prices in Seville? Mercado believed that demand, purchases from foreign merchants, and speculation were the prime reasons. [94] The latter held particular weight in Mercado's analysis. "I saw," he said, "Granadan velvets selling from 28 to 29 reals when an impudent Seville merchant bought up all there was and in the space of fifteen days the price of velvets rose 35 to 36 per cent." Speculation was as common an occurrence in Seville as in the rest of the peninsula. Some, like the Genoese, specialized in the monopolization of the agricultural products of the Sevillian region. "In August and September the regraters buy large quantities of must; in November and in December the oil of Aljarafe; and in May and June all the wheat that they can lay their hands on." On many occasions, the activities of speculators attracted the attention of city officials. At a *cabildo* meeting in May, 1598, Juan Ponce de León, Mayor of Seville, reported that "although this province is one of the most fertile in the world, wheat and barley sell at excessive prices due to regrating, that is, many people buy up all the wheat before the harvest . . . and by monopolizing it, force the city to make agreements with them at exorbitant prices." [95] In this manner, the monopolists increased the prices of the products to be sent to the Indies "of the mercery from Flanders, the cloth of Segovia and Toledo, and the wine and oil of Aljarafe."

Monopolistic speculation was also an important feature of American business life.[96] "Some buy up all the wine that has arrived or all the ironware or all the silk goods, and since there is a great scarcity of all this merchandise, they make the purchasers pay as much as they can for it." In Vera Cruz it was customary for the merchants, in alliance with those of Mexico City, to purchase all the wine brought by a fleet and to hold it so as to profit from a situation of scarcity. A second factor that raised prices in America was the buying on credit in Seville from foreigners on long terms of payment. Clothing and manufactured goods, usually of foreign origin and brought to Seville by foreign merchants, were the articles most desired in the New World; merchants took advantage of the difference between the cost of production abroad and the selling price in Spain, buying cheap and selling dear. As a result, foreign goods that had been originally solicited for their low prices became more expensive than Spanish products. Despite the fact that merchandise purchased on credit cost more than that paid for with cash, buying and selling on time was characteristic of business transactions in the sixteenth century.[97] In the trade with the New World payments were due either in Seville or at the fairs of Medina del Campo after the return of the fleet.[98] Ordinarily the sum was divided into three parts: the first payment was due at the fair that coincided with the arrival of the fleet, while the other two were divided between the two following fairs.

In addition to credit purchasing, Mercado mentioned two other well-established sixteenth-century forms of trading used in the American trade. The most common practice was "payment with money and part time." "Sometimes," noted Mercado, "the total cost of a shipment is so large that it cannot be paid in cash or credited." In this case, one third or one fourth was paid in cash and the rest credited. In the Indies, prices varied according to the size of the cash payment and the length of time desired for payment.

Barter (*baratto, barata*), a vestige of medieval commerce, also maintained a place in Sevillian commercial life. In spite of its doubtful reputation, it remained honorable.[99] Barter, according to a sixteenth-century definition, was "no other thing but to deliver or change one manner of ware for another with hope to receive profit thereby." [100] Yet the barter described by Mercado was far more complicated. The origin of this transaction, he wrote, "is and was the need which many have for ready cash that they cannot borrow due to the short terms of repayment, and fearing that they will lose more by delaying the payment from fair to fair, they decide to barter. They buy a quantity of goods on credit and sell it immediately for cash, at less than its value. Thus, losing 25 or 30 per cent, they obtain money at a time when they need it most." Even this, the simplest form of barter known to Mercado, was not free from fraud in the hands of Sevillian merchants, because the man who credits the goods invariably asked more for them than they were worth. When he saw a poor man desperately in need he increased the price almost as high as would a regrater, and sometimes the creditor gave "ruined merchandise or that which could not be sold."

A second variety of barter, involving repurchase by the creditor of the same merchandise at 25 or 30 per cent less than the original sale price, was considered by Mercado to be "infernal." Many times it was merely a paper transaction, since the "goods did not leave his house or store." In a third manner of bartering brokers acted as intermediaries between buyers and sellers. Their objective was to gain a percentage over that of their normal brokerage commission. To obtain this extra profit the brokers took goods bought on credit and "looked for persons in need of money and who desired to barter." To the latter they sold the specified merchandise at a 20 to 30 per cent loss and then offered their services to find a merchant willing to accept the barter. To this individual they resold the goods, not losing more than 15 to 20 per cent. Their net gain was 5 or 6 per cent in addition to brokerage fees.[101]

The custom of trading on time and crediting the payment for the fair protected merchants from inconveniences and dangers caused by the frequent delays of the return fleets carrying the funds necessary to satisfy the debts. Pirates, enemy squadrons, storms, and the difficulties involved in transporting the treasure obstructed the scheduled sailings. But shipping on time increased the cost of the merchandise in America. Mercado gives a concrete example: "A vara of velvet worth 1,000 maravedís in Seville would cost 2,000 maravedís in the Indies. When it was bought on credit its price became 1,400 maravedís in Seville and 2,800 maravedís in the New World. . . . And if the price of some merchandise is lowered, it is only by 2 or 3 per cent." In America the goods coming from Spain were also sold on credit. "Formerly in Tierra Firme," noted Mercado, "they sold for cash . . . but now there are so many people and the quantity of the goods so great, that not even Peru with all its wealth could supply the funds to pay for a fleet composed of such a large number of ships." Regardless of the size of the fleet or the amount of merchandise, cash purchases were impossible, as there was little ready money.

The manner of selling in the Indies was "different from that used in Seville, the rest of Spain, outside the Kingdom, in Flanders, and Italy." At the fairs of Medina and in the other parts of the peninsula merchandise was sold at retail. "When a large quantity of goods is purchased by a merchant, it is by pieces," [102] while in the Indies the shipments, containing all the salable goods, from linens and mercery to ironware and wax, were sold together. "In one sale an investment of 8,000 to 10,000 ducats is disposed of." Nor was it unusual for American traders to purchase an entire cargo even before it was unloaded. These purchases in bulk offered definite compensations in price, and Mercado was quick to recognize the advantages in this mode of selling. "Evaluating each piece for itself, one arrives at a large sum," he noted. Moreover there was a great demand in the Indies for all kinds of manufactured goods, "even for brushes and hourglasses which are all brought from Spain." If such articles were sold individually they would cost more, but "by selling them together, some goods augment the value of others, while diminishing their own."

Upon the arrival of a fleet in Cartagena, Vera Cruz, or Portobello, a fair lasting from twenty to thirty days was opened. All purchases and sales were concluded during this period of time. Even before the fair began, the terms upon which the goods were to be sold were settled by mutual agreement between American and European traders and made public. After this, everyone began to dispose of his merchandise more or less in conformity with the established prices.[103] The average interest taken on all shipments was 60 per cent, which was to be paid, along with the total sum, in three installments. Interest rates, however, could run as high as 65 per cent or as low as 58 per cent, "depending upon the scarcity or abundance of some merchandise, particularly linens, silk, or paper." Although Mercado, as a theologian, was anxious to point out instances of usury, he considered even the 65 per cent interest rate to be just. "But if the purchaser asks to credit his goods at four-sevenths [that is, for payments of one-seventh each time], the interest rate on his purchases will rise to 80 per cent and even more for longer installments." This placed the American traders at the mercy of the merchant-monopolists of Seville.

In the New World prices were not influenced by the number of buyers or the availability of ready money; such conditions as the inland demand and the size of the fleet were far more important. The expectation of another fleet within a short period of time could reduce prices by half. Aside from these factors

46

prices were set freely, for government policy ruled against fixing prices or interfering with the practices of the market except for the imposition of custom duties and other taxes. A royal cedula of April 8, 1538, decreed that "the authorities should not set standard prices on the wine, wheat, and other provisions and merchandise that the merchants of this kingdom ship to the Indies . . . and we permit them to sell wholesale or retail." [104] Fifteen years later this law was applied to the American merchants. Nevertheless, prohibitions against trading in some articles existed and were maintained throughout the century. An ordinance of the Casa de Contratación in 1504 prohibited the shipment to the Indies of gold, silver, money, horses, mares, slaves, arms, or base gold (guañines) without a license and without paying the taxes and customs prescribed.[105] As the century progressed the specific list of things that could be exported freely was always several times as long as those for which a license was required. The objective of the government was not to monopolize the trade in those articles, but to regulate it and to draw revenue from it.

The profit of the Sevillian merchant who bought on credit and sent his merchandise on consignment to be sold at the best price in the American fair was unusually large. Mercado believed that it could be as high as 100 per cent, but if the cost of transportation, the travelling expenses of the merchant or his factor, and the damages to the merchandise are considered, the total would probably amount to half. In any event, it was the American trade that brought the Sevillian merchants, and especially the Genoese, the extraordinary wealth that created their city's "Golden Age" during the sixteenth century, and their own fame and prosperity.

CHAPTER III

The Opening of the New World

THE Genoese colony of Seville played a principal role in the sixteenth-century trade between Spain and Spanish America. No group was better prepared to participate in the newly opened commercial relations between the Old and New Worlds. Established in Seville since the reconquest, the Genoese had built up large reserves of capital through their combined activities of commerce and moneylending.[1] In the sixteenth century, this ready capital enabled them to assume a commanding position in the American trade. As they had successfully joined commerce and finance in the Middle Ages, they continued to do so in the sixteenth century. The aggressiveness, opportunism, and covetousness, which had for so long characterized their economic endeavors, ruled out any kind of specialization. All members of the Genoese colony of Seville were both merchants who traded with the New World and capitalists who financed the trade of others.

No separation can be made between the commercial activities of the Genoese in Seville and their financial relations with the Spanish monarchs. Since the fourteenth century members of the Sevillian colony had loaned money to Castilian sovereigns, and they continued this tradition in the sixteenth century.[2] A large part of the fortunes made in the American trade was loaned to Charles V and Philip II. Throughout the century Sevillian Genoese shared their position as royal creditors with their relatives at the Spanish Court, in Genoa, and in Antwerp. But unlike their Ligurian compatriots, they did not abandon trade in order to concentrate on finance.[3] In the early years of the century, those who participated in financial dealings with Charles V, such as Agustín de Vivaldo, traveled back and forth between the court and Seville.[4] By the 1550's, several of the most prominent Sevillian Genoese—for example, Andrea Spínola and Hector Doria—had taken up permanent residence at court (see Table 1). They did not discontinue their commercial

Table 1. Members of the Sevillian Genoese colony at court during the sixteenth century *

Name	Year
Alejandro Cataño	1550
Jácome Cataño	1550
Cristóbal Centurión	1551
Hector Doria	1550
Constantín Gentil	1554
Juan Batista Gentil	1577
Carlos Jufre de Lercaro	1551
Cristóbal Lercaro	1551
Hector Picamelías (Piccamiglia)	1580
Esteban Salvago	1527
Andrea Spínola	1580
Antonio Spínola	1550
Jácome Spínola	1580
Agustín de Vivaldo	1526

* This table is based solely on the Sevillian Protocols, and includes only those Genoese who are recorded as residents of the court. It does not exclude the possible existence there of others not mentioned in the notarial registers. As such, only an approximate value can be given to this table.

activities in Seville, however, but simply placed the management of their investments in the hands of partners or agents.[5]

Loans and credits played a vital part in the relations between Seville and America. In particular, the Genoese made loans to persons departing for the New World, helping them to arm their ships or to cover the cost of merchandise. Under the terms of the sea loan they accepted the risk of safe arrival in return for a considerable compensation in the form of interest. As early as 1509, interest rates were so high that the Archbishop of Seville tried to prohibit these transactions but was deterred by King Ferdinand, who sanctioned the loans on the grounds of economic necessity.[6] By mid-century, 80 to 90 per cent was taken from shipmasters, and 50 to 60 per cent from passengers in need.

Often, the Genoese agreed to deliver merchandise on credit instead of furnishing cash.[7] In this arrangement the interest was included in the higher valuation of the goods, which ostensibly served to compensate the delay in repayment. The borrower counted on the profit from the sale in America to enable him to repay the debt. If in the original operation the credit contract was different from the loan, both terminated in the same way.[8] In general, the majority of the Genoese merchants of Seville preferred to grant loans rather than sales credit, although one of the richest members of the colony during the first decades of the century, Jácome de Grimaldo, was involved in a considerable number of such credit dealings (see Table 2). Lucas Pinelo and Batista Cataño also divided their investment between loans and credits.

In the beginning, the settlement of loans and credits took place in Seville after the return of the borrower. As closer economic ties were established between the Old and the New Worlds, such debts were more and more frequently redeemed in America.[9] The Genoese were interested in recovering their investment at the earliest possible moment, not wanting to prolong an operation that distance and dishonesty made dangerous. Moreover, they looked for the possibility of additional profit on a ship that might be returning with precious metals.

From 1513 to 1517, Juan Francisco de Grimaldo and Gaspar Centurión were among the most active Genoese capitalists in Seville. They worked together in a regular fashion but, in accordance with the Genoese custom of individual enterprise, were not joined by any bonds of partnership. As Tables 3 and 4 indicate, the majority of their sea loans were granted for the dispatch of merchandise rather than for the provisioning of ships. Their most active borrowers were Spanish merchants who did not have funds to cover the costs of shipment and were thus completely dependent on the Genoese capitalists.[10] More of the profits from the trade with the New World accrued to such

Table 2. Loans and credits granted by
Jácome de Grimaldo in 1508

Date	Amount	Type
14 Feb.	62,300 mrs. *	loan
29 Feb.	59,910 mrs.	loan
22 Mar.	90 ducats	loan
24 Mar.	92,450 mrs.	loan
— Mar.	15,000 mrs.	credit
14 Apr.	11,500 mrs.	credit
19 Apr.	23,500 mrs.	credit
27 Apr.	10,200 mrs.	loan
29 Apr.	15,400 mrs.	loan
4 May	300 ducats	loan
8 May	90 ducats	loan
8 May	150 ducats	loan
29 May	30 ducats	loan
22 Sept.	31,950 mrs.	credit
16 Nov.	32,000 mrs.	credit
16 Nov.	30,030 mrs.	credit
5 Dec.	150 ducats	loan
16 Dec.	336,000 mrs.	credit

* 375 maravedís (mrs.) = 1 ducat.
Source: The Sevillian Protocols.

capitalists rather than to the merchants who were crushed by high interest rates or by the heavy advances they were forced to make.

Another important part of Genoese participation in the transatlantic trade was the shipment of goods to America. As early as 1500, Francisco de Riberol and the Aragonese Juan Sánchez de Mercadería sent out two caravels to Hispaniola with provisions for the starving colonists, but those vessels never reached the New World. The Catholic kings claiming that the two businessmen had not secured proper royal license, forced the

51

Table 3. Investment in sea loans for 1513—Juan Francisco de Grimaldo and Gaspar Centurión

Date	Amount	Purpose	Borrowers	Ship	Destination
13 Feb.	142 ducats	dispatch of merchandise	Francisco de Jerez, money changer	*San Cristóbal*	Santo Domingo
20 Aug.	3,812 mrs.*	dispatch of merchandise	Pedro Fernández de Córdoba, merchant	*Santa María de la Luz*	Santo Domingo
25 Aug.	70 ducats	dispatch of merchandise	Juan de Campo, "vecino de Puerto Real en las Indias", and Alonso de Velasco, master of ship *Trinidad*	*Trinidad*	Santo Domingo
7 Sept.	8,400 mrs.	dispatch of merchandise	Juan de Campo, "estante en Indias" Francisco de Olaso, "vecino de Buenaventura en las Indias" and Alfonso de Velasco as guarantor	*Trinidad*	Santo Domingo
7 Sept.	278 ducats	dispatch of merchandise	Bernardino de Santa Clara and Antonio de Santa Clara	*Buen Jesús*	Santo Domingo
10 Sept.	70 ducats	provisioning and dispatch of ship	Alonso Fernández, master	*Santiago*	Santo Domingo
14 Sept.	12,600 mrs.	dispatch of merchandise	Vicente Yáñez Pinzón	*San Francisco*	Santo Domingo
14 Sept.	15 ducats	provisioning and dispatch of ship	Francisco Fernández, master	*Santiago*	Santo Domingo
16 Sept.	6,800 mrs.	dispatch of merchandise	?	?	Santo Domingo
5 Oct.	35 ducats	dispatch of merchandise	Pedro de Espinosa, apostolic notary	*Santa María de la Antigua*	Santo Domingo
5 Oct.	70 ducats	dispatch of merchandise	Diego Fernández, merchant	Ship of Ambrosio Sánchez	Santo Domingo
7 Oct.	138 ducats	dispatch of merchandise	Fernandez de Berrio, notary public of Seville and Cristóbal Suárez, master	*Santa María de los Remedios*	San Germán P.R. and Santo Domingo
7 Oct.	14 ducats	dispatch of ship	Cristóbal Suárez, master	*Santa María de los Remedios*	Santo Domingo
14 Oct.	14 ducats	dispatch of ship	Cristóbal Suárez, master	*Santa María de los Remedios*	Santo Domingo
15 Oct.	246 ducats	provisioning and dispatch of merchandise	Ambrosio Sánchez, master and Fernando de Berrio, notary public of Seville	*San Francisco de Buenaventura*	Santo Domingo
Total	1,194 ducats				

Table 4. Investment in sea loans for 1517—Juan Francisco de Grimaldo and Gaspar Centurión

Date	Amount	Purpose	Borrowers	Ship	Destination
Date missing	10 . . . ?	provisioning of ship	Cristóbal Sánchez, owner of ¼ of ship San Francisco and master of it and Bartolomé Díaz, owner of ¾ of it	*San Francisco*	Santo Domingo
6 Mar.	100 ducats	provisioning of ship	Bartolomé Fernández Franco, master	*Santa María del Antigua*	Cuba
6 Mar.	13 ducats	provisioning of ship	Cristóbal Sánchez, master	*San Francisco*	Santo Domingo
20 Mar.	21 ducats	provisioning and dispatch of merchandise	Fernando Gallego, master and Pedro de Medina, merchant and Martín de Escalante	*Caravel Santa Cruz*	Santiago de Cuba
22 Apr.	65 ducats	dispatch of merchandise	Luis de Aranda, merchant and Juan Carrillo	*Santa María del Antigua*	Santo Domingo
2 May	16,900 mrs.	dispatch of merchandise	Pedro Camacho	*Santa María*	Santo Domingo
2 May	30,000 mrs.	dispatch of merchandise	Gaspar de Montalbán, merchant, "vecino de Santo Domingo" in the name of his father Lope de Montalbán	*San Juan*	Santo Domingo
7 May	250 ducats	provisioning of ship	Cristóbal Valles, master	*Santa María del Antigua*	Santo Domingo
8 May	130 ducats	provisioning of ship	Juan Martínez, master and Francisco de Canaria, merchant	*San Andrés*	Santo Domingo
19 May	32½ ducats	provisioning of ship	Cristóbal Suárez, master	*Santa María de los Remedios*	Santo Domingo
25 May	6,850 mrs.	provisioning of ship	Juan Martínez, master	*San Andrés*	Santo Domingo
3 June	100 ducats	dispatch of merchandise	Antón Rodríguez, owner and Martín de Solís	*San Francisco*	Santo Domingo
8 June	82 ducats	dispatch of merchandise provisioning of ship	Juan Ramos, master and Francisco Rodríguez Zarco, as guarantor	*San Miguel*	Santo Domingo
15 June	15,000 mrs.	provisioning of ship	Pedro . . . ?	*Caravel Santa María de las Nieves*	Hispaniola

Table 4 (Continued)

Date	Amount	Purpose	Borrowers	Ship	Destination
15 June	252 ducats	dispatch of merchandise	Diego Méndez "vecino de Santo Domingo" and Martín Núñez, master	*Santa María del Antigua*	Santo Domingo
29 June	26 ducats	dispatch of merchandise	Don Juan de Santa María, archpriest of the Ch. of Santa María de la Concepción de la Vega and Alonso de Guadix, merchant	*Santa Catalina*	Santo Domingo
3 Aug.	30 ducats	dispatch of merchandise	Fernando Pinto	*La barca de Santa María*	Santo Domingo
17 Aug.	13 ducats	dispatch of merchandise	same as 29 June	same as 29 June	Santo Domingo
19 Aug.	214,000 mrs.	provisioning of ship	Juan Rodríguez, master	*La barca de Santa María*	Santo Domingo
22 Aug.	26 ducats	dispatch of merchandise	Alfonso de Guadix, merchant	*Santa Catalina*	Puerto Rico
5 Oct.	30 ducats	dispatch of merchandise	Cristóbal de León, merchant	*Santa María*	Darien
14 Oct.	9 ducats	dispatch of merchandise	Juan de Villacosta, servant of the Adelantado Juan Ponce de León, "vecino de la isla de San Juan."	*San Francisco*	island of San Juan
18 Nov.	32½ ducats	dispatch of merchandise	Gonzalo Fernández, royal notary	*San Francisco*	Santo Domingo
Total	1,946 ducats				

* 375 maravedis (mrs.) = 1 ducat.
Source: The Sevillian Protocols.

ships to return to Spain and ordered an embargo on their goods.[11] Although this first attempt by a member of the Genoese colony of Seville to trade with the Indies was unsuccessful, by 1504 the Governor of Hispaniola was obliged to inform King Ferdinand that most of the merchandise entering the island belonged to Genoese and foreigners.[12] Life in America during the first decades of the sixteenth century was such that demand existed for only the most necessary foodstuffs and clothing. Domestic animals, wine, oil, cheese, flour, and all kinds of cloth and clothing made up the overseas cargoes. The following shipment, sent to Hispaniola in 1508 by Lucas Pineolo, is typical: it included "6 casks of vinegar, 240 porcelain cups, 149 arrobas of oil, 400 pairs of shoes, 15 fanegas of chickpeas, 6 bales of paper, 4 rolls of coarse cloth, 36 arrobas of soap and 8 calves." [13] By the second half of the century the growing self-sufficiency of the New World caused a gradual decline in the trade of food products, whereas the development of a wealthy class in America created a demand for European manufactured goods and luxury items. After mid-century ships bound for Vera Cruz, Portobello, and Cartagena carried all kinds of fine manufactured items, the products of French, Flemish, and English industry.[14]

There were also traces of a regular traffic in Negro slaves, an enterprise that enriched many Genoese families by mid-century. In the years following the discovery of America, licenses to export Negro slaves to the West Indies were frequently granted to courtiers, explorers, colonists, and royal functionaries. The government insisted only that the slaves be Christians, meaning that they had either been born in Spain or had resided there long enough to be baptized, because the Spanish monarchs were anxious to keep the settlements free from religious taint.[15] In 1501, for example, Governor Ovando was specifically authorized to take over Christianized slaves born in the Peninsula, but this permission was withdrawn by Isabella two years later at the Governor's request, for he reported that the Negroes fled and corrupted the Indians. After Isabella's death in 1504, however, Ferdinand, less zealous in religious matters than his wife and more interested in augmenting royal revenues, occasionally sent out a few to labor in the mines. In 1510 he gave permission to ship slaves from Seville to a maximum of two hundred, for sale to the settlers or for work on the royal properties. He also frequently allowed the inhabitants of the islands to take a limited number of slaves with them to America for their own personal service, but he prohibited their sale.[16]

Until 1513, royal permits, or licenses to transport slaves to America, were distributed by the government to favored individuals as free gifts, but in July of that year King Ferdinand decided, as a fiscal measure, to impose a charge of two ducats on each license so granted. The King's objective was to gain additional government revenue from a more liberal distribution of licenses. In line with this new policy he issued a decree in 1514 fixing an export tax of 120 maravedís on each slave, to be paid by the recipient of the license. Although the King was careful to limit the number of licenses available for purchase, they were, at this time as later, freely bought and sold on the market, and at competitive prices.[17] In fact, their very scarcity immediately increased their value and favored the development of a speculative market.

Among the first to buy and sell licenses for speculative purposes were the Genoese. Just three months after the July cedula, on October 12, 1513, Jácome de Grimaldo sold a license to send a slave to Hispaniola for the exorbitant price of fifteen ducats to a Sevillian notary, Juan Aguado. The Genoese were apparently taking full advantage of the speculative boom in licenses that followed the 1513 decree. Under these circumstances it is not surprising that they preferred to deal in licenses rather than undertake the difficulties involved in transporting and selling slaves in America. By 1514, however, the boom had passed, and we begin to find more references to their actual participation in the shipment and sale of slaves in the colonies. A series of notary deeds issued in June gives us some idea of their role in this early trade. On June 10th Francisco de Garay, a councilman of the city of Santo Domingo, authorized Niculoso

Cataño to obtain for him twelve Christian slaves to be transported to Hispaniola. Two days later, the Councilman sold Cataño one of these slaves—"an adult male Negro from Guinea" —for 3,000 maravedís, and on June 13, Cataño made an agreement with Lope Sánchez, master of the *San Francisco,* to carry this slave to the Indies. In a subsequent deed issued on the same day the Genoese businessman empowered Sánchez to take charge of the sale of this slave in the New World.[18] No price was set in the document, but it was assumed that Sánchez would dispose of him at a price high enough to cover his own commission and bring a profit to Cataño. Other members of the Genoese colony of Seville involved in the slave trade were Juan Francisco de Grimaldo and Gaspar Centurión; these two versatile businessmen sent a small, but steady stream of slaves to Hispaniola during this early period.[19]

The limited but profitable trade in slaves between Seville and America during the reign of Ferdinand came to a temporary halt in 1516 with the death of the king. The Cardinal-Regent Cisneros suspended the traffic, pending a thorough investigation of the license system which he held unsatisfactory from the fiscal point of view. Cisneros believed that the slave trade should be taxed more heavily and thus bring the government larger revenues.[20] But the Cardinal's thoughts and actions were contrary to those of the new king, Charles I of Spain, later Emperor Charles V, who, while still in Flanders, was persuaded by his courtiers to grant licenses for the importation of Negro slaves into the West Indies, to the number of six hundred or more.[21] Notwithstanding the protests of Cisneros, Charles allowed the Lord of Chièvres, the recipient of these licenses, to send the specified number of slaves to Santo Domingo. Moreover, the King soon received recommendations from the Hieronymite Friars governing the island at that time, from the "Apostle of the Indies," Bartolomé de las Casas, and from the clergy of Santo Domingo, all urging him to spare the Indians by a more general substitution of Negro labor.[22]

In 1518 Charles issued the first license to transport Negroes in quantity directly from Africa to America, to a Flemish favorite, Laurent de Gouvenot, Master of the Royal Household. It involved the sole privilege for eight years of introducing African slaves into the Indies, to a maximum of 4,000, free of all fiscal obligations.[23] Gouvenot, desirous of obtaining quick profits, and unwilling to become involved in the difficulties of obtaining and disposing of these slaves, immediately sold his privilege for 25,000 ducats to the Genoese-controlled firm of Fernán Vázquez, Domingo and Tomás de Forne, and Agustín de Vivaldo.[24] We do not know how many slaves they actually sent to the colonies during the first year of their monopoly, or if indeed they sent any, but it is clear that they resold many of the licenses at speculative prices, ranging from 8 to 12½ ducats apiece. Eventually in this manner and through the sale of their slaves in the New World, they were able to make a profit of nearly 300,000 ducats on their original investment.[25]

One year after purchasing the Gouvenot privilege, Vázquez, Forne, and Vivaldo decided to exploit their monopoly with greater efficiency by putting it on a more organized basis. Since the members of the firm spent most of their time at the royal court, they found it difficult to control their affairs in Seville, particularly those related to the slave monopoly. They needed a trustworthy associate in that city, and they soon found one—in the person of Gaspar Centurión. In 1519 the firm commissioned Centurión to take charge of the shipment of their slaves to America. This Sevillian Genoese and his associates were determined to sell their slaves at the highest possible prices, but they realized that the sudden introduction of large shiploads of Negroes into the New World would immediately lower their value. Therefore, in order to keep up the price level, they decided to create a fictitious shortage in the colonies by sending out only small groups of slaves at a time, and by allowing long intervals to elapse between shipments. In this way, they believed that they could maintain maximum prices, and keep their profits high during the whole period of their monopoly.[26]

To oversee the sale of their slaves in the New World the firm chose as their American agent, Melchor Centurión, a brother of their Sevillian partner Gaspar, and a merchant of long-standing in Seville.[27] They realized that the proper functioning of their business depended to a large degree on their colonial representative, and so great care was taken to select a person who would be clearly identified with their interests. Melchor's close business association with his brother and his experience and connections both in Seville and America determined their choice. It was further agreed that he would reside in Santo Domingo for the duration of the monopoly, and that he would personally receive and arrange for the disposal of all slaves sent by the company to the island.[28] It was also his duty to establish and maintain contact with the firm's other agents in Puerto Rico and Cuba and to keep his European partners informed of market conditions throughout the colonies.

The success of the firm's manipulations was soon apparent. From 1519 on, royal officials on Hispaniola complained to King Charles, by now Holy Roman Emperor, that there was a critical shortage of African slaves on the island, and that prices were unusually high. In a letter written from Hispaniola in July 1520, Licentiate Figueroa claimed that no shipments of slaves had reached the island for about a year.[29] For this reason he advised the monarch to limit Gouvenot's privilege to four years, and to open the trade to the colonists. Subsequent communications from the members of the *cabildo* of Santo Domingo urged him to pay the Genoese their 25,000 ducats and to revoke the monopoly. Regardless of all these protests, the Emperor allowed Gouvenot's privilege to run its full eight years, and even renewed it before the end of its term, at the latter's request, for a similar period of time.[30] Nevertheless, the colonists complained so bitterly about the renewal that Charles V was finally forced to revoke the monopoly in 1526. From this time until the end of the century, with the exception of the years 1528 to 1532, the government administered the supply of slaves to the colonies under the license system.[31]

Although the revocation of the Gouvenot grant brought an

59

end to the monopolization of the slave trade by Vázquez, Forne, and Vivaldo, it did not cause the firm to suffer any serious financial loss, for they had long before obtained their profits from the venture.[32] Indeed, both the firm and the Sevillian Genoese gained from this action; it opened the way for full-scale participation in the Afro-American slave trade by all the members of the Genoese colony of Seville, for it made possible the purchase of licenses at will from the government. As for Vázquez, Forne, and Vivaldo, it meant that they no longer had to limit their shipments so as to maintain prices, but could now, under the new competitive conditions, expand their activities and profits. In the 1530's and 1540's most of the slaves sent out by the firm went to supply the needs of the expanding sugar industry on the islands of Hispaniola and Puerto Rico. Since the millowners were usually in debt because of costly initial outlays and high operating costs, they paid for these slaves in sugar rather than cash.[33] By mid-century the firm's principal business in the New World consisted of the exchange of slaves for sugar.

Besides Vázquez, Forne, and Vivaldo there were many other members of the Genoese colony of Seville who were especially active in the slave trade during the years 1520–1540. Among the most prominent was Pedro Benito de Basiñana. In 1526 Basiñana formed a partnership with the clergyman Álvaro de Castro, a resident of the town of Concepción on Hispaniola, who had just received royal permission to introduce 200 slaves into that island.[34] These slaves were destined for the farms, plantations, and sugar mills of Concepción where Castro had large holdings. According to the terms of the agreement between the clergyman and the merchant the latter agreed to take charge of the whole operation, that is, the purchase of the slaves in Africa, their transport to Hispaniola, and their disposal on the island. Basiñana, in turn, commissioned Esteban Carrega, a compatriot and well-known Sevillian shipmaster, to sail along the African coast, gather a cargo of 100 slaves and carry them, as a first shipment, to Santo Domingo. A member of Basiñana's family, Esteban, was to accompany Carrega on the voyage, and to supervise the sale of the slaves upon their arrival in Hispaniola. He was also to remain in the New World as Pedro Benito's agent.[35]

It seems that Carrega made several runs between Seville, Africa, and Hispaniola under the Castro license. Moreover, the success of their arrangement with Castro encouraged the three Genoese to think in terms of expanding their business; therefore when the Castro-Basiñana agreement lapsed, Pedro Benito secured several new licenses from Charles V permitting them to ship slaves not only to Hispaniola but to the other islands as well. One of these licenses permitted them to send a total of 80 slaves to Cuba. On their first trip to that island Carrega and Esteban Basiñana disposed of 40 slaves, but on their second trip they brought in 75, thus making a total of 115 slaves of which 35 were clearly illegal under the terms of their license.[36] The Genoese offered to pay the customs duties on the illegal 35 slaves in return for their acceptance. This was the usual procedure in such cases, for the critical labor shortage in the New World had for a long time forced royal officials to countenance the illegal introduction of slaves into the colonies. Permission was therefore given to the Genoese to dispose of their whole human cargo on the island. Shortly afterwards, however, Basiñana had certain differences with the Governor of Cuba, Gonzalo de Guzmán, who suddenly seized the Genoese and imprisoned him. Basiñana eventually escaped from jail and took refuge in the town church, claiming the right of asylum under the prevailing ecclesiastical privilege.[37] A series of unfortunate incidents soon followed in which Basiñana became the "cause célèbre" of a scandalous conflict of jurisdictions between the Governor, cabildo of the town of Santiago, and the Church. The Basiñana case is surely one of the most curious episodes involving a member of the Genoese colony of Seville.

Although Basiñana, in taking refuge in the Santiago church, was following an accepted and traditional practice of the sixteenth century, Governor Guzmán, for reasons that he never made clear, refused to recognize the right of asylum in this

61

case.[38] Determined therefore to remove the Genoese from his sanctuary, the Governor eventually appeared, accompanied by a group of armed followers, at the church. When it became apparent to the clergy that Guzmán was actually going to seize Basiñana, and thereby break the inviolability of church sanctuary, one of the priests rushed up to the altar and seized the monstrance containing the consecrated Host. Holding it up before the Governor, he entreated him not to proceed any further out of respect for the presence of the Lord. Guzmán was then reputed to have said: "Our Lord is in heaven and not here," and with these words, proceeded to remove the prisoner from the church, ignoring the consternation of an astonished and frightened clergy. From there Basiñana was transferred to the city jail where he was placed under heavy guard.

The Governor's next move was just as surprising as his first. With the Genoese safely locked behind bars, Guzmán and followers then went over to the City Hall where the members of the municipal council were holding one of their regular meetings. Entering into the room in which they were assembled, Guzmán, in an apparent rage, walked over to the constable Bernardino de Quesada and "attacked him, tearing his shirt and breaking his staff [of justice]." He then arrested all of them, claiming that they had conspired to protect Basiñana and had refused to help him remove the Genoese from the church.

Reports of the Governor's actions soon found their way to Hispaniola and to the attention of the members of the Audiencia. Disturbed by these rumors, the royal judges decided to send a special commissioner (juez pesquisidor), accompanied by a constable and notary, to Cuba to make a thorough investigation of the situation. When these officials arrived in the island, they found that the church authorities, in the person of the Vicar-General Sancho de Céspedes had already condemned Guzmán for his disregard of their privileges and had subjected him to penance.[39] After conducting their inquiry, the royal agents returned to Santo Domingo and made an unfavorable report about Governor Guzmán to the Audiencia. The judges then wrote to Charles V informing him of the circumstances of this strange case.[40] At the same time, the Governor, aware of their report, sent an appeal to the monarch in which he claimed that his original imprisonment of Basiñana was justified, on the grounds of "the gravity of the crimes that the latter had committed," and that his later seizure of the prisoner from the church was necessary in order "to uphold and enforce royal justice.[41] As for his presumed blasphemy on the occasion of the church incident, he claimed that he had never made such a statement, and that the clergy had invented it to discredit him.

Although Charles V and the Council of the Indies were faced with conflicting evidence in this case, it was clear to them that more than the apparent conflict between the Governor and the Church over their respective rights and privileges was involved here. This unpleasant episode was a direct result of the lax attitude taken by the Governor and the royal officials of Cuba toward the illegal entrance of slaves into the island. The Emperor, therefore decided to take stronger measures against the underlying causes rather than the results of the controversy. A stern reprimand was sent to Governor Guzmán instructing him to respect the immunities of the clergy and to obey the decrees of the Audiencia. This was followed by a royal cedula ordering the immediate confiscation, without exception, of all Negro slaves introduced illegally into the Indies, that is, without royal license.[42] The prohibitory legislation of 1528 thus owed its origin to the actions of a Genoese merchant in Cuba.[43] As for the principal protagonist in the drama, he was eventually released from prison, and in the 1530's could be found in Santo Domingo where he continued to devote himself to the slave trade in association with his relative Pedro Benito de Basiñana.[44]

In the 1540's and 1550's numerous other Sevillian Genoese began to turn more actively to the Afro-American slave trade. The growing self-sufficiency of the New World, the resulting decline of the staple trade, and the increase in slave prices, all combined to influence many of the Genoese to concentrate more of their efforts on the slave trade. Prices had risen steadily during the first half of the century, and slaves that sold for 45 ducats in 1528 brought 100 ducats in the islands and 120 ducats in Mexico by 1556. This trend continued in the last quarter of the century stimulated by a growing demand, the result of the continued territorial expansion on the mainland and the official ban against enslaving the Indians.[45]

Two families, the Cataño and Negrón, were particularly active in the trade around mid-century. Not only did they send large numbers of slaves into the colonies, but they also extended their control over the vessels engaged in the trade. The ownership of slavers by members of the Genoese colony coincided generally with their new interest in the ships that plowed the Atlantic between Seville and America.[46] Members of the Cataño and Negrón families owned several of the vessels that ran slaves between Africa and Vera Cruz—one of the main ports of entry for slaves on the mainland. Among the Cataño was Nicolás, whose ship, the *Trinidad,* made numerous slave runs during the 1540's and 1550's. In 1541, within a six month period, Nicolás, in partnership with his relative Jerónimo and with Juan Francisco de Vivaldo, sent 350 slaves to Vera Cruz.[47] As for the Negrón, Licentiate Carlos de Negrón owned two important slavers, the *Santa María de Gracia* in the 1540's and the *San Salvador* in the 1550's.[48] Both ships made yearly voyages transporting their human cargo from Africa to the islands and Mexico.

Royal financial demands contributed to the increased participation by the Cataño, Negrón, and other Sevillian Genoese in the slave trade. Many of the licenses that they obtained came into their hands not through purchase, but were granted them by the government in return for confiscated American bullion. Although dispossessed persons were usually compensated with *juros,* slave licenses were also given in return for these forced loans. Such a license granted to Jerónimo Cataño in 1536 is typical of its kind. According to its provisions, Cataño received permission to ship 76 slaves to the New World in return for a sum of 226,400 maravedís that the government had confiscated from him in that same year.[49] One third of these slaves were to be women and all were free from fiscal obligations including the customs duty.

Other Sevillian Genoese involved in the slave trade were Tomás de Marín and Leonardo Lomelín. In 1540 these two businessmen formed a partnership dedicated to the trade of slaves and sugar between Seville and Mexico. Two years later, in return for a loan of 6,300 ducats, Charles V granted them a license to send 900 slaves to the colonies.[50] Many of these slaves were transported to Vera Cruz on Nicolás Cataño's *Trinidad*. Cataño was closely associated with Lomelín, and in 1550–1551, when Lomelín was not in Seville but at the royal court, he served as Lomelín's proxy in a lawsuit before the officials of the Casa de Contratación.[51]

The majority of the slaves sent to Mexico by Lomelín and Marín were sold to Hernando Cortés for use on the sugar mills that he had established at Tuxtla near Vera Cruz and at Tlaltenango in Cuernavaca.[52] In 1542 the relations between the Genoese firm and Cortés were placed on a firmer basis when the latter signed two contracts with them, looking toward the exchange of his sugar for their slaves. One of these contracts called for the immediate shipment to Mexico by Lomelín and Marín of 500 slaves worth 75 ducats a head. Delivery was to be made in Vera Cruz through the firm's representatives in that city, Juan Bautista de Marín and Juan de Camilla. Under the terms of the other agreement, Lomelín and Marín pledged themselves to purchase all of the sugar from Cortés' mills of Tuxtla and Tlaltenango, and to arrange for its transport to Vera Cruz, and from there to Spain.[53] Juan Bautista de Marín and Juan de Camilla were again placed in charge of this transaction. Accordingly, on August 16, 1543 the two agents accompanied by Antonio Fiesco, another company representative recently arrived from Spain, presented themselves at the Tlaltenango mill. There they collected 131 arrobas of sugars (almost 52 toneladas) divided into three kinds: white sugar, browns (panelas), and muscovado (*moscabado*), all of which made up the first ship-

65

ment sent to Seville under the Cortés-Genoese contract.[54]

During the years 1545–1547 the Lomelín-Marín factors sent five shipments of sugars to Spain that eventually brought 7,976,789 maravedís in profits. One of the last shipments was dispatched in 1548 on the ship *Victoria* and consisted of 63 wooden boxes containing 132 arrobas of white sugar.[55] Cortes' death in 1547 and the financial difficulties that he had experienced with Lomelín in the months preceding his decease influenced his heir, Martín Cortés, not to renew the contract. Besides, the firm's capable factor, Juan Bautista de Marín, was now in Cortés' own employ as central treasurer and principal assistant to Pedro de Alumada, the administer of the Cortés estates in the New World.[56] Yet Don Martín's dissatisfaction with Lomelín and Marín did not, on the other hand, prejudice him against the Sevillian Genoese. In 1550 he apparently entered into another agreement with a Sevillian Genoese company, for their factor, Tolomeo Spínola, took charge of Cortes' sugar shipments from Vera Cruz in the following year.[57] There exists, among the documents in the Archivo de Protocolos, a partnership contract dated January 29, 1550, between Tolomeo and several leading Genoese—Constantín and Luis Spínola, Lucas Pinelo, Octaviano de Negrón, and Antonio Fiesco, the former Lomelín-Marín agent—for the trade of merchandise and slaves between Seville and New Spain. It is quite possible that Fiesco was the leading spirit in organizing this partnership, and that it was formed with the objective of entering into a contract with Cortés through the good offices of Fiesco. The new partnership represented a total capitalization of 12,000 ducats of which Tolomeo invested one third, the remaining two thirds being contributed by the others. Under its provisions, Tolomeo was "to accompany the investment (slaves and merchandise) to New Spain and sell it there" [58] and to share equally with the others in the division of the profits. One year later, Tolomeo, by this time in Vera Cruz, sent 1,521 arrobas of sugars from Cortés' Tuxtla mill to Spain in two shipments. In 1554 the *San Esteban* carried 340 arrobas of sugars from the Orizaba mill recently

66

purchased by Cortés and 180 arrobas from Tuxtla. A year later 790 arrobas of sugars from the Tuxtla mill arrived in Seville.[59]

By the second half of the sixteenth century the trade of sugar and slaves had become, for all practical purposes, a single enterprise. They were completely dependent on each other, for without a steady stream of fresh slaves, the sugar plantations and mills of the New World could not operate, while sugar production provided the *raison d'être* for the trade itself.[60] Genoese interest in the American sugar trade did not, however, develop out of the slave trade, but rather grew up alongside of it. In the first quarter of the century, the Genoese invested in sugar production on both Hispaniola and Puerto Rico and imported sugar from both of these islands in exchange for European goods. In fact, a document from the Archivo de Protocolos indicates that what historians claim to be the first sugar sent from the New World to Spain was destined for a group of Genoese merchants of Seville, but that the ship on which it was being carried fell into the hands of the French pirate Jean Florin. The five Genoese businessmen—Pedro Juan de Riberol, Franco Leardo, Pedro Benito de Basiñana, Esteban de Forne, and Leonardo Cataño—who in December of that year appeared before a Sevillian notary to legalize their claims to "all the gold, pearls, sugar, hides and other items"[61] that were on the ill-fated vessel, were among the most important Genoese merchant-capitalists of the first half of the century. And in the following years the rapid expansion of the sugar-cane culture in the Antilles and Mexico meant that these men and their compatriots would import an ever-increasing quantity of American sugar. Moreover as the century wore on, sugar, because of its important resale value, stimulated by growing demand, became the second most important New World export, that is, after precious metals. The latter was, without a doubt, the most solicited American product throughout the colonial period.[62]

Besides sugar and precious metals there were other American exports that held an important place in Genoese trade during the whole century. Such agricultural and forest products as hides,

67

cotton, dyewoods, medicinal plants, and cochineal were all imported into Seville by the Genoese. Indeed, in 1528 two of the largest importers of sugar and hides, Franco Leardo and Pedro Benito de Basiñana, went so far as to obtain a monopoly of the balsam and *cañafístola* trade of Santo Domingo.[63] In addition to American drug products, the Genoese, after mid-century, began to import large quantities of cochineal from New Spain. Contemporary opinion held that Mexican cochineal was the best, and it was therefore a particularly solicited item on the European market. During the last quarter of the century, normal cochineal imports into Seville ranged from 6,000 to 8,000 arrobas, and in 1594 reached their high point for the century— 16,000 arrobas.[64] Almost all of this cochineal was re-exported from Seville to Antwerp for use in the cloth industry of the Low Countries.

To obtain American products, to recover the capital they had loaned, or to get the return on their merchandise and slaves, Genoese creditors found it necessary to establish business relations with agents in America. This was done by granting a power of attorney, either specific or general. At first the Sevillian Genoese preferred to delegate specific powers to trustworthy shipmasters, travelers to the Indies, or residents there. In 1514, for example, four different people served Juan Francisco de Grimaldo and Gaspar Centurión in this capacity.[65] Later it became customary to send individuals under partnership contracts (*compañías*). In its simplest form the *compañía* was an association between two individuals in which one party furnished the capital and remained at home while the other carried the investment to its destination. Since the traveling partner (*compañero*) contributed only his services, he received a percentage of the profits, usually one fourth. When "all invested both money and labor," the profits were divided.[66]

Once in the New World, the traveling *compañeros* became for all practical purposes commission agents. The role of the commission agent in America was a difficult one, not only because of the physical hardships that it entailed, but also because of the opportunities for fraud and graft in the colonies. "He who goes to the Indies . . . earns a great deal," remarked Padre Mercado.[67] As early as 1514, there was a flood of complaints against such abuses committed by the agents of the Sevillian traders as refusals to send in accounts and malversations of funds.[68] To further complicate the situation, those who left for America entered into several advantageous contracts with different merchant-capitalists, making it difficult to determine the gains and losses of each investor in case of fraud.[69] The Genoese were well aware of the fraudulent operations that could be entered into by their American agents, and for this reason they never entrusted any associate or factor with full power for too long a period of time. This distrust is reflected in the actions of Grimaldo and Centurión. In February and March of 1516 they drew up company contracts with two Spanish merchants for the sale of merchandise in the New World. These Spaniards were also given general power of attorney to settle all debts owed to the merchant-capitalists in America. Yet in October, Grimaldo and Centurión again found it necessary to grant a power of attorney to a Sevillian merchant about to leave for the Indies.[70]

One of the ship captains who served as an agent for Grimaldo and Centurión was a Genoese named Juan Rodríguez, whose career at sea spanned the first quarter of the century. For twenty-five years Rodríguez served as the master of various ships plying the Atlantic between Seville and America (see Table 5). We know almost nothing about Rodríguez personally except that he was a denizen of Seville in 1514 and for many years maintained a residence in the traditional seamen's district of Triana. In 1524 he was mentioned as a resident of the Santa María quarter, an indication of the increased wealth and social status that he had acquired by that time.[71]

Like all Sevillian skippers engaged in the *carrera de Indias*, Juan Rodríguez was forced to seek funds from interested capitalists to outfit and provision his ship under the terms of the sea loan. His search for ready cash brought him into contact with his compatriots, the members of the Genoese colony of Seville.

He soon gained their confidence and they began to ship their goods on vessels that he commanded.[72] They also empowered him, on many occasions, to collect debts for them in America. Their trust in him culminated in 1514, when Juan Francisco de Grimaldo and Gaspar Centurión granted him "full powers to take charge of all their business in the Indies." Three years later these same two businessmen outfitted and provisioned his ship, *La barca de Santa María,* loaded their merchandise aboard her, and underwrote the cost of the whole voyage.[73]

Table 5. Juan Rodríguez, Sevillian Genoese shipmaster, 1504–1529

Ship	Date	Position
Santa María	1504	Master
San Cristóbal	1506	Master
Santa María de la Rábida	1507–1508	Master
Santa María de Loreto	1511–1512	Master
Santa María de la Antigua	1513–1515	Master
La barca de Santa María	1516–1521	Master
Santa María de la Merced	1524–1526	Owner and Master
Santa María de la Regla	1526–1529	Owner and Master
La Trinidad	1526	Part owner

Source: The Sevillian Protocols and Chaunu, *Séville et l'Atlantique,* II.

Although Rodríguez was by profession a seaman and by choice an agent of his compatriots, this did not prevent him from trading on his own. In the early years of the sixteenth century it was common practice for shipmasters to buy merchandise in Seville to take to America to sell.[74] As yet few merchants wished to venture to America on a regular basis, thereby giving the skippers their opportunity to become *de facto* merchants. Rodríguez was one of those who gained considerable profits from this side-line trading. In 1508, for example, he purchased a quantity of "velvet, camlet cloth, and 10 dozen caps" from Jácome de Grimaldo, which he later sold in Santo Domingo.[75] As his fortune improved, he even began to grant small loans, mostly to those who had booked passage on his ship, to cover their fare and the maintenance and often the transport of their goods. He also lent money to merchants and returning residents of the New World who were unable to pay freighting costs.[76] Although the profit from these loans was small, it enabled him, in addition to his commercial investments and service to the Genoese merchant colony, to purchase the *Santa María de la Merced* in 1524. Two years later he bought the *Santa María de la Regla* and served as her master until 1529. At the same time he was a co-owner of the *Trinidad* along with her master, Juan de los Pinos.[77] It appears that Rodríguez made his last trip in 1529 and probably died in that year, since his name disappears from the *registros* of the Casa de Contratación and we have no further record of him in the Sevillian Protocols.[78]

Although most of the Genoese merchants of Seville were content to remain at home consolidating their fortunes in the American trade, a few ventured to the New World as agents.[79] This group was largely made up of the younger members of the various families. The brothers Rafael and Juan Cataño were the first Genoese to serve as agents for their compatriots on the island of Hispaniola. Rafael accompanied Columbus on the Second Voyage as his accountant, but remained on the island of Hispaniola after the Admiral's return to Spain.[80] By 1503 Rafael's brother Juan had joined him in the new colony. Although the Catholic kings ordered the brothers to leave the island, in February 1504 they were granted permission to stay until they had completed all of their business for Columbus. Regardless of the royal will, the Cataños did not return to Spain; both remained on the island, establishing themselves in the city of Santo Domingo as commission agents for the Sevillian Genoese. By 1512 Rafael had become a denizen of the city, and in the *repartimiento* (division) of the Indians in 1514 he received eleven *naborías* (household servants). Two years later he made a brief trip to Seville where he bought a large quantity of merchandise which he took back with him to sell in Santo Domingo.[81]

Besides the Cataño brothers there were other Genoese agents on Hispaniola during the first decade of the sixteenth century.

In 1508 Bernaldo de Grimaldo sent his nephew Jerónimo to manage his affairs in Santo Domingo, and before leaving Seville, Jerónimo received powers of attorney from eight other members of the Genoese colony.[82] In 1509 Tomás de Castellón left for the New World with merchandise belonging to his father, Bernardo, and to Batista Centurión.[83] A year later he was followed by his brother Jácome, who carried the goods of Esteban Centurión. In later years Benito Centurión, Jácome Spínola, Esteban Basiñana, Jerónimo de Riberol, and Esteban Justinián—among others—traveled to the Indies as agents or associates of their families or compatriots (see Table 6). Most of these New World agents remained permanently in America, becoming citizens of Santo Domingo, Puerto Rico, Cuba, and Mexico. One—Juan Batista Pineolo—returned permanently to Seville. Some, such as Tolomeo Spínola and Valián de Forne, returned briefly to Seville after many years away, only to depart once more for America.

The dissatisfaction of the Genoese with their representatives in the New World was not relieved by the establishment there of their fellow countrymen. Their confidence in their compatriots was often badly misplaced. This was particularly true in the case of Jerónimo de Grimaldo, who, along with Antonio Italián (Italiani), was their principal representative in Santo Domingo during the first decades of the century.[84] For four years Jerónimo's uncle Bernaldo de Grimaldo and six other Genoese merchants of Seville sent him large quantities of merchandise to sell on the island. They granted him full power to supervise their business in the Indies. Jerónimo faithfully carried out his duties for two years.[85] By 1509, however, distance and the opportunities available in America proved too great for him. He began to manipulate for his own benefit the funds he had collected for the Sevillian merchants. Much of the money went into the construction of houses in the city of Santo Domingo, which he subsequently rented. To cover his activities, he simply stopped sending the records of his transactions back to Seville. In 1511, after several unsuccessful attempts to force Jerónimo to

Table 6. Members of the Sevillian Genoese colony in America during the sixteenth century *

Name	Location	Dates of residence	Status	Returned to Seville
Esteban Basiñana	Santo Domingo, Cuba	1526–	*vecino*	1511
Jácome de Castellón	Santo Domingo	1510–1511, 1512–1535 †	*vecino*	
Tomás de Castellón	Santo Domingo	1509–1513	*residente*	
	San Juan	1513–1527 †	*vecino*	
Juan Cataño	Santo Domingo	1503–	*estante*	
Rafael Cataño	Santo Domingo	1492–	*estante*;	
			1512 on, *vecino*	
Benito Centurión	Santo Domingo	1527	*estante*	
Lucián Doria	Santo Domingo	1530	*residente*	
Valián de Forne	Santo Domingo	1535	*estante*	
Gaspar Gentil	Panama	1580	*vecino*	
Jerónimo de Grimaldo	Santo Domingo	1508–1516, 1517–1536	*vecino*	1516, 1536
Antonio Italián	Santo Domingo	1507–1515 †	*estante*	
Esteban Justinián	Santo Domingo	1523–	*vecino*	
Juan Batista de Negrón	Mexico	1584	?	
Juan Batista Pinelo	Indies	1525	returned permanently to Seville	1527
Jerónimo de Riberol	Santo Domingo	1520–23	*estante*	1523
Jácome Spínola	Santo Domingo	1525	*vecino*	
Tolomeo Spínola	Mexico	1550, 1580	*vecino*	1580

* This table is based solely on the Sevillian Protocols. The dates are those on which the individual appears as such in the notarial instruments, and do not exclude the possibility of previous residence.
† Indicates date of death.

send his account books to Seville, his uncle sought the aid of the crown. The King directed the governor of Hispaniola "to investigate all persons in the Indies who have debts pending with Bernaldo de Grimaldo and order that they be paid." [86] The intervention of the King accomplished the desired result. Jerónimo saved himself from punishment by his ability to replace the missing sums, and returned to Seville in 1516. His favorable economic position, and his suggestions for profitable investment to his uncle and other members of the community, restored him to their favor.[87] Once more they gave him merchandise to sell in America and general power to take charge of their overseas affairs. That he betrayed their confidence again is quite obvious. Just a year after his departure, both Bernaldo and Agustín de Grimaldo petitioned the governor of Hispaniola to force Jerónimo to show his account books to their representative from Spain.[88] At this point Jerónimo's name disappears from the Sevillian Protocols, but it seems likely that the events of 1511 were repeated. Nineteen years later he returned to Seville as a wealthy man. Whether he remained there or returned to America is not known, since no further trace of his career can be found among the notarial deeds.

In the first decades of the century, the most active members of the Spínola, the largest Genoese family in Seville, were the brothers Ambrosio and Nicolás. Ambrosio, who was often in Cordova during the last years of the fifteenth century, moved to Seville at the opening of the sixteenth century, as did so many other Genoese who had lived in neighboring Andalusian cities. Although he remained permanently in Seville, he did not become a denizen as did Nicolás.[89] Their participation in the American trade combined—as was typical of Genoese merchants in Seville—both capitalistic and commercial ventures. Both were particularly active in sea loans and the shipment of goods.[90]

In spite of the general scarcity of information about families of the Sevillian Genoese merchants, it is possible to reconstruct, at least partially, the life of Cristóbal, one of Nicholás' sons. Cristóbal received the usual commercial education given the

74

sons of Genoese merchants. At eighteen he was married to Francisca Cataño, in accordance with the Genoese custom of intermarriage. Cristóbal soon rejected his business career for a military one, and in 1539, eager for adventure, he joined the De Soto expedition. Five years later he was among the survivors of that ill-fated enterprise who reached Pánuco in Mexico.[91] He wanted to remain in Mexico, but since "in order to serve His Majesty he had sold all his property," he petitioned the Viceroy in 1549 to grant him a concession of Indians in encomienda.[92] Whether his petition was granted is not known, but in 1565 he returned to Seville, and within the year emigrated to Mexico with his family.[93]

One of the wealthiest members of the Centurión during the early years of the century was Esteban. Although a denizen of the city of Granada, he spent several months a year in Seville. During the rest of the time his business in Seville was managed by his brother Melchor. Both brothers sent large amounts of merchandise to America and invested heavily in sea loans. In addition, Esteban was the owner of a ship, *La Victoria*, which made regular runs between Seville and the island of Hispaniola. Like their compatriots, the brothers found it difficult at first to find agents to represent them in America. In 1507, they entrusted merchandise to Jerónimo de Grimaldo and granted him full power to conduct their affairs in the New World; as a result, they suffered the same difficulties as the elder Grimaldo. Three years later they sent Jácome de Castellón to America as their agent, with much better results. Finally, in 1520, their business had so expanded that a third brother, Benito, was sent to Santo Domingo as their permanent representative in America. Unfortunately, this profitable business arrangement came to an end only five years later with Esteban's death. His single heir was a minor daughter who, along with his property and investments, was placed under the guardianship of a Spanish merchant, García de Castilla.[94]

During the first half of the sixteenth century, profits from the American trade were assured to Genoese capitalists who gave either credit or cash in the form of the sea loan. Sevillian merchants and shipowners were much less sure of making substantial gains, as they had to accept more unfavorable conditions in their contracts with the capitalists.[95] In addition, the possibilities for dividing the risk were limited. By the middle of the century the situation had changed radically. The gradual enrichment of the Sevillian merchants began to limit the role of the pure capitalist. Sea loans became less frequent, as there was no longer an urgent need for ready cash. Insurance contracts could be had on easier terms and served to cover the risk.[96]

It was at this time that the Genoese began to show a greater interest in the vessels engaged in the *carrera de Indias*. During the first decades of the century, very few members of the Seville colony owned such vessels, the majority of them being in the hands of the Sevillian magnates whose prime interest in the American trade centered around the ownership of such ships.[97] As for the Genoese, there were specific reasons for their limited participation in this aspect of the transatlantic trade. In the first place, the cost of maintaining these ships was high and the Genoese, with their varied investments and nonspecialized attitude, did not want to invest so much capital in one single enterprise. Even a merchant-capitalist of the caliber of Gaspar Centurión owned only one quarter of the *Santa María del Antigua* in 1517.[98] Secondly, they found it easier and more profitable in the long run to finance voyages rather than assume the problems and risks involved in ships undertaking long and dangerous trips.[99] Only when conditions in the second half of the sixteenth century limited their capitalistic role in the trade with the New World, did they change their opinion.

In the 1540's and 1550's the growing volume of the slave trade encouraged the Genoese to purchase vessels used primarily for carrying slaves. They found it advantageous to control not only the sale of slaves in the colonies, but their transport as well. Prominent Genoese such as Carlos de Negrón and Nicolás Cataño owned several slavers that made regular runs between Africa and America.[100] In the last quarter of the century Genoese investment in transatlantic vessels reached its highest point: In the 1590's, ten members of the Genoese colony of Seville controlled twelve ships of the *carrera de Indias,* and it was not unusual for several Sevillian Genoese to own two ships at the same time. One of the most typical of these Genoese-owned ships was the *Salvadora* of Teodoro Spínola, a vessel of 300 tons. She crossed the Atlantic every year for eight years until she was finally wrecked in the Caribbean in 1599.[101]

The decline of capitalist participation in the overseas trade also tended to draw the Sevillian Genoese further into imperial finance. In the first half of the century only a few of the wealthiest Genoese engaged in financial transactions with the Spanish monarchs; by the second half, such loans were a general practice among the members of the colony. As the number of loans increased, so did their size, although they never reached the proportions of those contracted by relatives and compatriots in Genoa or at the Spanish court. The investments of the Sevillian colony, with few exceptions, never exceeded a total stake of 100,000 to 200,000 ducats, while those of their compatriots rarely went below 200,000 ducats for individual loans.[102]

The documents do not allow us to reconstruct the participation of the members of the Sevillian colony in royal finance. Only scattered evidence is available. Thus, we have the notarized drafts received by the Sevillian Genoese from officials of the Casa de Contratación as reimbursements for their loans to the monarchs.[103] The use of drafts on American treasure was one of the most convenient and, in many instances, the only way of compensating the bankers, particularly those in Seville. Table 7 lists the drafts they received in this manner from August 1550 to February 1551. The largest loan amounted to only 58,750 ducats (22,031,250 mrs.); the average loan ran between 40,000 and 50,000 ducats. If we subtract the interest—sometimes as much as 13 per cent—from these sums, the original investment of the Sevillian colony is of course considerably reduced.

Some additional light is shed on the role of the Sevillian Genoese as royal financiers by two treasury reports compiled in

77

Table 7. Reimbursements from crown treasure by members of the Genoese colony of Seville, August 1550–February 1551 *

Date	Collector	Recipients	Total sum	Payment
10 Aug.	Pedro Batista Spínola	Andrea and Constantín Spínola	19,912,500 mrs.	15,045,000 mrs.
13 Aug.	Nicolás Cataño	Himself	19,912,500 mrs.	6,637,500 mrs.
25 Aug.	Luis Spínola	Andrea Spínola and Cristóbal Centurión	19,912,500 mrs.	6,637,500 mrs.
29 Aug.	Nicolás Fiescorragio	Juan Antonio Pallavicino †	15,000,000 mrs.	10,076,000 mrs.
12 Sept.	Nicolás Cataño	Himself	19,912,500 mrs.	6,637,000 mrs.
14 Sept.	Luis Spínola	Andrea Spínola and Cristóbal Centurión	19,912,500 mrs.	6,637,000 mrs.
16 Sept.	Pedro Batista Spínola	Andrea Spínola, Tomás Spínola, and Hector Doria	53,100 ducats	12,980 ducats
30 Sept.	Nicolás Cataño	Himself	19,912,500 mrs.	6,637,000 mrs.
17 Oct.	Pedro Batista Spínola	Andrea Spínola, Tomás Spínola, and Hector Doria	19,912,500 mrs.	6,637,000 mrs.
19 Oct.	Pedro Batista Spínola	Himself and Juan Antonio Spínola	6,637,000 mrs.	2,000,000 mrs.
22 Oct.	Nicolás Fiescorragio	Juan Antonio Pallavicino †	15,000,000 mrs.	10,501,676 mrs.
5 Nov.	Nicolás Cataño	Andrea Spínola and Ambrosio de Negro †	10,501,676 mrs.	8,404,296 mrs.
6 Nov.	Pedro Batista Spínola	Andrea Spínola, Tomás Spínola, and Hector Doria	22,031,250 mrs.	10,401,984 mrs.
21 Feb.	Galeazo de Negrón	Himself	8,112,500 mrs.	7,500,000 mrs.
23 Feb.	Galeazo de Negrón	Himself	8,112,500 mrs.	8,112,500 mrs.

* 375 maravedis (mrs.) = 1 ducat.
† Not members of the Sevillian colony.
Source: The Sevillian Protocols.

1554.[104] Their value for our purposes is limited, however, as they do not indicate when the original debt was contracted. According to the first of these statements, which, although undated, must have been drawn up during the first weeks of the year, Galeazo de Negrón and his partner Cristóbal de Lercaro were creditors of the king to the tune of 61,560 ducats, to be paid in April of that year. Cristóbal Centurión was to receive 100,000 ducats plus 3,000 ducats of interest. The participation of Constantín Gentil was carefully itemized. Of his total investment of 166,825 ducats, 20,160 came from a loan due on January 15, 1554, and 46,665 ducats from a loan due on April 15 of the same year. An additional 100,000 ducats that he loaned the Duke of Alba was to be raised through the sale of offices in the religious-military orders of Santiago, Calatrava, and Alcántara.

The second treasury statement, compiled in September 1554, shows several additional loans credited to the three bankers, an indication that they were contracted in the intervening months. Galeazo de Negrón and his partner Lercaro were credited for a loan of 41,560 ducats that was to draw interest until paid. Their total investment for the year then totaled 103,120 ducats. As for Gentil, the King now owed him an additional 50,000 ducats "on account of various loans," [105] which gave him an investment of 316,845 ducats, considerably above the usual range. He was by far the most important and the wealthiest of the royal bankers from the Sevillian group. And his audacity was astonishing. Four months after the royal bankruptcy of January 1557, he risked lending Philip II 600,000 escudos, to be repaid partly from the American treasure and partly from the revenues of Castile. At Gentil's death in 1576, 600,000 ducats, the balance of loans made during the years 1573–1575, remained to be paid to his heirs.[106]

In finance as well as commerce, the Cataño was one of the most successful of the Genoese houses of Seville. Alejandro Cataño spent most of his time at court conducting financial operations with the Spanish rulers.[107] In 1550 he concluded an *asiento*[108] with Charles V, in which he promised to pay 200,000 ducats annually for the maintenance of Prince Philip's household. The banker was to be repaid from the American treasure, with the interest rate set at 13 per cent a year. His commercial investments in Seville were managed by his two brothers, Nicolás and Visconte, who drew the greater part of their wealth from the slave trade. Nicolás was the owner of the vessel *La Trinidad* that ran slaves between Africa and Vera Cruz in the 1540's and 1550's.[109] Nicolás and Visconte were also engaged in royal finance. In 1551 Nicolás loaned 30,000 escudos to Philip II's sister Mary and her husband, Maximilian, the sovereigns of Bohemia, who ruled Spain in the absence of the King.[110]

Nicolás collaborated with his relative Jerónimo Cataño on many occasions. Jerónimo carried on an active trade in merchandise and slaves between Seville and Mexico. In the decade 1540–1550, this trade increased to such a degree that he found it necessary to send his brother Juan to represent him in Mexico City. He also invested heavily in insurance and for several years, along with two Spanish merchants, held the farm of the import-export tax of Seville.[111] In finance most of his loans went to members of the Sevillian aristocracy to sustain their rather expensive personal habits.[112] The Genoese had loaned money to the regional nobility since the Middle Ages; these transactions reached a high point by the 1550's as the nobility, tied to their fixed incomes, attempted to weather the storm of the price revolution.

By the second half of the sixteenth century, a decisive change in business organization had been adopted by the larger Genoese merchants of Seville. The customary Genoese method of individual cooperation among investing capitalists without ties of partnership was no longer suitable for those members of the group who desired to carry on large-scale monetary operations with the government while also investing in the American trade. Imperial finance demanded the ready availability of large quantities of capital, but the funds of the average Genoese were tied up in trade, and returns from America were slow in arriving. A fluid cash reserve could be assured only through a merger of funds, and in the sixteenth century, partnership was the usual device for uniting two or more persons in an enterprise that could not be handled satisfactorily by one person.[113] The companies formed among the Sevillian Genoese at mid-century were nonfamily partnerships of unlimited liability, based on the real partnership (*vera societas*) of the Middle Ages. As in the real partnership, each member put in a share of capital and helped to carry on the business; the partners agreed to work together for a fixed number of years—generally from three to seven—under conditions set down in a formal contract; and each member accepted unlimited liability, since he invested both money and labor.[114] Table 8 lists the companies of Sevillian

Table 8. Genoese companies of the second half of the sixteenth century

Name	Year in which operations began
Polo Centurión, Constantín Spínola, and Lucas Pinelo	1539
Juan Antonio Spínola, Jerónimo and Pascual Cataño	1549
Luis Spínola, Cristóbal Centurión, and Carlos Jufre de Lercaro	1549
Juan Jácome Spínola, Nicolás Cataño, and Angel de Marín	1551
Pedro Batista and Andrea Spínola, and Hector Doria	1551
Galeazo de Negrón, Jácome Calvo, and Cristóbal de Lercaro	1551

* The company of Jerónimo Centurión is omitted for lack of the names of his partners.
Source: The Sevillian Protocols.

Genoese operating during the last years of Charles V. As can be observed, the rule of three was applied to them.[115]

As for the growing trend toward greater specialization and increasing separation of trade from finance, the Sevillian Genoese accepted the former to a certain degree, but they completely rejected the latter: they continued to trade in both goods and money. Within this broad range, however, there was some tendency to concentrate on specific activities. Several companies, like that of Juan Antonio Spínola, Jerónimo and Pascual Cataño, invested most of their capital in insurance operations. Others were more active in the trade of merchandise or slaves.[116] Some concentrated on loans to the regional nobility or to the Spanish rulers.[117] Yet even a cursory glance at the activities of an important firm like Centurión, Spínola, and Pinelo shows the variety of their interests and the broad span of Sevillian Genoese investment. The slave trade, insurance, merchandise, public banking, loans to nobility, city, and monarch all formed a part of the daily business of the company.

There is also evidence of a considerable amount of division of labor and responsibility in the Genoese companies. The partnership of Luis Spínola, Cristóbal Centurión, and Carlos Jufre de Lercaro is a good example. Of the three associates, only Luis Spínola was a denizen of Seville. As such, he preferred to remain there to manage the firm's investments in the American trade and its mercantile and financial business in the city. Carlos Jufre de Lercaro resided continuously at court, where he arranged the company's financial operations with the government. The position of Cristóbal Centurión was less clearly defined—during the first years of the firm's existence he spent most of his time in Seville engaged in commercial activities, and from 1551 to 1553 he could be found at court, where he negotiated several large loans for the firm. His success at court influenced him to turn more and more toward finance. In the years after the termination of the partnership in 1554, he reduced his commercial investments in Seville and established himself permanently at court.[118] By the end of the century, he was one of the most outstanding royal bankers from the Genoese colony of Seville.

The career of Cristóbal Centurión, however, is not truly representative of the majority of Sevillian Genoese in the last decades of the sixteenth century. They did not abandon Seville for the court, nor did they place royal finance above trade. Like their ancestors, they successfully combined both activities. The outstanding Genoese of Seville, as Galeazo de Negrón, Lucas Pinelo, and Luis Spínola, were first and foremost merchants and only secondly royal financiers. They realized that their economic position was based on the American trade, which alone could provide them with the steady flow of capital necessary to meet their commitments to the Spanish monarchs and to take care of their other monetary business in Seville.

CHAPTER IV

The Sevillian
Money Market

GENOESE monetary operations in Seville were varied and extensive. Besides engaging in the ordinary business of money-lending and the trade in bills of exchange (with the customary practices of Ricorsa and arbitrage), they operated banks of deposit and transfer. During the sixteenth century Spain was one of the few countries in Western Europe in which private transfer banks continued to exist, and Seville, due to its commercial and financial importance, contained the largest number of them. These banks were an integral part of the financial life of the metropolis, and therefore it is not surprising to find the Genoese deeply involved in their operations.[1]

The Sevillian banks, like those elsewhere in the country, were typical private banks of deposit and transfer, primarily serving the business community. The bankers accepted deposits payable on demand and undertook to make payments by transfer, even when the parties involved did not have accounts with the same bank. The latter operations were effected through the clearing accounts which the bankers had with one another. Transfer orders were given orally, the debtor and the creditor both being present while the banker made the entry in his journal.[2] As in the medieval period, this action discharged the debtor from further obligation and a written document was not necessary.

The main business of the Sevillian banks was, in effect, the acceptance of deposits on current account. Mercado gives a precise description of these operations. "The bankers of Seville," he said, "are the treasurers and depositaries of the merchants because as soon as the fleet arrives each one places in the bank all that was sent to him from the Indies. Once they [the merchants] have deposited their money in the bank they go withdrawing and assigning while the bankers charge and discharge." [3] Moreover, the bankers frequently advanced credit to their customers by allowing them to overdraw their accounts. In this case, some type of security was usually necessary, either the personal guarantee of a depositor's bondsman or, in cases of doubtful solvency, some kind of salable property solicited as collateral security for the loan.[4] These overdrafts were particularly utilized in Seville by the silver merchants. Though at times the Casa de Contratación was paid for the metals in cash, the usual procedure was for the stipulated sum to be paid in advance by the mint to which the silver merchant had contracted to deliver the bullion. The mint was repaid on time through the accounts of the silver merchants in one of the city's banks.[5]

The Sevillian banks operated within a system of sureties. All bankers were required to furnish bondsmen, which meant that several individuals had to make themselves liable for stated sums as guarantors. The amount of the guarantee varied throughout the century, depending on the given circumstances, but could run as high as 200,000 ducats. Regardless of the size of the surety, it represented, in the case of failure, only a part of the total capitalization.

The number and the wealth of the bondsmen were of great importance to the reputation of the banker and the success of his enterprise. The merchants who patronized these establishments valued the name and the credit of the guarantors even more than that of the banker.[6] Sevillian bankers were therefore anxious to attract the wealthiest members of the city's business community, and since the Genoese were among the most outstanding of this group, they soon became the bondsmen of the largest Sevillian banks.

In contrast to their colleagues in other parts of Spain, the

Sevillian bankers did not charge their customers for their services.[7] Mercado jestingly called this practice "gentlemanly" (*ahidalgado*), but then shrewdly pointed out that there was no need for them to charge a commission to earn a profit because, "since all [the merchants] deposit their funds there [in the bank], the bankers have large sums to utilize in their other enterprises, such as trade and moneylending."[8] The investment possibilities available to the bankers were so extensive, according to the theologian, that they were tempted to overinvest, thus bringing about their own ruin.

Direct investment by bankers in other forms of business enterprise was one of the basic faults of the banking system of the period, and the principal reason for the numerous failures. Throughout the century, both royal and municipal authorities prohibited this practice, but in Seville the laws were apparently ignored.[9] After all, the demand for capital and the opportunities for easy wealth made Seville into one of the most speculative market places in sixteenth-century Spain, and the bankers were in an excellent position to benefit from this. All kinds of business ventures attracted them, but they were particularly active in the local traffic in agricultural goods, the transatlantic trade, and the negotiation of bills of exchange.[10] Documents from the Municipal Archives of Seville give us some idea of their activities as regraters. In 1554 a group of depositors sent a petition to the city council in which they complained that they "could not obtain the withdrawal of their deposits in either large or small amounts" because the bankers used their money to purchase merchandise with the intention of reselling it at a higher price through the medium of retailers. When similar complaints continued to reach the members of the council, they decided to ask the bankers for an official reply. In their defense, the bankers of Seville—Alonso and Pedro de Espinosa, Juan Iñíguez, Octaviano de Negrón, and Pedro de Morga—denied that the difficulties charged by the depositors were the result of what they called their ordinary business, the trade of merchandise and exchange. To the bankers, the protestations of the depositors were nothing more than exaggerations and errors.[11]

The diversification of the bankers' interests and the availability of the depositors' funds proved to be, in most cases, a fatal combination. Banking failures were all too common in Seville, and in fact, the city had the reputation of being an "unsafe place."[12] As Simon Ruiz wrote in 1592, "I have known Seville for fifty years and I have seen many banks established there. None have avoided failure."[13] Indeed, Margaret of Parma's comment about Antwerp—"there is always a feeling of failure in the air"—could also be applied to the Sevillian money market, dependent as it was on American bullion.[14] Any delay in the arrival of the silver fleets caused such tightness on the money market that the solvency of the bankers was severely threatened. Moreover, the repayment of debts in annuities rather than in ready money deprived the bankers of the fluid capital needed to effect their payments and transfers. The failures of several of the oldest and most important banks in Seville, from 1553 on, were closely related to the confiscation policies of the government.[15] Although insecurity and risk governed the bankers' existence, success, even though temporary, brought enormous profits, and this explains the willingness of many to invest in this kind of enterprise.

It was the lure of large rewards that initially drew the Sevillian Genoese into public banking. Their numerous monetary commitments as traders and financiers demanded large and constant capital reserves, which, under the conditions of the American trade, were difficult to maintain. As public bankers, they would have at their command unlimited funds that they could dispose of at will. Furthermore these additional sums would enable them to extend the range of their investments and, in the long run, to increase their hold over the Sevillian money market.[16] Traditionally, the Genoese had always combined trade and public banking. Since the Middle Ages, the most important commercial houses of Genoa, like the Centurione, had practiced trade and all forms of banking simultaneously. The Genoese businessman was never specialized, and the Genoese colony of Seville was particularly characterized by the diversity of its activities. All aspects of the trade of goods and money interested the Genoese.[17]

No better example of the Genoese practice of combining trade and banking can be found than the careers of Juan Francisco de Grimaldo and Gaspar Centurión. We have already described their joint role in the American trade as merchants in their own right and as capitalists who financed the trade of others during the period 1513–1517. Although the Sevillian Protocols of the years 1513 and 1514 refer to them as merchants (*mercaderes*), those from 1515 on call them bankers (*banqueros*). In 1518 we find the first reference to Juan Francisco de Grimaldo as "public banker of Seville" (*banquero público de Sevilla*), and in the following year, the same designation is applied to Gaspar Centurión. It is clear then that by 1519 both Centurión and Grimaldo had opened banks and were engaged in the usual activities of such establishments. On the other hand, can we assume that they originally entered the banking business in 1515 when they were first called "bankers" in the notary deeds, or that they were merely designated bankers because their operations in the American trade had "taken on the character of an employment of money," as Sayous believed?[18] The evidence suggests that they practiced public banking as early as 1515, but it was not until 1518 that they were licensed by the city and therefore could officially use the title "public bankers." Regardless of whether they entered banking in 1515 or 1518, Centurión and Grimaldo are the earliest known public bankers in Seville in the sixteenth century, and most likely the first to operate under the system of municipal appointment. Carande's assumption that the "Sevillians must have learned banking from the Genoese" seems then to be justified.[19]

Our knowledge of the banking operations carried out by Grimaldo and Centurión is very limited indeed. We do not know, for example, whether they functioned as individuals or were united in a partnership. On the basis of their commercial relationship, it would seem that they were not partners, but worked together closely. They maintained accounts in one another's banks as was customary among the Sevillian bankers, and probably served as each other's bondsmen. In addition to their regular deposit and transfer business, they dealt in bills of exchange, and engaged in large-scale lending operations with the local aristocracy.[20] Among the most important recipients of their loans were members of the Columbus family, especially Diego and Ferdinand, sons of the Discoverer.[21] We also know that Juan Francisco de Grimaldo was closely associated with his relatives Nicolás and Juan Bautista of Genoa, who were among the most prominent royal creditors as well as residents of the royal court.[22] Bills drawn on Seville by the two court Genoese were payable in the bank of Juan Francisco, who joined his relatives in several loans involving the Columbus family.[23] Unfortunately, the Grimaldo bank came to an abrupt end with the death of its founder in 1523. As for Gaspar Centurión, he was still functioning as a "public banker" in 1525, and we do not know how or when his banking career ended.[24]

During the 1530's and 1540's the names of several Sevillian bankers appear in the documents preserved in the Archivo de Protocolos; among these were Cristóbal Francesquín and Diego Martínez, who were active between 1537 and 1542, and whose partnership extended over into joint investment in the trans-atlantic trade. Like all Sevillian bankers, they shipped goods to America and maintained factors there. Moreover, they were among the most important slave traders in Seville. In 1535 they received royal permission to transport 1,000 slaves to the New World, and twelve years later, they were permitted to ship 1,500 slaves to the colonies.[25] Juan Iñiguez was another well-known Sevillian banker; he began in 1536 and was still in the banking business in 1554. During all of those eighteen years Iñiguez actually performed the duties of public banker although there were, in reality, several banks that operated under his name representing different partnerships that he formed during the period. In 1553–1554, for example, he was in partnership with the Genoese Octaviano de Negrón.[26] The bank of Iñíguez and Negrón failed in 1554 as a result of the tightness of the Sevillian money market that year. Thomas Gresham, then visiting the city, noted the disappearance of this bank, which he called "one of the oldest in Seville," [27] obviously referring to the operations of Iñíguez rather than the short-lived enterprise of Iñíguez and Negrón.

One of the most important bankers from 1537 to 1550 was Franco Leardo, a wealthy and prominent member of the Genoese colony of Seville during the first half of the century. He began operations in 1537 in partnership with a compatriot, Bautista de Brine. A few years later Brine withdrew and Leardo established a new bank in his own name.[28] This second enterprise was in full operation during the 1540's, but must have failed sometime before 1553 because it is not included on the official list of the city's banks drawn up in that year. Banker Leardo was a typical representative of the Sevillian Genoese group with their broad interests and varied investments. He was primarily a merchant, and as such he participated in almost every aspect of the trade with the New World. In the early years of the sixteenth century, his activities consisted of sending goods to America and granting sea loans. In 1508, for example, he formed a partnership with a Sevillian merchant, Juan Gómez, for the "trade of merchandise between Seville and the Indies." During the 1520's he invested heavily in the slave trade in association with Silvestre de Brine, a relative of his future banking partner. In 1524 Leardo and Silvestre de Brine helped to finance the Sebastian Cabot expedition, and Leardo served as the spokesman of the investing group.

Like so many of the other members of the Genoese colony of Seville, he maintained close financial relations with the Columbus family. Diego Columbus' daughter and her husband, Don Jorge de Portugal, were deeply indebted to him for large and constant loans.[29] Ferdinand Columbus was his personal friend as well as one of his best customers.[30] Shortly before his death,

Ferdinand named Leardo an executor of his will along with three other Sevillian Genoese—Gregorio Cataño, Leonardo Spínola, and Pedro Benito de Basiñana—with whom he maintained both personal and business relations.[31] All four men must have occupied seats of honor at the requiem mass for Ferdinand Columbus, held by the Sevillian authorities on the day following his death, which was attended by "all the Genoese [of Seville], compatriots of Don Ferdinand."[32]

Another member of the Leardo family to practice public banking in Seville was Pedro Juan Leardo, a denizen of the city in the San Salvador quarter, who during the 1540's appears in the Sevillian Protocols as an active participant in the American trade. In 1549 the designation "public banker of Seville" is first attached to his name, and it seems likely that he opened his bank in that year.[33] His bank was guaranteed by several influential Genoese, including his nephew, who was a member of the Palavicino family. Another important bondsman was Jácome Boti, a well-known Florentine merchant of Seville. His customers included some of the most prosperous Sevillian merchants, both native and foreign, in addition to his colleagues, the bankers Pedro de Espinosa and Juan Iñíguez, all of whose names appear on the official list of his creditors drawn up by the city officials after his failure in August 1552.[34]

Leardo's sphere of influence was not confined, however, to the merchant community, but extended over into the circle of the powerful city nobility. The banker's close association with the Sevillian aristocracy came as a result of the marriage of his daughter to Antonio Farfán de los Godos, a scion of one of the oldest noble families of the city. Farfán joined his father-in-law in several commercial undertakings, and may have even been a secret partner in his bank. In 1549 the Duke of Veragua, nephew and heir of Ferdinand Columbus, initiated a lawsuit against both Leardo and Farfán over the ownership of his late uncle's residence. It seems that the beautiful home built by Ferdinand Columbus near the Puerta de Goles had in this year come into the hands of Leardo and his son-in-law by default, but that their claim to the property was contested by the Duke. This case, involving a mass of litigation, was not resolved until 1563 when the Duke of Veragua renounced his rights in return for 600 ducats compensation. By this time, however, Leardo had died and the house had become the residence of Farfán. It remained in the possession of the Farfán family until 1594 when "it was seized for debt and sold at public auction."[35]

The Genoese were not only public bankers in their own right in sixteenth-century Seville, but they managed to interfere in the operations of almost all the city's banks. Their role in the bank of Domingo de Lizarrazas is an excellent example of the extent of their influence and control over the Sevillian banking system. Lizarrazas, a Guipuzcoan, was operating as a public banker in 1545, and enjoyed considerable reputation among the business community precisely because of his close association with the Genoese.[36] Two of the wealthiest Sevillian Genoese during this period, Jerónimo Cataño and Juan Jácome Spínola, had guaranteed his bank and were his secret partners.[37] Both businessmen had deposited their large personal funds in the bank and had encouraged several other prominent compatriots— Luis and Francisco Spínola, Cristóbal Centurión, and Nicolás Cataño—to do the same. In all, at the time of the bankruptcy in 1553, the Genoese had six million maravedís deposited in the bank.

Secured as it was with Genoese money, the bank of Lizarrazas attracted a larger clientele than usual. Important New World shippers, farmers of the municipal and royal taxes, slave traders, and foreign merchants all patronized his bank. Even the officials of the Casa de Contratación became so impressed with Lizarrazas that they allowed the silver merchants to use the bank in making their repayments to the mint. As a result, more than fifty million maravedís of royal treasure was in the bank when it failed in 1553.

Although several versions of the bankruptcy appear in the reports prepared by the officials of the Casa, all of them stress the decisive role played by the Genoese in the failure of the bank.

According to the attorney of the Casa in December 1553, ten months after the event, "the Genoese were the cause of this bankruptcy and the secret partners of Lizarrazas." They had precipitated the failure "by removing 80,000,000 maravedís from the bank when they knew that the funds of His Majesty had been deposited in it."[38] They had also demanded a penalty of 20,000 ducats interest on sums that they had deposited in the bank and which Lizarrazas had not sent to the fair at Medina del Campo as they had ordered. Therefore, when the treasurer of the Casa drew an order of payment for 60,000 ducats on the bank, Lizarrazas, as a result of the actions of the Genoese, could not pay and this brought down the bank.[39]

As for the attitude of the Genoese after the failure, the Casa officials believed that they were purposely obstructing justice in collusion with the city government. "They [the Genoese] are preventing a satisfactory conclusion of this affair, and there is no way of acting against them due to their control over the municipal council" reported the Casa attorney reported in early December 1553.[40] Because of these circumstances he suggested that the case should be turned over to a special investigator sent down from Madrid. At the end of the month, Juan de Sarmiento of the Council of the Indies arrived on the scene and opened a new investigation, but the documents do not reveal whether he uncovered any new details or was able to discover any way of punishing the Genoese. We know, however, that neither the Casa de Contratación nor any of the other creditors of Lizarrazas ever regained the total of their deposits.[41] The public auction of all of Lizarrazas's property, including two galleons of 300 toneladas each, only covered a part of the sums that he owed.[42] As for the banker, he died just a year after his disgrace, his health broken by the hardships he suffered during his imprisonment for debt.

With the failure of Lizarrazas in 1553 there still remained two other important banks in Seville, neither of which belonged to the Genoese. One of them was founded just five months after Lizarrazas' bankruptcy by Pedro de Morga, a Biscayan, while the other, the Espinosa bank, was a family enterprise that had been in existence for many years. Although the Genoese did not own either of these banks, they patronized both, and were associated in one way or another with each of them. Morga had several partners, including such prominent Sevillian merchants as the brothers Luis and Juan Sánchez Dalvo, and Alonso y Rodrigo de Illescas. Alonso de Illescas, on the other hand, worked closely with Jerónimo Cataño—they farmed the *almojarifazgo* together from 1549 to 1551—who was eventually brought into the Morga bank as a secret partner. Both Morga and his partners shipped merchandise to the New World and invested in the slave trade and insurance. For several years Morga and Rodrigo de Illescas also farmed the *almojarifazgo*. The varied activities of the Morga bank brought severe criticism from the Sevillian authorities and as a result of pressure from them, Morga was forced to dissolve the company in 1557. At the same time he established a new bank that would concentrate purely on banking operations.[43] We do not know how long this second banking company lasted, but we can assume that Morga entered into many such partnerships during the following nineteen years that he practiced public banking in Seville, and that the Genoese played a role in these companies. In 1576 the Morga bank failed as a result of the second royal bankruptcy, which had such disastrous consequences in Seville and all over Spain.[44]

The Morga bank enjoyed an excellent reputation for solvency and dependability. In fact, Morga was so well known in Seville that the street on which he lived was popularly and even officially called by his name, and his home was considered to be one of the most attractive residences in the city. After his bankruptcy, the property was sold to a newly-rich merchant, Hernando de Paz, who in 1587 turned it over to the Carmelite Nuns for 13,000 ducats.[45]

The year 1576 also witnessed the failure of the Espinosa bank, the oldest in the city. Three generations of the Espinosa family had performed banking operations in Seville. The founder of the Sevillian bank was Pedro, a New World shipper of the first decades of the sixteenth century, who was styled "public banker" in the Sevillian Protocolos for the first time in 1525. These documents further indicate that a certain Domingo de Çornoza and two of Pedro's relatives, Juan de Espinosa and Juan de Espinosa Salado, all "merchants," were "officials of the bank." Pedro's brother Alonso was also a partner. In 1537 a nephew, Melchor, became a member of the firm, and from this time until Pedro's death in 1543 the bank bore the names of both Pedro and Melchor. At Melchor's death in 1545, Melchor was succeeded by his brother, Alonso. In 1553 Alonso joined with his younger brother, Pedro, to establish the "Bank of Alonso and Pedro de Espinosa, heirs of Pedro de Espinosa." [46] Both Alonso and Pedro were deeply involved in commercial ventures outside of the operations of their bank. Alonso, for example, formed a company for trade with the Indies with his cousin Juan de Espinosa and relative Gaspar de Espinosa, a judge in Panama. [47] The total capitalization of this partnership was 2,000,000 maravedís.

In the first half of the century the Espinosa bank was one of the few in Seville free from Genoese control, due primarily to its establishment as a family firm and also to the Espinosas' long tradition in trade and finance. Moreover, they had the financial basis that many of the other Sevillian bankers did not have, and were forced to obtain from the Genoese. By the third generation, however, the situation had changed. Under the direction of the heirs of Alonso and Pedro the Espinosa bank became involved in royal financing. As royal creditors, their need for large capital reserves increased to such an extent that they were forced to seek the aid of the Genoese. Juan Fernández de Espinosa, Royal Treasurer from 1574 and an important government creditor, drew his funds from the family bank, which in turn obtained funds from the Genoese merchants of Seville. At the time of the second royal bankruptcy, he refused to support his relatives' claims against the treasury, alleging that he had only acted as their agent. [48] The Sevillian bank failed as a result and its owners were jailed.

The royal bankruptcy of 1575–1576 almost completely destroyed the Sevillian banking system. It is not until the 1580's that we begin to find references in the documents to the existence of any new banks. During those years the bank of Diego de Albuquerque and Miguel Ángel Lambías operated in the city.[49] Albuquerque, like other members of the Sevillian aristocracy, participated in the American trade and also held a seat on the city council. His partner, Lambías, was an active New World shipper and moneylender.[50] The bank of Albuquerque and Lambías survived several serious crises and a near failure in 1585. They were eventually drawn into royal financing and in 1584, in return for a large loan to the king, they were granted a monopoly of the banking business in Seville for ten years.[51] The grant of a monopoly gave the bankers enormous advantages, while the monarch received immediate aid for the treasury and realized his desires to stabilize the banking system.[52] Ten years later this privilege came into the hands of the bankers Gonzalo de Salazar and Juan de Carmona of Medina del Campo, who had decided to open a branch in Seville.[53] Within one year financial difficulties forced them to transfer their rights to the Genoese Adán de Vivaldo. On April 28, 1595, Philip II granted Vivaldo and the person "with whom he would associate license and authority to establish a public bank in Seville." This privilege was granted to him for ten years during which time he was to enjoy the exclusive right of operating "the only bank allowed in Seville." For his part, Vivaldo promised to lend the crown 300,000 ducats. Vivaldo, however, was only acting as an intermediary for the brothers Juan Castellanos de Espinosa and Pedro de la Torre Espinosa, descendants of the founder of the original Espinosa bank, to whom he transferred his privilege several days later.[54] After Pedro's death, his widow ceded the bank to the Genoese Jacome Mortedo and Bautista Serra,[55] who in 1600 joined with Juan de Castellanos Espinosa to establish the bank of Mortedo, Castellanos, and Co. The life of the new bank was indeed short, for just one year after its establishment it failed, largely as a result of the fraudulent dealings of Juan de Castellanos.[56]

The transfer of the Espinosa bank at the beginning of the seventeenth century to Jacome Mortecho and Bautista Serra represents another victory for the Genoese. More significant, however, is the opposition that this transaction aroused among the members of the Sevillian city government. A group of aldermen, under the leadership of Francisco Mexía and Bartolomé de Hoces, contested the grant of a banking monopoly to Mortecho and Serra on the grounds that they were unnaturalized foreigners.[57] Although the final decision in this case was favorable to the two Genoese, it is quite clear that the climate of opinion was changing in Seville by the opening of the seventeenth century. A less tolerant attitude was now being taken toward the activities of foreign merchants not only in Seville but also in the rest of the country. Although native feelings of hostility toward the Genoese had been expressed throughout the sixteenth century both in the petitions of the Cortes as well as in the literature of the period, it is not until the seventeenth century that we can perceive the formation of definite anti-Genoese sentiments. This trend is reflected in contemporary literature, where the writers of the period, Quevedo, Tirso, and Gracián, among others, lampooned and satirized the Genoese businessmen and finally succeeded in creating a stereotype of the avaricious, unscrupulous, and materialistic Genoese that was both comic and vicious.[58] Nor were these writers satisfied with mere ridicule and caricature. They also concluded that the Genoese were one of the main causes for Spain's declining fortune in the seventeenth century. It was their opinion that Spain was the prey of the profit-seeking Genoese who, through their commercial and financial machinations, had succeeded in stealing that nation's American treasure and in crippling her economy. Gracián, states their position very clearly when he exclaims: "If Spain would not have had the drain of Flanders, the blood-letting of Italy, the gullies of France, the leeches of

97

Genoa, would not all of her cities today be paved with gold and incased in silver?" [59]

The conversion of the Sevillian nobility to commerce during the course of the sixteenth century is another factor to be considered when viewing the changing Sevillian scene at the beginning of the seventeenth century. Once the Sevillian aristocrats had broken the barrier of tradition and entered trade, it was only a matter of time before they would interest themselves in other commercial and financial activities outside of the American trade. The Albuquerque bank is an indication of their new orientation.

As for the Genoese, it is clear that in 1600 they were still interested in investing in private transfer banks in Seville, although at this time such establishments were being replaced in other parts of Europe with public banks.[60] With their experience and knowledge of European business affairs the Sevillian Genoese must have realized that the day of private banks was over. Nevertheless, the Genoese stayed in banking because they needed the banks as agencies through which they could control the Sevillian money market, and in the last analysis maintain their position in the American trade. After all, the Genoese colony of Seville was primarily interested in the opening of the New World, and all their economic activities in Seville were directed to that end.

CHAPTER V

Investment in Discovery and Exploration

THE role of the Genoese in the discovery and conquest of the New World began with the Columbian voyages. The discoverer of America, who had worked for the Centurione in his youth and undertaken a commercial voyage for them to Madeira in 1478–1479, turned to his former business associates and other Genoese merchants in Seville when in financial need. We have already noted the participation of Francisco Pinelo in the first and second voyages, but there were other members of the Seville Genoese colony who contributed funds to the voyages of their compatriot. One of the most notable among them was Francisco de Riberol, who, during the years that he aided Columbus, was also financing the conquest of the Canary Islands.[1] At the time of the First Voyage, Riberol, with three other Genoese merchants—Francisco Doria, Francisco Cataño and Gaspar Spínola—in addition to the Florentine Juanoto Berardi, loaned Columbus the 250,000 marvedís that the Discoverer himself invested in the venture.[2] Merchant Riberol also advanced funds to Columbus for the Fourth Voyage, and the Admiral held him in such high esteem that he left his personal papers and copies of his royal privileges with Riberol for safekeeping before departing on that last adventure.[3] As for the Centurión, several members of that family resident in Seville intervened in the financial arrangements for the Third Voyage, but were more active as personal creditors of the admiral and his descendants than as financial backers of the Columbian voyages.[4]

For the Genoese the discovery of the New World by their compatriot Columbus meant the opening of new trading areas and the opportunity for large profits from commercial enterprise. As has been pointed out repeatedly, the Genoese were primarily merchants and as such interested in expanding their trade. But they were also moneylenders and like modern-day capitalists were willing to invest their money in speculative ventures, particularly if there was any hope of large or immediate profits.

Circumstances in Seville at the end of the fifteenth century and during the first half of the sixteenth century gave the Genoese ample opportunity to invest in overseas exploration. The city fairly hummed with activity as explorers and future conquerors went about outfitting ships and gathering their followers.[5] Stories of fabulous riches to be found in the New World circulated throughout the town, arousing the hopes of high and low, and particularly of the business colony. For the Genoese conditions could not have been more favorable: With surplus capital available in their strongboxes they stood ready to contribute to the launching of the era of Spanish overseas exploration. The situation was particularly advantageous for them because of the limited role played by the Spanish sovereigns in financing these voyages. In general, explorers and conquistadors had to finance their own expeditions, which meant that they were forced to seek funds from interested Sevillian capitalists, the most important being the Genoese.[6]

Nevertheless, we know very little about Genoese investment in exploration during the first two decades of the sixteenth century, and have only one example of Genoese participation in a company organized for overseas exploration. In 1500 Rodrigo de Bastidas, a notary of Seville, obtained royal permission to undertake a voyage of exploration and discovery in the New World.[7] To finance his expedition Bastidas entered into a partnership with a group of moneyed Sevillians among whom was the Genoese merchant Luis de Negro. De Negro, a denizen in the district of Santa Catalina, invested 14,000 maravedís in the venture—although far from being the largest contribution, this sum represented a sizeable investment. The total capitalization of the company amounted to 377,547 maravedís, and the venturers were assured a return of 100,000 maravedís in addition to one third of the profits.[8] In October 1500 Bastidas, with the cooperation of Juan de la Cosa, the famous pilot and map maker, set sail from Spain; they proceeded to the northern coast of South America, which they explored as far as the Isthmus of Panama.[9] Although they suffered severe hardships, including the loss of their two ships off Santo Domingo on the return voyage, the expedition obtained enough treasure to cover the costs of the enterprise and to bring profits to the sponsors.

Although we have very little information about Genoese investment in exploratory ventures during the early years of the sixteenth century, the documents of the Archivo de Protocolos are full of insights as to their relations with the early explorers and conquerors. The names of the most important participants in the Spanish overseas expansion appear in the notarial deeds as debtors of the Genoese. In particular, they borrowed funds from the Genoese in the form of a sea loan to outfit and provision their ships. In December 1513, for example, Martín Fernández de Enciso, ready to depart for Panama with the Pedrarias expedition, received 225 ducats from Juan Francisco de Grimaldo and Gaspar Centurión to equip his caravel *Santiago* and to cover the cost of the merchandise that he had loaded on her. The two Genoese businessmen also outfitted the *Concepción*, another vessel included in the 1514 fleet, and partially owned by Enciso.[10]

Often New World adventurers solicited money from the Genoese to purchase merchandise to sell in America. Vicente Yáñez Pinzón obtained 12,600 maravedís for this purpose from Juan Francisco de Grimaldo and Gaspar Centurión in 1513 when that veteran navigator planned to accompany the Pedrarias fleet. For similar reasons Pedro Vaz, Pedrarias' major-domo, received a like sum from Agustín de Grimaldo. Moreover, explorers and conquerors looked to the Genoese for personal loans. Among the better-known figures who received funds from the Genoese at various times were Hernando de Soto. Ponce de León, Martín Fernández de Enciso, and Gonzalo Fernández de Oviedo.[11] As for the lesser adventurers—soldiers who took part in the conquests, early settlers, and royal functionaries—who obtained financial aid from the Genoese, the list is so long that it defies presentation here. A special study would be necessary to deal with them all.

Besides their loans, the Sevillian Genoese colony had other business dealings with several prominent New World captains. Gaspar Centurión, for example, gave Pedrarias full powers of attorney to collect certain debts for him just before the new Governor-General departed for the New World.[12] The close relations between the Genoese and Pedrarias and their interest in the 1514 expedition to Panama stems from their long-range goal of reaching the east through the western route, which at the time seemed possible due to Balboa's discovery of the Pacific Ocean. In fact, two influential Genoese businessmen, Agustín de Vivaldo and Nicolás de Grimaldo, prevailed upon King Ferdinand to waive the prohibition against admitting foreigners to the Indies, and to allow them to send factors of their own nationality along with the fleet.[13] We do not know whether or not any Genoese factors actually accompanied the Pedrarias expedition, but it is clear that there were numerous Genoese agents of the Seville colony in Panama during this period. A royal cedula of 1520 that prohibited the passage of any Genoese to Tierra Firme took note of the fact that there were quite a few of them already in residence there.[14] During these years the Genoese had frequent business contacts in Panama with Enciso and Fernández de Oviedo. Both men, it appears, worked for the Genoese during their residence on the Isthmus. Oviedo, in particular, was a close friend of Franco Leardo, who entrusted him with funds to invest in mining and other profitable enterprises in that region. In addition, Oviedo carried out other commissions for Leardo including the sale of goods and the collection of debts owed to the merchant-banker on the Isthmus.[15]

Bastidas and V. Y. Pinzón were two other early New World adventurers who had numerous business relations with the Genoese. Both allowed the Genoese to arrange their private financial matters in Seville, and Bastidas had dealings with Genoese factors like Juan Cataño in the New World. As for Diego Velázquez, the Conqueror of Cuba, he owned real estate and land-plots on that island in association with Juan Francisco de Grimaldo and Gaspar Centurión. We have already noted that even Hernando Cortés did business with the Genoese, selling them sugar from his Mexican estates.[16]

Regardless of their close contacts—personal, commercial, and financial—with the New World discoverers and conquerors, it is not until the Sebastian Cabot expedition of 1525 that we find the Genoese investing as a group in a company organized for overseas exploration and conquest. The time could not have been more propitious for them to make such a move. The Magellan voyage had opened the possibility of reaching the Moluccas and the Orient by the western route, and had stimulated the appetite of the Sevillian business community for eastern goods. Not long after the return of the heroic ship *Victoria*, therefore, a group of Genoese merchants decided to organize a commercial expedition to the Moluccas. The Genoese decision to sponsor this venture, however, had more to it than the apparent desire for immediate profits that contemporary observers believed had stimulated the majority of the investors.[17] In this instance, the members of the Genoese colony of Seville thought in larger terms and had greater expectations. They believed that the contemplated voyage would bring about the realization of one of their long-cherished dreams—the establishment of a permanent western route to the Spice Islands and the Far East. Through this channel, they expected to tap the riches of the Orient. There was also the hope that this new voyage would result in the discovery of a shorter alternate route to the Molucca Islands.[18] Several prominent Sevillian navigators including Sebastian Cabot, the pilot-major of the Casa de Contratación, had expressed the opinion that a shorter route could be found, and that there were other islands besides those already discovered which were scattered over those seas, and not less deserving of exploration.[19]

To assure the success of the expedition, the Genoese thought of giving the command of it to the Pilot-Major himself. When approached Cabot quickly accepted their offer, but at the same time was determined to obtain more glory and fame than that which would come from directing a company of merchants. He sought, therefore, to draw the king into the enterprise, and to change it from a mercantile- to a government-sponsored expedition. With this idea in mind, he proceeded to the royal court and setting forth the great advantages of cooperation with the merchants of Seville, asked the governments for ships and equipment.[20] On March 4, 1525, the conditions of the government's concurrence in the venture were agreed on. Cabot was to "arm and equip not less than three or more than six ships with provisions for 150 men for two years." [21] He was ordered to sail by the Strait of Magellan to the Moluccas and other islands in those regions. From there he was to go in search of the islands of Tarshish and Opir, of Eastern Cathay and of Cipango, loading at each of these places and others that he should discover along his passage, all the gold, silver, precious stones, pearls and the like, that he could find.[22] For its part, the government promised to supply 4,000 ducats for the voyage with the rest of the cost to be carried by the sponsors. As a special favor to Cabot, Charles V promised to allow "merchants and other foreigners to invest in the enterprise without any restrictions as to amount." [23]

Eventually sixty-five subscribers came forward, and in their own names, or as representatives of commercial partnerships offered to finance the expedition. Seventeen of these investors were Sevillian Genoese, including the four original promoters of the venture (see Table 9). Indeed, the largest investment in the expedition was made by Franco Leardo and his partner Silvestre de Brine. Leardo's share in the venture and his prominent place in the Sevillian business world led to his selection by the investors as their spokesman, along with another well-known native merchant, Francisco de Santa Cruz. The second largest single contributor was Leonardo Cataño who invested 407,880 maravedís on his own, and 509,850 maravedís with the English merchant Robert Thorne.[24] In general, the contributions of the Genoese were far above those of the other investors. Their total

Table 9. Genoese investment in the Sebastian Cabot
expedition of 1526

Name	Amount
Pedro Benito de Basiñana	305,910 mrs.*
Silvestre de Brine and Franco Leardo	610,760 mrs.
Luis de Castellón	50,985 mrs.
Leonardo Cataño	407,880 mrs.
Leonardo Cataño and Robert Thorne	509,850 mrs.
Niculoso Cataño and Co.	321,400 mrs.
Gaspar de Cazaña	37,500 mrs.
Juan Francisco de Frucises and Jerónimo Spínola	88,125 mrs.
Gaspar de Negro	38,625 mrs.
Pedro Juan de Riberol	127,472 mrs.
Pedro Juan Salvago and Nicolás de Forne	254,925 mrs.
Total	2,998,057 mrs.

* 375 maravedís = 1 ducat.
Source: Medina, *Sebastián Caboto*, II, 70-73.

investment in the venture amounted to 2,998,057 maravedís (7,994 ducats) or 15 per cent of the capitalization of the expedition (see Table 10).[25]

With so much at stake, the Genoese decided to send one of their members along on the expedition to watch over their interests. Silvestre de Brine's son Octaviano was selected to be their agent and later was joined by another young Genoese, Gaspar Cazaña, when the Genoese felt that it was necessary to entrust two of their own for this mission. Both men were to share the position of *veedor* (overseer for the investors) on the ship *Trinidad*. Cazaña had already invested 37,500 maravedís in the venture and Brine followed his example by pledging 20,000 maravedís of his prospective salary.[26] As investors in their own right, and as representatives of the sponsors, Brine and Cazaña found themselves in a rather strong position. Cabot, on the other hand, resented their presence, and considered them nothing more than spies for the Genoese. Furthermore, he believed that their strength reduced his own powers as captain general. His resentment and suspicion of them eventually turned into open enmity, particularly toward Brine.

The departure of the fleet was set for August 1525, but a serious controversy between Cabot and the merchant's company prevented it. Cabot wanted his friend Miguel Rifos made second

Table 10. Analysis of the capital invested in the Sebastian Cabot expedition

Investors	Amount	
	Maravedís	Ducats
Genoese	2,998,057	7,994
Non-Genoese	16,339,396	43,571
Total	19,337,453	51,565
Additional costs shared by the investors	257,000	685
Total	19,594,453	52,250
Crown	1,500,000	4,000
Total	21,094,453	56,250

Source: Medina, Sebastián Caboto, II, 70–73.

in command, but the sponsors insisted on giving that position to Martín Méndez, one of the honored survivors that returned with the Victoria. Cabot supported his selection of Rifos by pointing out that the latter had contributed both a caravel and additional funds to the fleet, which according to the Captain General gave him a claim of the second position.[27] There was more to this dispute, however, than the apparent conflict over the position of lieutenant. Basically, the sponsors distrusted Rifos and wished to prevent him from taking part in the expedition. Nor were they satisfied with Cabot's direction of the enterprise. They suspected that the Captain General would readily sacrifice their interests to satisfy his own personal ambitions, and they were disgusted with his contradictory attitude. They also disliked the interference of his wife, Catherine de Medrano, who because of her influence over her husband had by this time a large role in the preparations for the fleet. In such circumstances, the choice of a lieutenant became a matter of highest importance to the merchants, for to let Cabot have one who would be his tool would be the same as surrendering their interests to his will and whim.[28] Cabot, on the other hand, knew that if the sponsors selected the second officer his own position would be difficult and perhaps untenable.

The dispute became bitter and as neither side would yield to the other, the Genoese appealed to Charles V. Secretly, they dispatched Bachiller Francisco Salvago, son of one of the investors and also a subscriber in the venture, to ask the Emperor to remove Sebastian Cabot as captain general of the expedition. Salvago actually reached Charles V, who apparently listened favorably to his arguments and then sent him to speak to the Bishop of Osma, the president of the Council of the Indies. The Bishop, however, refused to hear of the removal of Cabot and in fact banished Salvago from court. But Salvago's mission was not a complete failure, for soon afterwards the Council of the Indies ordered Cabot to accept Méndez as his lieutenant and the investors to give up their opposition to Rifos and allow him to accompany the expedition.[29]

The sad effects of this arrangement were soon apparent. Cabot continued to dislike and mistrust Méndez, whereas the latter conspired against him. Cabot eventually claimed at his trial that Martín Méndez and several others, namely, Francisco de Rojas, Miguel de Rodas, Octaviano de Brine, and Alonso de Santa Cruz, held a secret meeting in Seville at the Monastery of San Pablo just before the departure of the expedition. There, according to Cabot, they bound themselves by oath to unite on every occasion against him for the purpose of depriving him of his command and of putting Francisco de Rojas in his place. Several witnesses supported his accusations. On the other hand,

Méndez' mother asserted that Cabot's wife, after trying to prevent her son's appointment, conceived a bitter hatred for him and employed a person to assassinate him.[30]

The quarrels between Cabot, the officers, and the sponsors delayed the sailing of the fleet until April 1526 [31] and by this time there was little enthusiasm or optimism among the investors for the expedition. The merchants had grave doubts as to the wisdom or the security of their investment. Cabot was well aware of their feelings and, seemingly, more than ever determined to make the venture a success. He is reported to have told several of the crew shortly before the fleet weighed anchor that "although the sponsors [of the expedition] believe that they have gambled and lost their money, we will return with great wealth." [32] The season was not far advanced enough to be favorable for the voyage, but one of the seamen left in the Moluccas by the Magellan expedition succeeded in reaching Spain and brought news of the cruelties practiced by the Portuguese on the survivors of that expedition. This news caused the order to sail to be given at once in order to carry provisions and reinforcements to those remaining on the islands.[33]

The fleet was hardly at sea before Cabot set Méndez aside and allowed Miguel Rifos to carry out the duties of Méndez' office.[34] By this act he added fresh fuel to the already burning controversy and gave his enemies further basis for their hostility toward him. When the ships stopped at the island of Palma in the Canaries to take on additional supplies, the same group that had met in the Monastery of San Pablo in Seville frequently visited and met together at the residence of Alonso de Santa Cruz, one of the Inspectors for the merchants. Cabot, at his trial, stated that they gathered for the same purpose as in Seville, but there is no proof of this. Santa Cruz was ill at the time and it is possible that these visits were on account of his illness. But even if they were not real meetings for conspiracy, most of the men in the expedition believed that they were. All of the witnesses called by Cabot stated that they did not know whether these meetings were directed against Cabot or not, but they were publicly looked upon as conspiracies against the commander of the expedition.[35]

From the Canaries the fleet sailed to the Cape Verde Islands and from there to Pernambuco on the Brazilian coast where contrary winds forced them to remain for three months. While the fleet was anchored at Pernambuco, two members of that Portuguese colony frequently visited Cabot and told him of the riches to be found in the south. They also told him of two Spaniards, survivors from the Solís expedition, existing on the island of Patos. We do not know whether Cabot was under their influence and decided at this time to abandon the voyage to the Moluccas or if he came to this conclusion when the expedition was already at the mouth of the Plata River itself in Saint Catherine's Bay.[36] In any event, he called his officers together and told them of the wealthy lands to the south as described by the Portuguese. According to the witnesses at the trial, he gave them the impression that if they followed the advice of the Portuguese they would find immediate wealth without risking the voyage to the Moluccas.[37] Prominent among those who opposed any change in the course of the expedition were Méndez, Rojas, Brine, and Rodas, but it was Rojas who aroused Cabot's anger most when he dared to remind the Captain General of his obligations to the king and the sponsors. Shortly after this meeting, Cabot suddenly seized and imprisoned Rojas without ever publicly stating the reasons for his action. After keeping Rojas confined on board the flagship *Santa María* for several days, he released him, apparently without any further explanation of the episode, but then imprisoned Méndez and Brine, accusing them of conspiracy against himself. For the time being, Cabot made no move against Rodas, for he badly needed the latter's services as pilot. It is probable that he allowed Rojas to go free for similar reasons, that is, he was anxious to set sail as soon as possible, and there was no one else to whom he could entrust the command of the *Trinidad*.[38]

As for Méndez and Brine, Cabot refused to lease them and to their protestations gave only elusive answers such as "they would soon be informed of the reasons for their imprisonment." [39] Although he never stated his motives for imprisoning them, there are several possible explanations for Cabot's actions. In the first place, Méndez was Cabot's archenemy and would be the center of any conspiracy against him, and Brine was the representative of the Genoese investors who had tried to remove Cabot from his command, and in his mind was nothing more than the tool and spy of the Genoese. Brine was particularly dangerous because both Rojas and Méndez had always shown great deference and respect to the Genoese and had publicly stated that he deserved more consideration than any other member of the expedition because of his position. If Rojas and Méndez were planning to revolt against Cabot's authority, or to seize the *Trinidad* and undertake a voyage to the Moluccas alone as Cabot suspected,[40] Brine's participation would be tantamount to official recognition of the plot by the Genoese investors. By keeping Méndez and Brine imprisioned he could separate the conspirators and render them powerless against him.

With Méndez and Brine still confined as prisoners, the expedition left Pernambuco on September 29, and sailed down the coast to the Bay of Saint Catherine where their flagship struck on a bank and was lost. With it went no less than half their supplies and equipment; a blow the expedition never got over.[41] To this loss was added another still greater, that almost all of the expedition fell ill and died. Brine was among those who died of sickness at Saint Catherine's Bay, still uninformed of the reasons for his imprisonment even though a little while before his death he had presented Cabot with a formal petition requesting him to "declare without any further delay why he was being held prisoner, and to free him since he had done nothing against His Majesty or the Captain General." Cabot ignored the request and after Brine's death confiscated his personal possessions and ordered them sold at a public auction where according to witnesses, he purchased them himself.[42] These unexplained actions later provided Brine's father with a perfect case against Cabot.

It was at Saint Catherine's Bay that the fleet encountered several shipwrecked Spaniards who had been members of the Loaysa expedition. There were in addition two others who had belonged to the expedition of Juan Díaz de Solís and were with him at the discovery of the Rio de la Plata. The latter reinforced what the Portuguese had told Cabot of the great treasures of the country and convinced him that ascending the "River of Solís" they would find gold, silver, and other metals "with which they might fill their vessels." [43] They urged the Captain to follow this route. According to several witnesss at the trial Cabot was at first reluctant, but the survivors were so persistent that they finally won him over and with him the majority of the men. [44] Finally, Cabot, convinced that the ships and the men were in such dire conditions that they could never arrive at the Moluccas, assembled his officers and tried to persuade them to keep the fleet in the Plata. To Cabot, the purpose of the expedition would be abandoned, but with the prospect of great wealth in the area, the object would be achieved. The most vocal opponent of the plan was once again Francisco de Rojas, who aroused Cabot's anger to such a degree that he decided to rid himself of this troublemaker and his friends, Méndez and Rodas. He soon accused all three men of attempting to organize a mutiny against him, had them arrested, tried, and after finding them guilty, abandoned them on Patos Island in Saint Catherine's Bay. After the disposal of Méndez, Rifos, who had always performed the duties of lieutenant of the expedition, now assumed the title as well. The fleet then put out to sea, sailing south to the mouth of the Plata. It entered the estuary of that river, and stopping at a small island called San Lázaro for a rest, came across another survivor of the Solís expedition, who confirmed the tale of the great wealth of the region. [45] Encouraged by his words and taking him on as a guide, they began their ascent up the river.

Cabot followed the course of the Plata, eventually entering into the River Paraná. Some thirty miles above the present day Rosario, he constructed a fort which he called Sancti Spiritus. Continuing upstream he obtained some silver from the natives, but met fierce opposition from them. In spite of skirmishes with the Indians he ascended the Paraná as far as the rapids of Apipé, and finding his course barred in that direction, explored the River Paraguay as far as its junction with the Bermejo.[46] By the time the expedition entered the Paraguay, their food had given out, and they were being subjected to constant Indian attack. The situation seemed so helpless that several of the men planned a mutiny, but it was discovered and the leaders were duly tried and executed.[47]

For three years Cabot explored the Plata region, but found little gold or silver to compensate his efforts. Finally, the arrival on the scene of a rival expedition under Diego García, and the desperate conditions that existed among his own party, influenced Cabot to send two of his most trusted men, Fernando Calderón and Roger Barlow, to Spain to report to the government the state of affairs and to ask for aid. He gave them a letter for Charles V in which he explained the sad events of the voyage and the causes which made him cut it short. He spoke of the great wealth of the region, and asked the Emperor for men and a means of settling the area. To support his account and his demands, he sent some samples of silver, gold, metals, and some Indians along with them.[48] In November 1528 the two men arrived in Spain and made their way to the Emperor at Toledo. The idea of colonization was well received by Charles V, who decided to invite the merchant sponsors to share in the expenses of the new enterprise. When the merchants became aware of the Emperor's plans, they immediately refused to contribute any more funds to the venture. Only under considerable royal pressure did they consent to meet to discuss the matter. They finally decided not to invest in the expedition, but agreed to lend the necessary funds to the Emperor to be repaid from the royal revenues. As one of their conditions for the loan, they insisted that the government reimburse them for their original investment since "they had invested their money for trade not conquest, and that they were only interested in the former." [49] After refusing the merchant's offer, Charles V, whose hopes had been raised by the report of Calderón and Barlow, and the objects that they had brought him as samples, decided to assume the entire cost himself. He gave strict orders that the funds should be supplied at once, but the financial difficulties of the Spanish government prevented this. So time passed, and before an expedition could be outfitted, Cabot had already returned home.

Meanwhile in the Plata, Cabot, unaware of the fate of his emissaries' mission, found himself in greater difficulties as the months passed. The final catastrophe was the destruction of his fort of Sancti Spiritus by a fierce Indian attack. With a decimated force and meager supplies in a region populated by hostile Indians, Cabot finally concluded that he would have to return home. At the end of 1529, therefore, after spending three years in the Plata region, Cabot sailed for Spain, arriving in Seville at the end of July 1530. He had returned home, according to a contemporary observer, "very wretched and poor . . . [and] brought no gold or silver, not anything of profit to those who outfitted the vessels and of the 200 men that he took with him he brings back less than 20." [50]

As soon as Cabot arrived in Seville, his enemies fell upon him. So great was the outburst of accusations that the officials of the Casa de Contratación decided to have him immediately arrested and imprisoned. In a report to the Council of the Indies the Casa officials claimed that they took this action "at the request of the relatives of the persons of whose death he is accused, as also of having abandoned others on the land, and on the orders of the Royal Prosecutor who charges him with neglecting to follow the instructions he had received." [51] Eventually a regular trial was opened at Cabot's expense by the Council of the Indies on the accusations preferred against him.

The first to begin legal proceedings against Cabot was the Royal Prosecutor, Licentiate Juan de Villalobos, in the name of the Emperor. Among the several charges that Licentiate Villalobos made against him were his removal of Méndez from a crown-appointed position, his abandonment of Méndez, Rojas, and Rodas on Patos Island, and the most serious one of them all, his failure to lead the expedition to its agreed-upon destination, the Moluccas.[52] The Prosecutor concluded that Cabot was guilty of grave criminal acts and should be imprisoned and heavily fined.

Shortly after the presentation of the prosecutor's case, Catherine Vázquez, mother of Martín Méndez, and Francisco de Rojas, who by this time had returned to Spain, the sole survivor of the abandoned group, initiated their suits against Cabot. Catherine Vázquez claimed that Cabot was guilty of her son's death because he had unjustly left him on an island in an area where he knew there were cannibals.[53] Cabot defended his actions against Méndez on the grounds of necessity, saying that Méndez was the leader of a plot against him and that Méndez' death was the result of strife among the Spaniards on the island, over which Cabot had no control. At the Bay of Saint Catherine, among many others that died, there was a brother of Martín Méndez, named Hernán. His mother accused Cabot of his death also, saying that Hernán died of a broken heart because his brother was deposed and abandoned. But several witnesses called by Cabot testified that Hernán Méndez was taken ill and died of the same disease as many others. She then produced witnesses who claimed that when Hernán was ill, he received, on Cabot's orders, a purgative that so weakened him that he died shortly afterwards. As for Francisco de Rojas, his case against the former captain general was undoubtedly stronger than that of Méndez' mother. He charged Cabot of depriving him of his ship and command, imprisoning him without just cause, of trying him on false charges, and finally of abandoning him on an island peopled by cannibals. Cabot, in his own defense, answered these charges by stating that his actions against Rojas were mild in comparison to the gravity of Rojas' offense—mutiny against the commander of the expedition—and that of his companions, Méndez and Rodas. Cabot produced witnesses who supported his theory of a conspiracy between Méndez, Rojas, and Rodas to overthrow his authority and escape with the *Trinidad*.

Charges were also pressed against Cabot by Silvestre de Brine, father of Octaviano. The elder Brine accused Cabot of imprisoning his son without cause, in this way bringing about Octaviano's untimely death. Although Brine held Cabot responsible for his son's death, his suit was concerned with the property left by Octaviano. Witnesses testified that shortly after Octaviano's death, Cabot had purchased his possessions at a public auction. These items included "a jewelled dagger and case, some tooled leather hangings [*guademecíes*], a silver cup, a few silver knives, and a quantity of wine. Brine demanded that they be returned or that he be compensated for them. At the trial, Cabot admitted purchasing these articles, but claimed that he no longer had them, "having disposed of them as his own property." [54]

While Cabot was involved in what seemed to be an endless mass of litigation, his companions found that they also had to resort to the courts. Almost all of them had incurred debts before their departure, fully expecting to repay them from their share in the expedition's profits, but they now found themselves without any resources. Unable to pay their debts and at the mercy of their creditors, they petitioned their ruler to release them from their obligations "because of the great suffering that they had undergone in the said voyage." [55] They also asked the Emperor to pay them their salaries. Charles V was perfectly willing to release them from their creditors, but the payment of their salaries was something else indeed. Since there were no funds available in the royal treasury for this purpose, the Emperor ordered the sale of the remaining ships and equipment, and profits from which were to be divided among the survivors and the heirs of the deceased members of the expedition. [56] The crew members, however, never received anything because of the opposition of the merchant sponsors, who maintained that the ships had been bought with their money and the profits from their sale belonged to them. [57] Caught between the merchants on the one hand, and the expedition survivors on the other, Charles V finally rejected any responsibility for the enterprise, claiming that Cabot "had offered to undertake the expedition and was solely responsible for it and that royal permission had been given for a voyage of discovery and trade to the Moluccas and not to other places." [58] When it became apparent that no money would be forthcoming from the government, the expedition members turned to the sponsors and began a suit against them that lasted six years. Although the Council of the Indies initially decided that the merchants had to pay a part of the men's salaries—for the outward voyage from Seville to the Plata and the return voyage from the Plata to Seville—the merchants appealed the decision and were eventually absolved from all payment. [59]

As for Cabot, by the summer of 1531 he was at liberty on bail, with the Council of the Indies still deliberating the various suits against him. In February of the following year the Council made its final decisions in the several cases against him. He was sentenced to two years exile in Oran for abuses committed during the course of his voyage and ordered to pay large sums of money to the heirs of Catherine Vázquez, who had by this time died, to Francisco de Rojas, Silvestre de Brine, and all the others who had sued him, except the government. But none of the sentences against Cabot were ever carried out because Charles V pardoned him and even restored him to his former position of pilot-major. Apparently, Charles was convinced that Cabot had no equal in the knowledge of matters pertaining to navigation and cosmography and felt that he could not afford to lose him. [60] Although reinstated in his position, Cabot was not satisfied, and secretly made plans to leave Spain. His opportunity came with the accession to the English throne in 1547 of Edward VI, whose reign marked a renewal of interest by the English in maritime exploration and discovery. In October of that year a royal ordinance invited Cabot to England and provided funds to cover the cost of his trip. A few months later, Cabot secured governmental permission to take a trip to Germany to see Charles V, and to bring him a "plan containing a method to solve the problem of longitude." [61] Under this pretence he left Seville for Brussels, and from there crossed over to England. Cabot's flight to England marked a fitting end to his controversial career in Spain and closed an unsuccessful episode in the history of Genoese investment in maritime exploration.

The failure of the Cabot expedition discouraged the Genoese to such an extent that we do not have any evidence of further large-scale investment by them for many years.[62] It was not until 1544 that they again decided to sponsor an expedition, this time to explore and conquer the Amazon River basin. Rumors of the wealth of this region—the legend of El Dorado—had been filtering back to Spain for some years, and Francisco de Orellana's remarkable eight month voyage down the Amazon River in 1540–1541 seemed to bring closer to reality the eventual penetration and conquest of the area.[63] When the news of Orellana's feat reached them, it moved the members of the Genoese colony of Seville to think seriously about investing in an expedition that would penetrate the Great River and find the Gilded Man. Unknown to the Genoese merchants, Orellana had also decided to follow up his exploits by returning to Spain and obtaining royal authorization to explore and settle the region. Arriving in Spain in May 1543, he proceeded to the court at Valladolid where he presented a formal description of his journey and petitioned the King and the Council of the Indies that he be appointed governor of the area he had explored.[64] Nine months later Orellana succeeded in getting the King to grant him, on February 13, 1544, the royal decree authorizing him to undertake the exploration and settlement of New Andalusia. In this document the Monarch, after recalling briefly the services rendered by Orellana, put upon him the obligation to take along on his new expedition 200 infantrymen, 100 horsemen and the materials required for the construction of the ships needed to carry the men and horses up the river.[65] Furthermore, it was stipulated that he should build two towns, one inside the entrance to the river and the other at some distance inland. For his services he was to receive the title of governor and captain general, a salary of 5,000 ducats derived from the profits of the country that he should conquer, plus one twelfth of the royal revenues from the same.[66]

Several other appointments were made at this time including those of treasurer, inspector, and revenue collector. For the last-named post the King selected a certain Vicencio de Monte, who received special separate instructions in regard to the discharge of his office and was named magistrate of the town that was to be founded. Finally a Dominican Friar, Pablo de Torres, was appointed inspector general, "so that he may observe how our Governor adheres to and carries out the articles of agreement which we ordered to be drawn up in his favor." [67] During the following months Friar Torres, in the discharge of his duties, wrote several letters to the King; these dispatches supply us with most of the information that we have about the expedition. [68]

Although Orellana saw his aspirations to lead an expedition to explore and conquer the Amazon River basin realized in his capitulation, this grant did not include any royal financial assistance. The whole weight of putting together the expedition was to fall entirely upon Orellana, who did not have the necessary funds and who was afraid of informing the King of his real economic situation for fear of losing all. In these difficult circumstances Orellana then transferred his headquarters to Seville hoping to raise the money for the expedition on his own in that city. Once in Seville he found that he had to inform the King of the true situation. In a letter written sometime prior to May 1544 he asked the Monarch to give orders that he should be provided with the guns needed to arm his ships, but in reply he was told that "there was no source from which they could be supplied." Nor was any better reception accorded to his petition to be permitted to press the sailors that he found into going along with him. [69]

Without becoming discouraged at these refusals, the Adelantado carried on the preparations for the fleet, but on the very day that he had set as a probable date of his departure, he found it necessary to write to the King about the bad treatment, so it was said, he was handing out to those who were associated with him. He was sure that this information had reached the King and he wanted to clarify his position and defend his honor. He further added, to show the extent of his total commitment, that he "had pledged his person to the amount of 4,000 ducats . . . for the sake of putting in complete order the affairs of the expedition." [70]

To these obstacles was added still another, the appearance in Seville at the end of August of Friar Pablo de Torres on orders from the King directing him to report on "what equipment Orellana has on hand and what ship-stores and other supplies he has procured and whether the enterprise is in a state [of preparations] such that he will be able to go ahead with it." [71] In answer to the Monarch, Friar Torres wrote on August 27, 1544, that provisions had begun to be put on board and that it was hoped that in the coming month of September everything would be ready for the departure, but he also noted that dissension had broken out between the men, particularly between Orellana and his former companion on the Amazon voyage, Cristóbal de Maldonado, who suddenly left the expedition.[72] Despite all Orellana's problems, however, the Dominican felt that the expedition would eventually become a reality.

Nevertheless, the King was by this time not content with merely receiving reports from Friar Torres, but asked the Casa de Contratación to look into the matter. The officials of the Casa called Torres, Orellana, and the other royal appointees of the expedition to a meeting at which they obtained a full account of the state of the expedition. With this information at hand, they reported that Orellana still owed more than one thousand ducats on the price of a ship and a galleon, and that when the passengers who kept coming in to take ship learned about this and the lack of sailors and supplies, they refused to book passage. Moreover, he had not found any merchants to provide him with the necessary funds nor did he have greater success in recruiting men for the expedition.

Orellana was in these straits when his step-father, Cosme de Chaves, came to his aid, pledging to raise 1,500 ducats through the sale of his annuities.[73] But according to Torres, all attempts to secure money constantly failed before the machinations "of a person or persons who are striving either to take charge of this expedition themselves, or have friends of theirs take charge of it." [74] Friar Torres had rightly guessed that someone was deliberately sabotaging the expedition and frustrating all the Adelantado's efforts to obtain funds. This person, unknown to the Friar, was none other than the revenue collector, Vicencio de Monte. We know very little about Monte except that he was of Genoese origin and had been a trusted employee of Ferdinand Columbus until the latter's death in 1539. For years he had conducted Don Ferdinand's business and was well known and apparently respected in Sevillian business circles. [75] Through his long association with Ferdinand Columbus he had made some influential friends at court who intervened with the King to secure his appointment as revenue collector of the Orellana expedition. Monte saw the venture as an opportunity to further his own interests and those of the Genoese merchants of Seville.

Realizing that Orellana did not have the capital to finance the expedition, Monte decided to use his influence and connections among the Sevillian business colony to ruin all the Adelantado's chances to obtain funds until the latter in desperation would solicit his aid. He then planned to suggest to Orellana the possibility of interesting the Genoese in the expedition and to offer his services to this end. As a reward for his timely intervention, he wanted the Adelantado to appoint him lieutenant of the expedition and to grant his brother the post of constable. With these two key posts in his hands he hoped to emerge as the most important figure in the enterprise. As for his compatriots—the Genoese merchants of Seville—they could take advantage of Orellana's desperate need for funds and strike as hard a bargain as possible. [76] In this way, both Monte and the Genoese would profit from the venture.

In the fall of 1544 Orellana apparently reached the point of financial exhaustion that Monte was waiting for and fell in with Monte's plans. A secret agreement was arranged between them according to which Monte promised to bring the Genoese into the enterprise and the Adelantado, in his turn, to grant the revenue collector the positions that he desired. [77] From this time forward, Monte became Orellana's chief advisor and, in reality, the force behind the Adelantado.

The first indication of the success of Monte's plan comes in a letter of Friar Torres written on October 6. "To his surprise," the Friar wrote the King, "the Genoese merchants have themselves come forward with an agreement relative to the supplying of funds for the undertaking," and Torres added, unaware of the secret negotiations between Orellana and Monte and of Monte and the Genoese, "without being asked." [78] The manipulations of Monte and the Genoese can be discerned from the pages of the Dominican's letter of October 23. "The Genoese," says Torres, "have sent invitations to one another to get together for the purpose of helping out the expedition, and they requested as a method of dealing with them that Vicencio de Monte be sent to them in order that he might negotiate with them . . . and he [Monte] closed [certain] agreements with them without my seeing them . . . and when I did get to see them, they did not seem satisfactory to me." [79] Nor did these agreements seem acceptable to the treasurer of the Council of the Indies, Francisco de Ulloa, who arrived in Seville in November to see how far the preparations had gone toward the departure of the fleet. According to Ulloa, Orellana had closed certain transactions with the Genoese, but had accepted conditions which the Treasurer found to be too hard and which he was not willing to approve.[80]

The loan conditions laid down for Orellana by the Genoese and other details regarding their financial participation in the expedition emerge from the documents preserved in the Sevillian archives. The notarial deeds, particularly, give us a clear idea of the manner of Genoese investment. It seems that several of the wealthiest Sevillian Genoese bought up large blocks of shares in the venture amounting to a total of 3,000 ducats. These large shareholders then divided their holdings and sold them, at 100 ducats a share, to other members of the Genoese colony. We know, for example, that Ambrosio Spínola purchased 800 shares and that he sold 400 of them, at one share apiece, to Andrea and Francisco Lomelín, Cristóbal Lercaro, and Pantaleón de Negro. For every share so purchased, the investor was to receive the earnings of one member (peon) of the expedition.[81]

Among the special concessions granted the Genoese by the Adelantado was the privilege of sending a representative along on the expedition to look after their interests, that is, to collect their share of the profits. This individual was eventually appointed campmaster by Orellana, no doubt in accordance with a secret deal between the Adelantado and the Genoese. Torres described these events as follows:

He [Orellana] fixed his choice for a campmaster upon a Genoese, in defiance of the laws and the will of all, who are vexed at the setting of an Italian over these men, at first the plan as discussed was to have him go along merely as representative of the Genoese to collect the shares which they are demanding . . . on top of this he [Orellana] made him campmaster and they tell me that he handed some funds over to him; he said nothing to me about this.[82]

At the same time that Friar Torres was finding it more and more difficult to work with Orellana, Monte, and the Genoese, two unexpected events heightened the critical state of affairs. Rumors reached Seville from Lisbon that preparations were being made in Portugal for an expedition to the Amazon. The officials of the Casa de Contratación advised the King that they had heard that the King of Portugal was preparing a fleet of four ships for the Great River and the province of the Amazon," and they added that they were hastening as much as possible to get the ships under way, giving all the encouragement and assistance they could and working with certain merchants to get them to help Orellana as some had offered to do. Then suddenly, as Friar Torres wrote in his turn about this time, "the Adelantado has married despite my attempts to persuade him [not to] . . . because they did not give him any dowry whatsoever, I mean not a single ducat." [83] Furthermore, Orellana insisted on taking his wife along and also one or two sisters-in-law, all of which caused the Friar deep concern, but over which he had no control.

Finally in April 1545, after more than a year of struggles, quarrels, and vexations, Orellana succeeded in getting his ships as far as San Lucar, ready to sail. There the fleet was inspected by the royal officials who found that the "vessels lacked a certain amount of equipment and a certain number of guns and likewise certain supplies." [84] They also discovered that not all of the 300 men that Orellana was to take along were on hand, nor were there more than 24 of the 100 required horses. Finally, at least 1,000 ducats were still needed to purchase the last of the necessary supplies. As a result of what they considered the "unpreparedness of the fleet," the officials told the Adelantado that he could not leave port until the King should so order. This decision was communicated to him in complete secrecy "because, if the men had learned that we were ordering him to be held back," said the officials, "they would have all left him and the expedition would have been ruined." The King agreed perfectly with the opinion of his officials, commanding them "to let him go on his way as soon as he should have made up for what he lacked." [85] The monarch further ordered Orellana to remove Monte and his brother from their posts of lieutenant and chief constable respectively and not to give these positions to any foreigner whatsoever. [86]

One month after their first inspection, the royal officials asked Friar Torres, in company with the supervisor of all ships bound for the Indies, to make a second tour of the fleet in order to see if everything had now been put in order. Torres was cautioned, however, not to permit the fleet to leave if the equipment that they had prescribed was still lacking. On May 9, 1545, Torres and the other functionaries went on board the ships and, after completing their inspection, went to find Orellana to inform him that he should not leave until the officials of the Casa had seen the results of their investigation. But the Adelantado was nowhere to be found on that day or the next. [87] In view of this, on the day after the inspection, Friar Torres issued orders to the pilots whose duty it was to take ships over the bar not to lend their services, under heavy penalty, in taking the ships out, but this was to no avail, for on the morning of May 11, the four ships sailed two leagues outside the port.[88] There they remained anchored until the evening when they slipped out to open sea.

Several days after the fleet had departed, Friar Torres set down his impressions of the events of the preceding year in a final report to the King. In two letters written on May 19 and 20 respectively, the Dominican blamed Vicencio de Monte for the "infinite errors and frauds that have been perpetuated in connection with this expedition." "It is Monte who has made himself rich out of the money of the Genoese, through charterings, through deals." Moreover, "the Adelantado has been putting up with all this or else"—Torres had come to suspect the relationship between Orellana and Monte by this time—" they are dividing up the money and the profits." The Friar also accused Monte of falsifying the accounts to cover a sum of 1,200 ducats that he had illegally taken. Finally it seemed apparent to him that "there was collusion between Orellana and the Genoese," for neither party could account for the money intended to be used in chartering ships. "How can the fleet be fitted out," asked Friar Torres, "if to his own wife [Orellana's] they have given jewels and silks and embroideries and if the Genoese have not handed over the 3,000 ducats in 'numerata pecunia'; if Monte and the Adelantado have cash in their pockets while the rest of the expedition is perishing from hunger and thirst." As a result of all these manipulations and frauds, the fleet had slipped away without having taken on sufficient supplies and, in the opinion of the Friar, "no organizer of an expedition would let them go [even such a short distance as] from here to Naples." [89]

With poor equipment, few supplies, and unseaworthy vessels, the expedition thus sailed away from Spain on its mission to conquer and colonize New Andalusia.[90] According to his plan, Orellana steered his course for the Canaries where he remained for three months in the hope of procuring the supplies that he still lacked. From the Canaries he went on to the Cape Verde Islands where he was obliged to wait two months more. This delay was fatal to him, for he did not find the supplies he hoped for and the greater part of the persons on the ships became ill and many died. One of the ships had to be abandoned in order to refit the remaining ones with parts that they had lost. When the fleet again set sail, fifty more fighting men remained ashore, among them the campmaster and three of the captains.

Orellana, however, refused to abandon the enterprise, and in the middle of November the fleet headed across the Atlantic toward the coast of Brazil. During the crossing they met bad weather and the men would have perished from thirst if they had not run into tropical rainstorms. As a climax to their misfortunes, one of the ships, which carried seventy-seven persons, eleven horses, and a brigatine that was to be used to go up the river, was lost. Finally, after sailing for some 100 leagues within the sight of the Brazilian coast, they came upon fresh water, a sure indication that they were near the mouth of the river that they were seeking. On December 20, 1545, they entered the Amazon and started up it, covering a distance of 1,000 leagues past flooded lands and uninhabited regions until they arrived at some Indian huts. There the Adelantado ordered his men to stop and begin the construction of the brigatine, a task which took up the months of January, February, and March 1546.[91] As soon as the brigatine was finished, Orellana sent it off in search of food supplies, the lack of which had already caused the death of fifty-five men. The efforts of the brigatine were fruitless and after being attacked by the Indians, the survivors returned to camp. The brigatine and the ship then started out together in search of the principal arm of the river, but scarcely had they gone twenty leagues when the ship was wrecked, its crew being forced to take refuge on an island, one league from the scene of the catastrophe. Under these circumstances Orellana decided to leave twenty-eight or thirty of his men on the island while he set out again in the brigatine in search of the main branch of the river. After wandering about in vain for twenty-seven days, he returned to the camp and found it deserted.[92]

While the Adelantado was engaged in his search, his companions who had remained on the island, not knowing the whereabouts of their commander and fearing death at the hands of the Indians or from hunger, decided to build a boat from the wreck of their ship and to go find Orellana. After weeks of constant toil, they finally launched their craft on the river and although it was of such faulty construction that it let in water in all parts, they began to move up the river in search of Orellana. After having traveled for several days without finding any trace of the Adelantado and having by this time exhausted their provisions, they resolved to return downstream. On the trip downstream, they lost ten men of the original party, and six decided to stay in the region where the river flows into the sea—because this area was thickly populated and well provided with food, they believed it to be part of the mainland. Four leagues farther down, four others ran away in a small boat which had been taken along "because they considered the country to be a good one." The remaining men continued their way downstream and finally managed to get out to sea again. Sailing close to the coast, bailing out day and night the water that came into the boat, they finally reached, in the last days of November or the first of December 1546, the island of Margarita off the coast of Venezuela. There they found twenty-five of their companions [93] and also Orellana's wife, "who told us," says Francisco de Guzmán:

that her husband had not succeeded in getting into the main branch which he was looking for and [that] consequently and particularly [on account] of his being ill, he had made up his mind to come to a land of Christians and [that] during this time, when he was out looking for food for the journey, the Indians shot seventeen of his men with arrows. From grief over this and from his illness Orellana died.

And with him disappeared the last hope of any profit for the Genoese sponsors.

The failure of the Orellana expedition seems to have put an end to the era of Genoese investment in exploratory ventures. In any event, there is no available evidence to indicate any further large-scale investment on their part. If their investments in overseas discovery were not successful and brought them few returns, their entrepreneurial activities in the New World made up for these losses. The El Dorado of the Genoese was not to be found in the jungles of the Amazon Basin or along the shores of the Plata River, but in the systematic exploitation of the lands of the Caribbean and the trade in their products.

CHAPTER VI

Genoese Entrepreneurs in the Caribbean

ANOTHER major contribution of the Genoese to the overseas expansion of Spain in the sixteenth century was their role in the development of colonial economic life. From the first decades of the century, members of the Genoese colony of Seville went to America as merchants in their own right or as agents for their compatriots. Although many of them were only transients who, after several trips and a few years of residence in the colonies, returned to Seville, there were others who settled down permanently in America. As merchants they were primarily interested in the transatlantic trade—the exchange of European goods and African slaves for American commodities—but as capitalists their desire for profits soon led them to invest in such colonial enterprises as mining, agriculture, stock raising, and the intercolonial trade. Gradually their wealth and control over the land converted them into powerful *hacendados* whose descendants, intermarrying with the creole aristocracy, formed a part of the ruling class of the period.

Although the Genoese invested in many New World enterprises, their most important investments were made in the Carribbean sugar industry. It brought them the largest returns and provided a basis for the fame and fortune of the most prominent Genoese settlers of Hispaniola and Puerto Rico. Genoese involvement in the sugar trade was of long standing.[1] For centuries they had traded in sugar, and in the fifteenth century they promoted the manufacture of sugar on the newly opened Portuguese and Spanish Atlantic islands. Members of the Lomellini family settled on the island of Madeira in 1471 where they bought land and began to produce sugar.[2] In a similar fashion, the Riberol and Justinián families were among the most important mill owners in the Canary Islands, and they also, along with many of their compatriots, carried on an active trade in slaves and sugar between the islands and Seville during the second half of the fifteenth century.[3] With the introduction of sugar into the New World, the Genoese again took the initiative. Sugar making was a costly process, requiring much heavy equipment, usually necessarily imported from Europe, and, to operate it, a large fixed number of skilled and manual laborers. It was definitely a rich man's business. The Genoese had the necessary capital and, through their participation in the Negro slave trade, control over a steady supply of laborers, both of which enabled them to assume a predominant role in the Caribbean sugar industry during the critical first years of its development.

The Genoese built and operated three of the most productive sugar mills on the island of Hispaniola; we do not know their exact dates of construction, but we can assume that they were set up in the second or third decade of the sixteenth century. All three of these mills represented a capital investment either by Genoese residents of the New World or by members of the Seville colony who maintained representatives on the island to look after their investment. In two instances wealthy Spanish settlers also contributed to the enterprise and were taken on as partners. A good example of such a combination of resident Genoese and Spanish capital was the *ingenio* (water-powered mill) built by the Genoese Esteban Justinián and his Spanish partner, Pedro Vázquez de Mella, on the banks of the Haina River, three leagues from the city of Santo Domingo.[4] Like most of the Genoese millowners on Hispaniola, Esteban Justinián came to the island originally as a factor for his Sevillian compatriots and spent his first years of residence in the New World collecting debts and selling goods sent to him from Spain.

Even after the construction of his mill, Justinián continued to serve the Sevillian colony as a commission agent and to engage in commercial activities on his own. In 1536, for example, we find him collecting debts for Jácome de Grimaldo and Agustín de Vivaldo. His association with the latter involved the sale of Negro slaves, which, as we have seen, was by this time one of the most valuable commodities that the Genoese sent to the island. All of the Genoese residents of the New World were in some way or another connected with the slave trade. As for Justinián, he acted as an agent for the Vázquez, Forne, and Vivaldo company in the late 1520's. He eventually formed his own company—Esteban Justinián and Co.—that dealt in slaves and land, the two most important investment opportunities on the island. We do not know who his partners were, but two of the most likely seem to have been Melchor Centurión and Valián de Forne with whom he was associated in several transactions. He also joined Jácome de Castellón in a few deals involving slaves.[5]

Even though his investments in slaves and land brought him increasing profits, Justinián suffered losses from his sugar mill. He wasted both time and money in several attempts to build a dam to utilize the available water power from the Haina River. After his death in 1535, his heirs abandoned the mill, "dividing up the lands, the slaves, the cattle, and the implements they could make use of, and gave up the making of sugar in order not to lose everything they had in the enterprise." Within a few years, however, Juan Bautista de Justinián "fixed it up and kept the house and built a horse-powered mill [trapiche]" which produced excellent sugar and remained remarkably prosperous during most of the century.[6]

The ingenio of Sancti Spiritus, located eleven leagues outside of Santo Domingo, was also built by joint Genoese and Spanish capital. Agustín de Vivaldo, the Sevillian partner of Vázquez, Forne, and Vivaldo, underwrote the principal cost in association with two Spanish residents of Hispaniola, Juan de Villoria and Hierónimo de Agüero. The shares of the two Spaniards were subsequently purchased by Vázquez, Forne, and Vivaldo, who took over the ownership and operation of the mill. In the opinion of Oviedo, "It was a very good mill," and the Sevillian protocols seem to bear out his contention. In 1526, for example, Vivaldo collected 1,200 ducats of insurance on a cargo of sugar from this mill. At Vivaldo's death his share in the mill and place in the company were taken over by Valián de Forne who had represented Vázquez, Forne, and Vivaldo on Hispaniola for several years.[7]

Valián de Forne arrived on the island of Hispaniola in the early 1530's. His chief responsibility as a company factor was to dispose of the slaves that his firm sent to the island and to arrange for the return cargoes of sugar. In this capacity he soon became involved in a series of lawsuits growing out of his firm's dealings with the numerous small cane growers on the island, who were completely at the mercy of the millowners, for the millowners could refuse to grind their cane or delay in order to limit their profits. In 1531 and again in 1536 Forne and several small planters sued the owners and the major-domos of the sugar mills for not milling their cane in time, causing them great loss.[8]

During the first years of his residence in America, Forne was closely associated with Esteban Justinián and, as suggested before, may have become a member of Justinián's company. In any case, he joined Justinián in several land deals and slave transactions and after Justinián's death served as an executor of his estate. Forne maintained close ties with the Justinián family in both Seville and Santo Domingo. In 1549, after a brief trip to Seville, we find him accompanying María Justinián to the New World where she was to join her husband, Mauro Fantoni, a Florentine associate of both Forne and other members of the Justinián family.

In the 1540's and 1550's Forne continued to work for the Vázquez and Forne firm, but he also began to invest his own funds in urban real estate and cattle. In 1550 he owned several houses on Miradero Street in Santo Domingo and other valuable parcels of land within the confines of the city. Much of this property he held in partnership with Fantoni—in addition to several cattle estates. By this time he had also arranged his permanent status in the New World by becoming a denizen of Santo Domingo. His increasing prosperity enabled him between 1542 and 1544 to farm the *avería,* a special tax laid on imports and exports to meet the expenses of defence against corsairs and rebellious Indians.[9]

As for the Sancti Spiritus mill, we do not know how it fared under Forne's management or what it looked like during this period, but it could not have been very different from the other mills on the island. We can, on the basis of the existent inventories of several mills, obtain a general idea of a sugar mill on Hispaniola at mid-century. Like all tropical plantation units, the sugar mill combined two functions: it was at once an agricultural processing plant and an agricultural estate.[10] In area a good plantation might hold outright 200 acres, one half cultivated and the other half left to natural forest to furnish lumber for the furnaces. On the cultivated half, a relatively small amount of land was given over to the production of sugar cane, most of the area being set aside for the cultivation of food crops to feed the mill population and to vineyards, orchards, or whatever else the planter desired. The average plantation contained little more that 25 or 30 acres of cane which, on the basis of contemporary estimates of 5 tons of sugar per acre, yielded an average annual production of 125 tons. In addition to this acreage the millowner often acquired the use of certain crown lands in the vicinity for pasturing the one to two thousand head of cattle in the mill herd. As for the population of the *ingenio,* it varied depending on size and productivity. A mill producing 125 tons of sugar a year required about two hundred workers, one hundred and fifty or more of these being adult Negro slaves and the rest, perhaps, fifteen or twenty families of white foremen, craftsmen, and sugar technicians.

The third mill controlled by the Genoese on Hispaniola—in the Azua region on the Bia River—represents one of the best examples of Genoese entrepreneurship on the island. It was built by Jácome de Castellón, the most famous of all the Genoese residents of the New World.[11] Castellón, son of a prosperous Genoese merchant of Toledo, moved to Seville at the beginning of the sixteenth century to take advantage of the opening of the New World. In 1510 he undertook a selling trip to Hispaniola for his father and for a compatriot, Esteban Centurión. A year later he returned to Seville, but remained in the city only long enough to settle accounts with Centurión and to purchase a large supply of merchandise to take with him to the Indies. The economic possibilities in America had so captured his imagination that he resolved to remain in the New World, and in the summer of 1512 he left Seville and Spain forever, aboard the *Santa María de Gracia*.[12]

Like the rest of the Genoese residents of Santo Domingo, Castellón was primarily interested in the transatlantic trade and served for many years as a commission agent for members of the Seville colony.[13] In this capacity he was particularly interested in slaves and sugar, but trade was only one aspect of his total entrepreneurial activity. He also invested in stock raising, one of the principal industries of Hispaniola. Oviedo noted that during his time herds of 42,000 head of cattle could be found on the island and that 20,000 head was not unusual. Hides, along with sugar, made up the chief exports from the Caribbean area during the whole colonial period, and a large number of those sent to Seville by Castellón came from his own herds. In addition, urban real estate attracted him. He constructed several houses in Santo Domingo that he subsequently rented, and he bought lots in the city for speculative purposes.[14]

The construction of the Bia River sugar mill brought him into still another enterprise. We know almost nothing about this *ingenio* except for the judgment of Oviedo that it was a "very fine property and profitable." After Castellón's death in 1535, his wife, Doña Francisca de Isásaga, and his children continued to operate the mill, but in the words of Oviedo, "it has not been looked after as it should be since the death of Jácome de Castellón."

In the spring of 1522 an important interruption occurred in the life of entrepreneur Castellón. At that time rumors reached Santo Domingo of another Indian uprising in Cumaná, the coastal region of Venezuela opposite the island of Cubagua, center of the pearl-fishing industry. This area had been the site of Father Las Casas' experimental agricultural colony,[15] but the priest's good intentions conflicted with the profit-seeking designs of the inhabitants of the offshore island of Cubagua, who depended on the mainland for water and slaves. Continuous slave raids by the islanders finally caused the Indians to rise up in a widespread rebellion in 1520 in which they burnt the monasteries, massacred the clergy and Spanish settlers, and eventually even launched an attack against Cubagua. The Indian assault was so strong that the islanders could not resist it and they fled for their lives to Santo Domingo. Nonetheless, the pearl fisheries of Cubagua were too profitable to be abandoned so easily; in 1521 an expedition from Santo Domingo under the command of Gonzalo de Ocampo put down the uprising, but in the following year the Indians again rose up against the Spaniards for the same reasons.[16]

As the months passed it became clear to the officials of the Audiencia that the Spaniards on Cubagua could not suppress the revolt without substantial aid from Hispaniola. They decided to send a new expedition and gave the command of this force to Jácome de Castellón. Our sources give us very little indication as to why the Audiencia chose Castellón to lead this expedition. It is likely that he solicited the position and received it in return for a promise to contribute to the expenses of the undertaking. In any case, we note that he invested 1,663 pesos (748,350 maravedís), which, along with the contribution of the inhabitants of Cubagua, made up three quarters of the total cost.[17] The government, for its part, contributed one quarter of the necessary amount.

As for Castellón's motives for becoming involved in a military enterprise of this kind, I think we can conclude that he was inspired by the same spirit of adventure and the hope of gain that motivated the majority of Spanish settlers in the New World. In the case of the Genoese, however, the latter factor was not just a blind desire for easy wealth, but rather it involved a rational calculation of the immediate and long range economic benefits to be gained from the penetration of the Cubagua-Cumaná area. The pearl-fishing industry was in its initial stages, a development which meant that capital for investment was urgently needed and profits were high. Indian slaves, vital to the operation of the enterprise, were scarce and a valuable commodity for trade. Moreover, the terrain of Cubagua was so dry that it could not be cultivated without intense irrigation, forcing the islanders to depend on imports of food and other necessities. Staples were shipped to the island from Hispaniola and Puerto Rico while manufactured goods came directly from Seville.[18] Most important among the food products were cassava and maize, much of which was traded to the Indians of the mainland in return for slaves. The slave and commodities trade presented excellent commercial possibilities for a merchant and landowner like Castellón. On the other hand, the pearl fisheries offered ample opportunities for capital investment. To Castellón, the Cumaná expedition was essentially a calculated economic venture, under the guise of a military intervention, that would lead to the opening of a new area for exploitation.

Early in September 1522, Captain Castellón left Santo Domingo for Cubagua where he added both men and supplies to his force. A short time later, in the words of the chronicler Gómara, "he corrected the errors of Gonzalo de Ocampo, Bartolomé de las Casas and others . . . defeated the Indians, recovered the land, re-established the pearl fishing, and replenished Cubagua and even Santo Domingo with slaves." [19] After crushing the resistance of the Indians, he began to rebuild the fortress of Cumaná, which was completed in May 1523. Then, within close proximity to the former settlement of New Toledo, he founded another town called New Cordova, a visible symbol of Spanish authority and domination.

Castellón's military exploits soon reached the attention of

Charles V, who, in reward for his services, appointed him warden of the Fortress of Cumaná. His new position gave him an opportunity to assume an important role in the local slave trade, which was regulated by the government and supervised by the royal officials. This trade was based on a system of barter (*rescates*) involving the exchange of staple food products for Indian slaves. Only Indians who had been captured and enslaved by their own people as a result of intertribal wars could legally be bartered as slaves to the Spaniards. Although the provisions of the law were strict and went so far as to call for the presence of the bishop of the area as the "protector" of the Indians at every transaction, from the beginning fraud and abuses characterized the *rescates*. Free Indians were often sold as slaves and sent off to work in the pearl fisheries.[20]

The proceeds from the *rescates* were to be used to maintain the Fortress of Cumaná.[21] This arrangement led to a later claim by the overseer of the royal foundries of Santo Domingo, Gaspar de Astudillo, that Castellón had manipulated these funds for his own profit. In a letter to Charles V in 1528. Astudillo claimed that the *rescates* from the years 1523 to 1528 should have totalled 5,000 pesos, but that "Castellón had taken them for himself and never gave any account of them." It is unlikely that Astudillo's accusations were true, considering the character of the overseer—"a loud-mouthed man of dubious background," according to the officials of the Audiencia—who just a few years after his attack on Castellón was himself accused of defrauding the royal treasury and imprisoned by the authorities in Santo Domingo.[22] Astudillo's charges did not have any serious effect on Castellón, who during these years solicited and received from Charles V a special coat of arms commemorating his pacification of Cumaná.[23] This act confirmed his new status of conqueror, and from this time forward he was officially entitled "Jácome de Castellón, conquistador de Cumaná."

Outside of his participation in the Indian slave trade, we know very little about his other economic activities while in Cumaná. He probably invested in the pearl fisheries that reached the height of their production during this period. By the time Castellón left the area, some seven years after his arrival there, careless and unscientific methods of exploitation had exhausted the oyster beds, and the boom was over. The settlement on Cubagua continued to prosper for a few years longer, but the discovery of new banks at Cabo de la Vela along the mainland to the west of Cubagua in 1538 led to the rapid depopulation of the island.[24]

In 1528 Castellón, with new fame and fortune, returned to Santo Domingo where he resumed his varied business career. During these years he was active, like so many of the businessmen of Santo Domingo, in the commodities trade between Hispaniola and Cubagua. He also went back into the Negro slave trade, serving at times as a commission agent for Pedro Benito de Basiñana, and eventually formed a partnership with Jerónimo de Grimaldo dedicated to the sale of slaves and European goods in the islands and mainland of Central America. As for his sugar mill, he devoted considerable time and energy to it until he made it one of the most productive on the island. At the same time, he wanted to expand his investment in the Antillean sugar industry by taking over the mill originally set up by his brother Tomás in Puerto Rico, which, because of the death of Tomás' daughter, was now in the hands of her husband. For several years Castellón engaged in a legal struggle with his belated niece's husband over the mill and in the end he lost the suit. Although this legal defeat disappointed him and embittered his last years, it proved to be unimportant in the end, for at his death in 1534–1535 he was recognized as one of the most prominant entrepreneurs in the New World and, what was more important, in Spanish society, a proved military leader and conquistador.[25] Like his medieval predecessors, Jácome de Castellón had shown that, for the Genoese, military exploits and economic endeavors could be successfully combined even though the majority of his compatriots in America did not follow his example, preferring economic to military undertakings.

Jácome Castellón's brother Tomás is another example of a

successful Genoese entrepreneur in sixteenth-century Spanish America whose wealth was based on investment in both trade and agriculture. Yet his career differed from that of his brother and the other Genoese residents of Hispaniola, for unlike his compatriots, he did not continue to work as a commission agent for the Sevillian Genoese once he had established himself as a prosperous planter and sugar mill owner in Puerto Rico. In fact, he had very limited contacts with either the members of the Seville colony or his fellow countrymen on Hispaniola. All of his entrepreneurial activities on Puerto Rico were undertaken independently or, toward the end of his life, in association with his Spanish son-in-law, Blas de Villasante, the treasurer of the island.

In 1509, preceding his brother by one year, Tomás de Castellón, age twenty, arrived on Hispaniola as an agent for the Sevillian Genoese. We know that he made the crossing on the *Santa Ana* and that she was laden with merchandise belonging to both his father and Batista Cataño. He also carried with him a small quantity of his own goods to sell in the New World. Before his departure from Seville he was granted powers of attorney by several Genoese merchants, including Cosme and Francisco de Riberol, who, during the following two years, sent him a steady stream of merchandise to sell on the island.[26]

Although he was quick to take advantage of all the opportunities open to a Genoese factor in Santo Domingo, particularly speculation in urban real estate and cattle lands, he was dissatisfied with his life in Hispaniola. Santo Domingo was too crowded with gold hunters and his own alert compatriots for the adventurous and ambitious Castellón. He longed for the opportunity to go to a new and unexplored area that he could exploit with little competition. During these years Puerto Rico, recently conquered and as yet sparsely settled, seemed to offer excellent possibilities. Castellón soon left Hispaniola for Puerto Rico, taking with him a sizeable fortune won during his short residence on Hispaniola. He used these funds to purchase a large tract of land near San Germán, which he turned over to the cultivation of cassava and to stock raising.[27] Within a few years his lands were producing some of the largest cassava crops on the island. In 1513, for example, it was not difficult for him to provision an expedition of fifty men with 500 cargas of cassava bread. During the next few years he began experimenting with sugar cane, and by 1523 he was so successful that he was able to set up the first sugar mill (*trapiche*) on the island.[28] Although there were, from the second decade of the century, a few molasses mills and some attempts to grow cane in Puerto Rico, Castellón was the first to manufacture commercial sugar on the island. The Genoese may therefore be credited with founding the sugar industry in Puerto Rico.

Castellón's mill had its own port on the Bay of Añasco— Puerto Castellón, later called Cinca. Through this port sugar and hides were shipped to Spain while cassava and other agricultural products went out into the intercolonial trade. During the years from 1523 to his death, his mill prospered, but Castellón's other investments overstrained his financial resources. His last venture—farming the *almojarifazgo* from 1524 to 1527 —proved to be too much for him. At his death in 1527, he was so deeply in debt to the royal treasury that the governing officials of the island ordered the confiscation of his mill, which he had left—with the rest of his property—to his daughter, Teodora de Castellón, and her husband, Blas de Villasante. But the confiscation order never went into effect, for Villasante obtained a stay of execution of judgment against the property because "such execution would entail loss to the community." [29] Instead, the mill was to continue to operate under the management of Villasante and his major-domo Sancho Darsas, who were charged with repaying Csatellón's debts from the mill's annual production.

While Treasurer Villasante was attempting to repay his father-in-law's debts, he became involved in serious difficulties with some of his colleagues on the San Juan *cabildo*. For several years the *cabildo* had been plagued with dissension as its members accused each other of defrauding the royal treasury and other misdemeanors.[30] These accusations and counteraccusations resulted in the formation of angry factions that kept the government in perpetual chaos and the island in turmoil. At the center of these disturbances was the accountant Antonio Sedeño, who while enjoying the favor of the Conqueror of Puerto Rico, Juan Ponce de León, was using his public office to further his personal fortune. His actions aroused the hatred and jealousy of many, among the most vocal Villasante. Specifically, the two men both claimed the services of certain Indians belonging to the Caçica of Caguas, Doña María Baguanamay.[31] When Sedeño was finally ousted from his government post, he also lost his claim to the Indians, which meant that Villasante was able to put them to work on his own estates. Sedeño subsequently left the island. but his supporters syated behind. They were determined to ruin Villasante at all costs.

In the winter of 1528 the anti-Villasante group found an opportunity to take revenge against their enemy. At that time the Bishop of San Juan, angered by the chronic disorder and immorality that plagued the island and anxious to exert his power as inquisitor, issued a pastoral letter denouncing disguised heretics, blasphemers, adulterers, and all those who complained against the Holy Office. Following this announcement Bishop Mansa inaugurated a campaign designed to destroy heresy and immorality on the island. Not long afterwards the Bishop received several anonymous letters accusing Villasante of having maintained illicit relations with both Doña María Baguanamay and her daughter, a change that had been made originally as early as 1519.[32] Others claimed that the treasurer was a grandson of a certain Alonso Rodríguez of Medina del Campo, who had been burnt at the stake in Spain for heresy. Faced with such charges, Bishop Mansa, on December 11, 1528, had Villasante seized and imprisoned in the jail of the Inquisition, where he remained for several months in spite of his protests of innocence. At the end of February he sent a direct appeal to Charles V in which he dismissed the charges against him as false. But the Holy Office wanted irrefutable proof of his innocence and until it was forthcoming he would be required to stay in jail. Just a month later, however, he fell gravely ill, an event which seemed to move the Bishop, for he allowed him to exchange his prison cell for house arrest. Within a few weeks Villasante, his health restored, was permitted to resume his duties as treasurer.[33]

By this time, however, Villasante had to face new charges emanating from another direction. Licentiate Antonio de la Gama had just completed his *residencia* of all the governing officials of Puerto Rico—including Villasante, whom he had interrogated in jail just a few days after the treasurer was imprisoned.[34] De la Gama found certain discrepancies in the treasury accounts for which be blamed Villasante. His unfavorable report on Villasante led to the eventual appointment of a new treasurer, Miguel de Lizarazo, who reached the island in November 1529. Just five days before Lizarazo's arrival, however, Bishop Mansa had given Villasante permission to visit his country estates "to arrange for the repayment of debts owed to the crown by his wife as heiress of Tomás de Castellón." [35] With Villasante out of town, the *cabildo,* considering him to be a prisoner of the Inquisition and therefore unable to exercise his duties as treasurer, received Lizarazo and officially accepted him as treasurer of the island. When Villasante returned to San Juan and discovered what had occurred, he immediately appealed to the Audiencia claiming that his difficulties with the Inquisition did not disqualify him from holding office, since Bishop Mansa had allowed him to do so and his case was still pending.

In March Lizarazo died, but the *cabildo* appointed an acting treasurer who performed the duties of the office until June, when the Audiencia decided in favor of Villasante and ordered the *cabildo* to allow him to continue in the position of treasurer, even though he was under the jurisdiction of the Inquisition.[36]

The reinstatement of Villasante and the assistance given to him by the Audiencia, which subsequently authorized him to collect his seven months' back salary, angered the Bishop, who now saw the case in terms of a direct challenge to his authority and power by the Audiencia. When in March 1530 the Council of the Indies, by this time well acquainted with the details of this case, ordered Villasante to return to Spain to appear before them, Bishop Mansa refused to allow him to leave.[37] He reportedly told the members of the *cabildo* who brought him the official order for the prisoner's release that, "if the Emperor wants him [Villasante] in Castile, he must write to me and not to you," and with these words he threatened to excommunicate them if they tried to remove Villasante.[38] Once again he imprisoned the treasurer in the jail of the Inquisition where he remained until he was finally absolved and freed.

Villasante emerged from one set of difficulties only to become involved in another. A short time after his release from prison, his wife died, leaving him all of the possessions that she had inherited from her father, but her will was contested by her uncle, Jácome de Castellón.[39] Castellón had acted as her guardian while Villasante was in prison and now claimed the sugar plantation and mill in the name of the Castellón family. The mill was by this time in a sad state of disrepair due to an attack on it by pirates in 1528 and the general neglect it had suffered during the period of Villasante's imprisonment.[40] The Genoese entrepreneur of Santo Domingo hoped to restore it to its former condition and to convert it once more into a profit-making enterprise. Soon Castellón and Villasante were involved in a series of lawsuits that remained unresolved in 1535, the year of both contestants' deaths, although the mill was still in Villasante's possession.

During the years in which he was engaged in a legal battle with Jácome de Castellón over the ownership of the mill, Villasante married again, this time to Catalina Suárez del Pozo. At his death his property passed to his widow and to their daughter Juana de Villasante, who continued the legal struggle with other members of the Castellón family, namely Jácome's mother in Spain and his sister in Santo Domingo.[41] While the court proceedings dragged on, Doña Catalina and her daughter returned to Spain and took up residence in Valladolid. In 1550 they arranged to rent the mill to a prosperous Sevillian businessman, Francisco Ruiz, for 1,000 ducats a year, but Ruiz sent his American factors to investigate the place and they reported that it contained less land than was included in the inventory and that it was in bad condition. He therefore refused to pay more than 700 ducats yearly rent, which the widow finally accepted along with the gift of a "chesnut-colored horse, saddled and bridled." We do not know to what degree Ruiz was able to restore the mill and make it prosperous, but in 1554 disaster struck the place. In that year French corsairs entered the plantation's port, killed most of its slaves, and destroyed so much of it that it was later described as a total ruin. During the following years, owners of surrounding estates tried to seize its lands for cattle ranches. By 1571 it was prized solely for the wild herds that pastured on its lands, for in that year Villasante's daughter and her husband, Don Juan de Velasco y Vallejo, asked the King to prohibit unauthorized persons from killing cattle from their property for hides.[42] By this time, however, the "mill of the Genoese" was just a memory and wild grass covered the fertile fields where Tomás de Castellón had once cultivated cassava and sugar cane.

The entrepreneurship of Tomás de Castellón and his compatriots in the Caribbean Islands was just one aspect of the total Genoese contribution to the creation of the Spanish-American Empire in the sixteenth century. The discovery and conquest of America was a gigantic undertaking in terms of financial resources which Spain, just emerging from a centuries long struggle against the Moslems, did not have. The members of the Genoese colony of Seville helped to provide much of the capital necessary for the creation of the Spanish Empire in the New World. Not only did they help to finance the exploration and conquest of America, but they also played a vital role in the establishment and maintenance of trade between Spain and her colonies. Wherever the Spanish conquistadores went, Genoese merchant-capitalists were not far behind, always ready to sell goods and invest capital. The New World challenged them and they met it with the same spirit that had motivated their ancestors to expand in the basin of the Mediterranean Sea centuries before.

While the Genoese were helping the Spaniards carve out their overseas empire, they were also financing the establishment of Spanish power in the Old World. Throughout the century members of the Sevillian Genoese colony invested capital drawn from their transatlantic trade in royal financing and shared the position of crown bankers with their relatives in Genoa or at the Spanish court. By the last quarter of the century the Genoese incontestably ruled the world of Spanish finance.

It might have been true, as Quevedo and many of his contemporary Spanish writers claimed, that the tomb of Spanish gold was Genoa,[43] but it is doubtful that the Spanish monarchy could have supported itself without the aid of the Genoese. Genoese loans held the empire together during the Golden Age but with each royal bankruptcy—six between 1557 and 1647— they moved closer to the brink of ruin. Nevertheless, they continued to participate in the gamble of Spanish finance and overseas trade. Motivated by their insatiable desire for enrichment, and by the pressure of their investments, the Genoese moved along with the Spanish monarchy until the bankruptcy of 1647 that completely destroyed their finances. It was only at this time, when there was no longer any hope of further gain, that they severed their relations with Spain and, as a result, lost their commanding place in the American trade and their position as international bankers. At the end of the seventeenth century, the bell tolled for the Genoese as well as for Spain.

Notes

CHAPTER I

1. Genoese commercial penetration of Spain began in the twelfth century. In the first quarter of that century, Genoese appeared in the north in Galicia, playing an important part in drawing the whole Spanish littoral of the Bay of Biscay into the orbit of international trade. In the south they had connections with the commercial centers of Lower Andalusia which were still in Moslem hands. After the reconquest of this region by the Christians, Genoese established permanent commercial colonies in various Andalusian towns (Charles Verlinden, "The Rise of Spanish Trade in the Middle Ages," *Economic History Review*, X [1940], 49). For a description of Genoese colonial expansion in the Middle Ages see R. Lopez, *Storia delle colonie genovesi nel Mediterràneo* (Bologna, 1938).

2. The Spanish dramatist Lope de Vega thus described Seville in his *El peregrino en su patria*, quoted in Miguel de Cervantes Saavedra, *Rinconete y Cortadillo*, ed. Francisco Rodríguez Marín (Madrid, 1920), p. 10.

3. It was the richness of the Sevillian countryside, particularly the oil of Aljarafe, that initially attracted the Genoese to Seville. They traded with the city while it was under Moslem control, but did not have any permanent settlement there until the reconquest in 1248. At that time they received special commercial privileges, including the right to have a "fondaco, houses, church, and oven . . . with their own laws except in cases of homicide" (J. González, *Repartimiento de Sevilla* [Madrid, 1951], p. 377. See also M. del Carmen Carlé, "Mercaderes en Castilla [1252–1512]," *Cuadernos de historia de España*, XXI–XXII [1954], 231).

The number of Genoese residing in the city during the thirteenth century was indeed small, but with the establishment of Seville as a port of call for Genoese galleys and carracks en route to Southampton and Bruges in the fourteenth and fifteenth centuries, there was a gradual increase in the resident population (A. Ballesteros, *Sevilla en el siglo XIII*

NOTES, PP. 1–2

[Madrid, 1913], 42; R. Carande, "Sevilla, fortaleza y mercado," *Anuario de historia del derecho español*, II [1925], 287).

4. A more precise estimate of the city's Genoese population during the fifteenth century could be obtained from a thorough investigation of the Sevillian Protocols for that period (See H. Sancho de Sopranis, "Los genoveses en la región gaditano-xerience de 1400–1800," *Hispania, revista española de historia*, VIII [1948], 356–357). By the mid-fifteenth century Seville had become one of the most important mercantile cities in southern Spain, and the Genoese recognized this fact by making the town the center of their commercial and financial activities in that region. All of their business in Andalusia, and to a large degree in Castile as well, was directed from Seville. Genoese trade in Seville and the surrounding area has been described by Jacques Heers, *Gênes au XV*ᵉ *siècle* (Paris, 1961), pp. 487–497. See also Robert Lopez, "Market Expansion: The Case of Genoa," *Journal of Economic History* XXIV (1964), 445–464.

5. In 1528 Andrea Doria, leader of one of the political parties in Genoa, seized power and brought the city, which had been vacillating between the French and Spanish, into the Spanish camp. As a result, many members of the opposition left Genoa (F. Casoni, *Annali della repùbblica di Gènova del sècolo dècimo sesto* [Genoa, 1799–1800], III, 9–11; Vito Vitale, *Breviario della storia di Gènova* [Genoa, 1955], I, 165–179). In 1547, with French aid, Count Gian Luigi, head of the Fieschi family, led a conspiracy to overthrow Andrea Doria's government. Gianettino Doria, adopted son and heir of Andrea, was murdered and Andrea was forced to flee. The conspirators had secured most of the city when Count Gian Luigi Fieschi was accidentally drowned and the movement collapsed (Camillo Manfroni, *Gènova* [Rome, 1929], pp. 169–170; Vitale, *Storia di Gènova*, I, 211–219.

6. Over one hundred names of Genoese businessmen appear in the Sevillian Protocols during the course of the century. In contrast, an important Andalusian port city such as Cadiz contained less than half that number (see H. Sancho de Sopranis, 'Los genoveses," pp. 374–375).

As Fray Tomás de Mercado, author of the most important treatise on Sevillian commercial life, said: "La casa de la contratación de Sevilla y el trato della es uno de los más célebres y ricos que hay el día de hoy, o se sabe en todo el orbe universal . . . arde la ciudad en todo género de negocios" (*Summa de tratos y contratos* [Seville, 1587], p. A2).

7. Among the first group were Ambrosio Spínola, Pedro de Grimaldo, and Martín Pinelo (see José de la Torre y del Cerro, *Beatríz Enríquez de Harana y Cristóbal Colón* [Madrid, 1933], App. XI), and in the second, Esteban Centurión, "vecino de Granada" (APS, 7 Nov. 1511, Oficio XV, libro II, Bernal González Vallesillo, fol. tercer tercio del legajo); Agustín

Italián, "vecino de Málaga," (APS, 17 Dec. 1516, Oficio I, Libro II, Mateo de la Cuadra, fol. 959); Francisco Doria, "estante en Cádiz" (APS, 4 Sept. 1507, Oficio XV, Libro I, Bernal González Vallesillo, fol. 444).

8. In 1528, Andrea Doria, in an attempt to end the inter-family strife that had brought turmoil to the city throughout its history, decreed that only those families of groups possessing at least six *case aperte* (open houses) in the city could remain under their own name. All others had to join one of the larger groups. Only twenty-eight families were able to meet the requirement (Manfroni, *Gènova*, p. 152; Vitale, *Storia di Gènova*, pp. 206–211).

9. Members of the De Franchi and Usodimare had settled in Cadiz in the fourteenth and fifteenth centuries, and their descendants were among the outstanding citizens of that city in the sixteenth century (Sopranis, "Los genoveses," p. 374).

10. The following statistics are based solely on data from the Sevillian Notarial Archives, and therefore only an approximate value can be given to them.

11. During the thirteenth century the small merchant and artisan groups (the *popolari*) who had enriched themselves in the Syrian and North African trade formed a political party in opposition to the ruling nobility. By the end of the century, they had gained the support of one of the rival noble factions led by the Doria and Spinola, who saw in the popular party an effective weapon against the Grimaldi and Fieschi (Manfroni, *Gènova*, p. 141; Vitale, *Storia di Gènova*, pp. 81–87).

12. In the fourteenth and fifteenth centuries the Genoese moved easily and often between the cities of southern Spain, Portugal, and North Africa. For the majority, the aim was to enrich themselves and eventually return to Genoa (Sopranis, "Los genoveses," p. 371; Heers, *Gênes*, p. 493).

13. Torre y del Cerro, *Beatríz Enríquez de Harana*, App. XI, 13 July 1486; 14 May 1486; 19 Oct. 1490.

14. Antonio Ballesteros, *Cristóbal Colón y el descubrimiento de América* (Barcelona–Buenos Aires, 1945), II, 259. The maravedí was a copper coin equal to the ninety-sixth part of a mark of gold (the Spanish mark [marco], equivalent to 230.045 grams); 375 maravedís made up 1 ducat (S. E. Morison, *Admiral of the Ocean Sea, a Life of Christopher Columbus* [Boston, 1942], I, xiv).

15. Pinelo guaranteed a loan of 5,000,000 maravedís which the Duke of Medina Sidonia made to the Spanish sovereigns. In 1493 he loaned the Catholic kings 1,000,000 maravedís to transport the last Moslem king of Granada to Africa (Ballesteros, *Cristóbal Colón*, II, 259). See also

Ernst Schäfer, *El consejo real y supremo de las Indias* (Seville, 1935), I, 9. As an official of the Casa, he could not engage directly in the trade with America (Clarence Haring, *Trade and Navigation between Spain and the Indies in the Time of the Hapsburgs* [Cambridge, 1918], p. 31). Nevertheless, the Sevillian Protocols disclose that he gave credit in the form of merchandise to those trading with the New World (for example, APS, 21 Feb. 1508–27 May 1509, Oficio IV, Libros I, II, III, Bernal González Vallesillo).

16. Santiago Montoto de Sedas, *Sevilla en el imperio, siglo XVI* (Seville, 1938), p. 195; APS, 27 Apr. 1508, Oficio XV, Libro II, Bernal González Vallesillo, fol. comienzo del legajo: "Francisco Pinelo . . . delegates power to Andrés de San Martín, his employee, to take charge of all his business matters in the Indies"; 27 May 1508, fol. primer tercio del legajo: "Lope Sánchez, master of the ship Santa María obligates himself to pay Francisco Pinelo 1,875 maravedís for 25 arrobas of white wine for the provisioning of his ship on the voyage . . . to Santo Domingo."

17. Gonzalo Argote de Molina, *Nobleza del Andaluzía* (Seville, 1588), p. 245. The Pinelo family tomb is in the Chapel of the Virgin of Pilar of the Cathedral of Seville. The memorial plate contains the following epitaph: "Esta capilla es de los muy nobles Señores Francisco Pinelo Ginovés Jurado Fiel executor desta Cibdad; primer factor de la Casa de la Contratación de las Indias, falleció a XXI de Marzo de M.D. IX y de María de la Torre su muger falleció a XXX de Octubre año de M.D. XIII años y del Reverendo don Gerónimo Pinelo Maestre Escuela y Canónigo desta Santa Iglesia su hijo falleció a X de Setiembre año de M.D. XX años el la cual están enterrados y es enterramiento para su linaje cuyas ánimas ayan gloria amen." On top of the vault are the words:

> "O mors quam
> terribilis et potens
> es: vitam claudis
> sepulcrum aperis."

18. Justino Matute y Gaviría, *Hijos de Sevilla señalados en santidad, letras, armas, artes o dignidad* (Seville, 1886), I, 335.

19. The best sources for a sketch of the lives of Carlos de Negrón and his family are Argote de Molina, *Nobleza del Andaluzía*, pp. 245–246, and Francisco Pacheco, *Libro de descripción de verdaderos retratos, de ilustres y memorables varones* (Seville, 1599), pp. 27–29v, 41–45, 245. See also APS, 10 Jan. 1551, Oficio XV, Libro I, Juan Franco, fol. 840; *Santa María de Gracia*, APS, 22 Sept. 1540, Oficio XV, Libro II, Alonso de Cazalla, fol. 751; *San Salvador*, APS, 23 June 1551, Oficio XV, Libro I, Alonso de Cazalla, fol. 729v.

20. Schäfer, *El consejo real*, I, 367; Argote de Molina, *Nobleza*, p. 245.

21. The stigma of trade was eliminated by ennoblement and intermarriage with the nobility. According to Mercado, "The ennobled and hispanized merchants are persons of honor and reputation in Seville and the rest of the country" (*Tratos y contratos*, chap. I).

22. Julio was "señor de la villa del Casar i de la Torres i Dagança en Extremadura" (Pacheco, *Verdaderes retratos*, p. 44). In his geneological poem, "Historia y sucesión de la Cueva," stanza lxiv, the Sevillian poet Juan de la Cueva describes his Negrón cousins as follows:

"Cinco hijo varones, cinco sines celestres . . .
contra Arrianos y Calvinos
Se opondrán con divino y santo zelo
De ellos serán en las legales leyes
Defensa de los Reynos y los Reyes"

(Francisco A. de Icaza, *Tragedias y comedias de Juan de la Cueva* (Madrid, 1917), xxi).

23. The Colegio mayor de Santo Tomás was founded in 1517 by Archbishop Diego de Deza. By 1575 its graduates enjoyed the same privileges and exemptions as those of Salamanca (Montoto de Sedas, *Sevilla*, p. 110).

24. In stanza xlv Juan de la Cueva speaks of Luciano:

"Contra el rebelde Apóstata, que huye
La verdadera Ley, que el verdadero
Legislador dió al Mundo que destruye
La cisma y pertinencia de Lutero
Calificando al ciego error, arguye
Luciano de Negrón"

(Icaza, *Juan de la Cueva*, p. xxi). As a humanist, according to Pacheco, "fué famosíssimo Astrólogo, Mathemático i filósofo: gran Retórico, estremado latino, Griego i Hebreo i mui general en las demás lenguas vulgares" (Pacheco, *Verdaderos retratos*, p. 27).

25. Argote de Molina, *Nobleza*, p. 145. See also Pacheco, *Verdaderos retratos*, p. 27: "Una famosa librería hecha a gran costa (donde fueron muchos los libros que en ella junto de todas Facultades i Lenguas) tan conocida i alabada en España."

26. For both portrait and sonnet see Pacheco, *Verdaderos retratos*, pp. 27 and 28v. The "escuela sevillana," a group of Sevillian poets led by Fernando de Herrera, were his frequent guests. Their poetry was characterized by grandiloquence, verbosity, and neologism. Other meetings were held in the palace of Columbus' descendant, the Court of Gelves, Don Álvaro Colón y Portugal (Federico Carlos Sáinz de Robles,

Historia y antología de la poesía española del siglo XII al XX [Madrid, 1955], p. 87).

27. Spanish medieval concepts completely separated riches from nobility. A rich man was ingenious (*capaz*), powerful, and above all, virtuous. The highest grade of medieval nobility was formed by the "ricos homes" and money alone did not allow one to belong to this class (Alfonso García Valdecasas, *El hidalgo y el honor* [2d ed.; Madrid, 1958], p. 71).

28. This change of ideas, reflected first in Seville, was soon felt in the rest of the country. Lope de Vega expressed the new feeling in his *La prueba de los amigos:*

> "No dudes que el dinero es
> todo en todo:
> Es príncipe, es hidalgo, es caballero
> Es alta sangre, es descendente godo"

(Félix Lope de Vega Carpio, *Obras escogidas,* ed. Federico Carlos Sáinz de Robles [Madrid, 1952], II, i, 1429).

29. Mercado, *Tratos y contratos,* p. A2.

30. The reference here is to Francisco de Quevedo's satirical poem, "Poderoso caballero es don Dinero" (see Francisco de Quevedo Villegas, *Obras en Verso "Obras completas,"* ed. Luis Astrana Marín [Madrid, 1952]), p. 82.

31. As Alarcón stated in his *El semejante a sí mismo:*

> "Es segunda maravilla
> Un caballero en Sevilla
> Sin ramo de mercader"

(Juan Ruiz de Alarcón, *Obras completas,* ed. Agustín Millares Carlo [Mexico, 1957], I, 298).

32. Mercado, *Tratos y contratos,* p. A2. The wealth of the Sevillian merchants was proverbial. "There are merchants," wrote the contemporary Sevillian historian, Alonso de Morgado, "who are so rich they they could easily purchase three good villas outside of Seville, provide a dowry of 240,000 ducats for their daughters while at the same time keep their arms free for greater concerns" (*Historia de Sevilla,* reprinted by the Sociedad del Archivo Hispalense [Seville, 1887], p. 172).

33. Jaime Vicens Vives, *Historia social y económica de España y América* (Barcelona, 1957), III, 112.

34. Further comments on the capitalistic attitude of the Sevillian nobility and their role in the transatlantic trade can be found in Ruth Pike, "The Sevillian Nobility and Trade with the New World in the Sixteenth Century," *Business History Review* XXXIX (1965), 439–465.

35. The growing spirit of materialism among the Sevillian nobility is

reflected in the poetry of Baltasar del Alcázar, who belonged to an old noble family that traced their origin to the original Christian knights who took part in the reconquest of the city from the Moslems and whose members went into trade in the sixteenth century. In his "Cena jocosa," for example, a detailed description of a luxurious banquet, he praised the pleasures of the full table and the good life (Baltasar del Alcázar, *Poesías*, ed. F. Rodríquez Marín [Madrid, 1910], pp. xl–xlii).

36. Carande, "Sevilla," p. 397.

37. B. Bennassar, "Facteurs sévillans au XVᵉ siècle d'après des lettres marchandes," *Annales: Économies, sociétés, civilisations*, XII (1957), 66.

38. In the summer of 1964 I discovered this manuscript, it was entitled "Representación de un vecino de Sevilla a fines del siglo XVI en favor de los comerciantes extranjeros que habían en dicha ciudad," in the Biblioteca Nacional de Madrid. It is identified as 6754– S–110. The demographic argument is interesting: The author felt that the existence of foreign merchants in Seville was one of the reasons why the city had not become "depopulated like many others in the kingdom" (p. 225v).

39. "Unos por los muchos años que aquí biven y residen en ella, otros por haber nacido en ella, otros por que están cassados con mugeres naturales della." The only group of foreign merchants that the author claimed were not well assimilated were the English "que cassi todos los estrangeros fuera de los de la nación ynglesa están muy naturalissados en essa ciudad" (*ibid.*, p. 226v).

40. *Ibid.*

41. It is indeed a misconception to assume that the French were able to dominate the Sevillian market throughout the seventeenth century. According to a French memoire of 1682, the galleons arriving from the New World in that year brought 22,808,977 piasters (Mexican pesos). Of this sum 4½ million went to the Genoese, while only 2½ million belonged to the French. Nine years later the Genoese were still holding their own, as their share of the returning fleet equalled 11 to 12 million livres as compared to the French share of 13 to 14 million livres (E. W. Dahlgren, *Les relations commerciales et maritimes entre la France et le côtes de l'océan Pacifique, commencement du XVIIIᵉ siècle* [Paris, 1909], p. 77).

42. This document is entitled "Lo que parece se debe proveer para poner en orden el negocio y contratación de las Indias es lo siguiente." Although it is undated, Schäfer believes that it must have been written in mid-1502 for it mentions the Bastidas voyage.

It would be difficult to understand the selection of Seville as the site

151

for the Casa without considering the role of Pinelo and the Genoese (Schäfer, *El consejo real*, I, 9). Clarence Haring, who wrote some seventeen years before Schäfer's discovery, also mentioned that the presence of "foreign merchants, especially the Genoese [who] had enjoyed privileges there [Seville] since the time of Saint Ferdinand" was an important factor leading to the choice of Seville (Haring, *Trade and Navigation*, pp. 7–8). From the point of view of accessibility and port facilities Cadiz would have been a far better location.

43. Direct exploitation of the transatlantic trade by the crown was originally intended and embodied in the decree of January 20, 1503, establishing the Casa de Contratación, but this soon proved impracticable. The Casa emerged as a government bureau, licensing and supervising all ships and merchants, passengers and goods, crews and equipment, passing to and from the Indies and enforcing the laws and ordinances relating thereto. It also received and cared for royal treasure remitted from the New World and collected the *avería* or convoy tax and customs and other duties. During the first half of the sixteenth century it gradually became a training school for navigators, makers of maps and devisers of nautical instruments. Besides being a commercial and nautical bureau, it was something more, a court of law with jurisdiction over all cases incidental to American trade. In sum, the Casa served as a zealous overseer of the business of the New World.

In 1535, in an attempt to placate the resentment of the merchants of Cadiz against Seville, Charles V appointed a permanent resident (*juez oficial*) at Cadiz, and ships and fleets returning from America were frequently allowed to make that city their port, provided cargoes and registers were transported intact to Seville. This institution was throughout the sixteenth and seventeenth centuries a source of perennial jealousy and dispute (*ibid.*, pp. 9, 23–25). See also Albert Girard, *La rivalité commerciale et maritime entre Séville et Cadix jusqu'à la fin du XVIII* siècle (Paris, 1932).

44. Haring, *Trade and Navigation*, p. 15.

45. José Antonio Saco, *Historia de la esclavitud de la Raza Africana en el Nuevo Mundo y en especial en los países Américo-hispanos* (Havana, 1938), I, 242.

46. Alonso de Castillo Solórzano, *La garduña de Sevilla y anzuelo de las bolsas* (Madrid, 1942), pp. 104–105.

For a description of Erminio Grimaldi see Robert Lopez, "Le marchand génois," *Annales: Économies, sociétés, civilisations*, XIII (1958), 509; of Ansaldo Grimaldi, see Matteo Bandello, *Tutte le òpere di Matteo Bandello*, ed. Francesco Flora (Milan, 1952), I, 1010, and Jacobo Bonfadio, "Annali di cose de'Genovesi," quoted in Richard Ehrenberg, *Das Zeitalter der Fugger* (Jena, 1896), I, 332.

47. Miguel de Cervantes Saavedra, *La gitanilla* in *Las novelas ejemplares* (Madrid, 1952), p. 50. See also Cristóbal Suárez de Figueroa, *El pasajero,* ed. Rodríguez Marín (Madrid, 1913), p. 6: "Los tiempos limitaron sus demasías, y deshicieron la pompa de criados, caballos y banquetes; puesto que profesa ya el de mayores negocios ser en recolección y parsimonia un anacoreta."

48. Cristóbal de Villalón, *Viaje a Turquia* in *Nueva Biblioteca de autores españoles,* II (Madrid, 1905), 102.

49. Pedro Mexía, *Diálogos o Coloquios de Pedro Mexía,* ed. Margaret L. Mulroney (Iowa City, Iowa, 1930), p. 21: "[Bernardo] Vamos y tomemos por essotra calle, porque esta muy embaraçada con la labor deste mercader." The first edition of Mexía's work was published in Seville in 1547.

50. Although many of the traits considered here to be characteristic of the Genoese could readily be found among the citizens of the other Italian city-states during the same period, the Genoese seemed to reflect them to a greater degree, according to their contemporaries, than did the rest of their Italian neighbors.

51. For a discussion of the influence of Genoa's geographic position on her commercial greatness see R. Doehaerd, *Les relations commerciales entre Gênes, la Belgique et l'outremont d'après les archives notariales génoises aux XIIIᵉ et XIVᵉ siècles,* "Études d'histoire économique et sociale," II (Brussels, 1941), 77 ff., and R. Lopez, "Aux origines du capitalisme génois," *Annales d'histoire économique et sociale,* IX (1937), 429–449.

Genoa's commercial career began with the First Crusade in 1097, when she sent a fleet of twelve galleys to aid the crusaders who were besieging the city of Antioch. After the city was taken by the Christians, Genoa received extensive trading privileges there (see W. Heyd, *Histoire du commerce du Levant au moyen âge,* trans. F. Raynaud [Leipzig, 1923], I, 134).

52. Y. Renouard, *Les hommes d'affaires italiens au moyen âge* (Paris, 1949), p. 100. In Genoa the nobles and non-nobles alike were merchants and sailors, separated only by their birth (J. Burckhardt, *The Civilization of the Renaissance in Italy* [New York, 1958], III, 356).

53. "Oh Genoese! men estranged from all morality and full of all corruption, why are ye not scattered from the earth?" (Dante Alighieri, "Inferno," *The Divine Comedy* [New York, 1950], canto xxxiii, p. 179).

54. A. Ruddock, *Italian Merchants and Shipping in Southampton, 1270–1600* (Southampton, England, 1951), p. 22. In these instances the phrases "the place where God would lead them" or "where they might prefer to go" were used. Other times a false destination was given (Renouard, *Les hommes d'affaires,* p. 96).

55. Lopez, "Le marchand génois," p. 510.

56. The fall of the Latin Empire of Constantinople in 1261 was, in part, the work of the Genoese. When faced with the choice of aiding either the Latin Emperor or the Byzantine pretender, who was a heretic in the eyes of the Western Church, the Genoese decided in favor of the latter because—according to the chronicler Martino da Canal—the Greeks were "more willing to replace the Venetians by the Genoese." On the other hand, there were several Genoese who were well known for their piety and good works, such as the Jurist Bartolomeo Bosco and Caterina Fieschi (1447–1510), canonized as Santa Caterina Fieschi-Adorno (Emilio Pandiani, *Vita privata genovese nel Rinacimento* ("Atti della Società ligure di storia patria," XLVII [Genoa, 1915], 28).

57. R. Lopez believes that Columbus was an exception. He says, "Ceux eux, les génois se montrèrent pieux, mais sans exaltation mystique. Le cas extrème de Christophe Colombe . . . fut exceptionnel" (Lopez, "Le marchand génois," p. 506).

58. Columbus worked for the Centurione in Lisbon in 1477, and the following year went to Madeira to purchase sugar for them. It also seems likely that they took him to Chios in 1474–75 (S. E. Morison, *Admiral of the Ocean Sea*, pp. 22–23).

59. R. Menéndez Pidal, *Los españoles en la historia* (Madrid, 1959), pp. 20, 33.

60. C. Colón, *Los cuatro viajes del almirante y su testamento*, ed. Ignacio Anzoategui (Buenos Aires, 1958), p. 219.

61. For example, a municipal decree of 1396 stated: "Against those who claim that bills of exchange and insurance [contracts] are illegal and usurious . . . according to the Scriptures . . . and resort to the ecclesiastical courts . . . after obtaining delays, since if these contracts are not honored . . . it will cause serious damage to the citizens and merchants of Genoa . . . that anyone who attempts such a thing . . . will be forced to pay a penalty of one-half a pound [Genoese] for each pound he refused to pay" (Lopez, Le marchand génois," p. 506).

62. For a description of Lutheranism in Seville, see M. Menéndez Pelayo, *Historia de los heterodoxos*, 2d ed. (Madrid, 1928), V, 75–116, and Montoto de Sedas, *Sevilla*, pp. 94–99.

63. At the last moment, Juan Ponce de León recognized his errors and was reconciled to the Catholic faith. In this way, he avoided being burned at the stake and was instead garrotted, the usual procedure in last-minute conversions, but his remains were burnt in the public auto (Menéndez Pelayo, *Los heterodoxos*, pp. 112–116).

Among the records of the Sevillian Inquisition preserved in the Archivo Histórico Nacional in Madrid are several documents relating to the case of Doña Catalina Sarmiento.

64. I could not find the names of any Genoese merchants of Seville among the Inquisition records that I looked over in the summer of 1963.

65. See Diego Ortiz de Zuñiga, *Anales eclesiásticos y seculares de la muy noble y muy leal ciudad de Sevilla, metrópole de la Andalucía* (Madrid, 1796), III and IV.

66. Jorge Manrique drew a distinction between what he called the three lives: temporal life, which perishes, the life of fame, which is more enduring and more glorious than the life of the body, and lastly, eternal life, which is the crowning of the other two (Menéndez Pidal, *Los españoles*, p. 48). In the second half of the fifteenth century the wealthy merchant-banker Federigo Centurione left sufficient money in his will for 1,000 masses for his soul, but only 100 pounds (Genoese) for the poor, and 20 pennies for an almshouse (Heers, *Gênes*, p. 559).

67. Another member of the Pinelo family was Valentina Pinelo, a nun in the convent of San Leandro and a well-known poetess whose talents were praised by Lope de Vega (Montoto de Sedas, *Sevilla*, p. 219).

68. In the first quarter of the seventeenth century the third Marquis of Estepa, Adán Centurión, patronized the Sevillian writer Rodrigo Fernández de Ribera, who dedicated his novel *El mesón del mundo* (1631) to him. The Marquis of Estepa was not, however, a descendant of the Sevillian Genoese group. His ancestor, Adamo Centurione of Genoa, one of the most important of the Genoese creditors of Charles V, received the town of Estepa (Cordova) and surrounding territory in return for a loan of 200,000 escudos to help cover the costs of the Emperor's expedition to Algiers. The title Marquis of Estepa was created in 1564 by Philip II and conferred on Adamo Centurione's son, Marcos Centurión. See R. Fernández de Ribera, *El mesón del mundo*, ed. Edward Nagy (New York, 1963), and Juan Moreno de Guerra y Alonso, *Guía de la grandeza* (Madrid, 1924), p. 335.

69. See Robert Lopez, "Hard Times and Investment in Culture," in *The Renaissance: A Symposium, Feb. 8–10, 1952* (New York, 1953). The entire sixteenth century may be described as a long wave of expansion, culminating in 1608. There was one intercyclical recession— beginning in 1550 and ending 1559/1562—it was followed by another long expansion phase (Hugette and Pierre Chaunu, *Séville et l'Atlantique*, VIII [Paris, 1959]).

70. J. Vicens Vives, *Manual de historia económica* (Barcelona, 1959), p. 314.

71. The Genoese did not have to immobilize their resources in land for symbolic reasons, since their nobility had been recognized for centuries. The conclusions reached in this paragraph and the following one are based on a study of the inventories of numerous wills, both Genoese and native, found in the Archivo de Protocolos.

72. The first sequestration, totalling 300,000 ducats, was made in 1523 and was brought on by heavy costs of the war with France. Altogether, about five million ducats were secured by this method during the reign of Charles V (Haring, *Trade and Navigation*, p. 169; Ramón Carande, *Carlos V y sus banqueros* [Madrid, 1943], pp. 357–358). See also Vives, *Historia social y económica*, III, 108.

In the second half of the sixteenth century, the successive bankruptcies of the government brought disaster to the annuity holders. When repayment was finally made, the *juros* had depreciated to about 50 per cent of their original value. Only the profits of the American trade prevented the ruin of the Sevillian mercantile aristocracy under these conditions (Fernand Braudel, *La Méditerranée et le monde méditerranéen à l'époque de Philippe II* [Paris, 1949], p. 397).

73. Vives, *Historia social y económica*, p. 108.

74. Heers, *Gênes*, pp. 487–491.

75. V. Vázquez de Prada, *Lettres marchandes d'Anvers* (Paris, 1960), pp. 93–109; Bennassar, "Facteurs sévillans," pp. 60–70. See Chap. III.

76. Heers, *Gênes*, p. 290; Torre y del Cerro, *Beatriz Enríquez de Harana*, pp. 165–177. The Genoese were also active in the wool trade in both the central and southern parts of Spain, but since it is not possible on the basis of the available documentation to determine the precise participation of the various members of the Sevillian Genoese colony, I have omitted it from the text. For a description of the Genoese in the wool trade of central and northern Spain see H. Lapeyre, "Le commerce des laines en Espagne sous Philippe II," *Bulletin de la Société d'Histoire Moderne*, LIV (1955), 5–8, and for the wool trade in general, Carande, *Carlos V*, chap. iv.

77. The frequency with which these natural catastrophes occurred in the Sevillian region during the sixteenth century can be seen in Ortiz de Zúñiga, *Anales*, III and IV. See also Vives, *Historia económica*, p. 315.

78. This riot, popularly called "de la Feria y Pendón Verde," is described in *Anales*, III, 325–326.

79. CDI, 1st ser., XL, 145, 146.

CHAPTER II

1. The notarial documents published by R. Doehaerd that deal with the trade between Genoa, Flanders, and England during the thirteenth, fourteenth, and fifteenth centuries mention 192 maritime transactions between Cadiz and Southampton, Sandwich, and Bruges, as compared to the 52 which specify Seville as a receiving or departing port. See R. Doehaerd, *Les rélations commerciales entre Gênes, la Belgique et*

l'outremont d'après les archives notariales génoises aux XIIeme *et XIV*^eme^
siècles ("Études d'historie économique et sociale," II–IV [Brussels,
1941]); R. Doehaerd and Charles Kerremans, *Les rélations commerciales
entre Gênes, la Belgique et l'outremont d'après les archives notariales
génoises, 1400–1440* ("Études d'histoire économique et sociale," V
[Brussels, 1952]); C. Haring, *Trade and Navigation between Spain and
the Indies in the Time of the Hapsburgs* (Cambridge, 1918), p. 8. The
Genoese firms established in Seville maintained resident factors in Cadiz
to take charge of their shipments (J. Heers, *Gênes au XV*^e^ *siècle* [Paris,
1961], p. 490.

2. Fernando de Herrera, "Soneto a Sevilla," in C. Sáinz de Robles,
Historia y antología de la poesía española del siglo XII al XX (Madrid,
1955), p. 648.

3. Luis Vélez de Guevara, *El diablo cojuelo,* ed. Francisco Rodríguez
Marín (Madrid, 1951), p. 144. Seville, according to Mateo Alemán,
author of the picaresque novel *Guzmán de Alfarache,* was a "patria
común, dehesa franca, ñudo ciego, campo abierto, globo sin fin, madre de
huérfanos y capa de pecadores, donde todo es necesidad y ninguno la
tiene" (Mateo Alemán, *Guzmán de Alfarache,* in Ángel Valbuena y Prat,
La novela picaresca española [Madrid, 1956], Pt. I, Bk. I, chap. ii, p.
254).

4. R. Carande, *Carlos V y sus banqueros* (Madrid, 1943), p. 38.

5. Illustrations of sixteenth-century Seville can be found in Georg
Braun, *Civitates orbis terrarum* (1576–1618), I, IV, V.

Peraza died before he could complete this work and the MS remains
unpublished today (see J. Pérez de Guzmán y Boza, *Discursos leídos ante
la Real Academia Sevillana el 26 de abril de 1892* [Seville, 1892], p.
10).

Alonso de Morgado was a native of Alcántara and a parish priest in
that city for six years when he suddenly decided to move to Seville,
where he became the pastor of the church of Santa Ana in Triana. He
describes the reasons for his departure from Alcántara in the prologue to
his work: "Que estando yo en la muy antigua . . . villa de Alcántara,
mi patria después de clérigo de missa, seys años avía . . . en la mayor
quietud de que yo se recordarme . . . me privó de una descansada vida
un tan forçoso desseo de residir en la muy famosa ciudad de Sevilla."
After residing some time in Seville, he decided to write a history of the
city because "ninguno otro que yo sepa osado commençar como es sacar a
luz la crónica de la noble y muy leal ciudad de Sevilla" (A. de Morgado,
Historia de Sevilla [Seville, 1587], Prologue).

6. Andrea Navajero described the city in 1526: "Seville, a city
situated on a flat plain on the left bank of the Betis now called the

Guadalquivir, has an extension of from four to five miles and resembles to a greater degree the cities of Italy than any other Spanish town" (Antonio María Fabié, ed. and trans., *Viajes por España de Einghen, del Barón de Rosmithal de Blatna, de Francisco Guicciardini y de Andrés Navajero* [Madrid, 1879], p. 200). The Monastery of San Francisco was located in the Plaza de San Francisco, which became the principal square of the city by the end of the century; the palace of the Dukes of Medina Sidonia was situated in the Calle de la Sierpe, the main business center (S. Montoto de Sedas, *Sevilla en el imperio, siglo XVI* [Seville, 1938], pp. 13, 32).

7. Luis de Peraza, "Historia de la imperial ciudad de Sevilla," quoted in Montoto de Sedas, *Sevilla*, p. 24.

8. The example of the fishermen may be cited. Of the fifty-six mentioned in a mid-fourteenth-century tax list, only six lived in the district assigned to them. The rest were distributed through the parishes of Omnium Sanctorum, San Martín, La Magdalena, and San Vicente, which is the nearest to the river, and in Triana (R. Carande, "Sevilla fortaleza y Mercado," *Anuario de historia del derecho español*, II [1925], 292).

9. In 1502, for example, the navigators residing in Triana formed a confraternity and began construction on their hospital of Espíritu Santo (Montoto de Sedas, *Sevilla*, p. 167).

10. Pedro de Medina, *Libro de grandezas y cosas memorables de España* (Sevilla, 1548), fol. li.

11. Morgado, *Historia*, pp. 173, 174.

12. L. Vélez de Guevara, *El diablo cojuelo* ed. F. Rodríguez Marín (Madrid, 1951), p. 223.

13. See F. Lope de Vega, *El Arenal de Sevilla*, in *Obras escogidas*, I (Madrid, 1952), Act I, scene 1, l. 1382.

14. Morgado, *Historia*, p. 173. On March 22, 1595, Francisco de Ariño noted in his diary that the Indies fleet had arrived and that its treasure was being hastily unloaded on the wharves near the Golden Tower to be transported from there in carts to the Casa de Contratación (Francisco de Ariño, *Sucesos de Sevilla de 1592 a 1604* [Seville, 1873], p. 22).

Miguel de Cervantes Saavedra, in his novel *Rinconete y Cortadillo*, relates how the two young thieves, Rinconete and Cortadillo, upon arriving in Seville, "se fueron a ver la ciudad, y admiróles . . . el gran concurso de gente del río, porque era tiempo de cargazón de flota. . . . Echaron de ver muchos muchachos de la esportilla que por allí andaban" (in *Novelas ejemplares*, ed. Francisco Rodríguez Marín, I [Madrid, 1952], 147).

15. Doña Laura—Famoso está el Arenal . . .
    No tiene, a mi parecer,
    todo el mundo vista igual.
    Tanta galera y navío
    mucho al Betis engrandece"
(Lope de Vega, *El Arenal de Sevilla*, Act I, scene 1, p. 1382).
    16. Vélez de Guevara, *El diablo conjuelo*, pp. 150–151. Morgado, who observed the construction of the Lonja, gives the following description of it: "La nueva Lonja de mercaderes que se va labrando a toda priessa, y se començó por el año de mil y quinientos y ochenta y tres. . . . El sitio que costó sessenta y cinco mil ducados se le dió en la más cómoda parte de Sevilla, y allí cerca de Gradas, que han servido y sirven de Lonja, en quanto acaba esta otra. Que comoquiera que no se junta otro algún edificio, va campeando más su gran sumptuosidad, con sus quatro Puertas principales, que tienen en cada lienço la suya, que salen a quatro Plaças" (Morgado, *Historia*, pp. 317, 172).
    17. Fabié, *Viajes*, p. 271.
    18. The hospital de la Sangre was built through the generosity of the Ribera family, particularly Don Fadríque Enríquez de Ribera, Duke of Alcalá and first Marquis of Tarifa, who according to Medina left a legacy of a million maravedís to the hospital (P. de Medina, *Libro de grandezas y cosas memorables de España* [Seville, 1548], fol. xlviii); the casa de Pilatos was built in 1533 by Don Fadríque Enríquez de Ribera in commemoration of his pilgrimage to the Holy Land in 1519. It was claimed to be a copy of the house of Pontius Pilate in Jerusalem. M. de Cervantes Saavedra, *Rinconete y Cortadillo*, ed. Francisco Rodríguez Marín [Madrid, 1920], p. 14).
    19. AMS, *Tumbo*, as quoted in Montoto de Sedas, *Sevilla*, p. 14.
    20. *Ordenanzas de Sevilla* (Seville, 1527), fol. lxxiii.
    21. According to Peraza there were more than eighty important plazas in Seville in addition to many other smaller ones, "que no hay caballero en Sevilla, que no tenga una placeta frente de su casa, ni iglesia que no tenga uno o dos" (quoted in Montoto de Sedas, *Sevilla*, p. 27).
    22. The important gates of the city were La Puerta del Sol, de Córdoba, Jerez, Carmona, de la Carne, Triana, Arenal, Real, Ossario, Nueva, del Almenilla, San Juan, del Aceite, del Oro, and del Carbón. All gates were locked at nightfall except the Arenal, Triana, and Meatmarket gates. The Meatmarket Gate opened into the district where the municipal slaughterhouse and meatmarket were located (Morgado, *Historia*, pp. 113, 134). Near the Arenal Gate, which led into the public walk of that name, could be found the Old Clothes Market (Cervantes, *Rinconete y Cortadillo* [1952 ed.], p. 146).

23. Cervantes' Rinconete and Cortadillo entered the river port through the Customhouse Gate in the company of a group of travelers. As Cervantes explains, "A la entrada de la ciudad, que fué a la oración, y por la puerta de la Aduana, a causa del registro y almojarifazgo que se paga" (*Rinconete y Cortadillo* [1952 ed.], pp. 145–146).

24. Vélez de Guevara, *El diablo cojuelo*, p. 146.

25. P. Mexía, *Diálogos o Coloquios de Pedro Mexía*, ed. M. Mulroney (Iowa City, Iowa, 1930), pp. 21–22.

26. Morgado, *Historia*, p. 448.

27. "Porque muy pocos hazen más de un alto, y assí quedan toda vía las casas humildes y de poca authoridad, y por eso a los estrangeros y a los que traen los ojos ceuados de Barcelona y otras ciudades cuyas casas tienen tres o quatro altos, nunca parescerán bien los edificios desta ciudad" (Mexía, *Diálogos*, p. 22).

It was from the roof (*terrado*) of an inn on the Calle del Agua that Don Cleofás and the Limping Devil viewed the city.

28. Cervantes, *Rinconete y Cortadillo* (1952 ed.), p. 162.

29. Morgado, *Historia*, p. 141.

30. According to Medina, "también bebe del agua del Guadalquivir, que es muy buena, el qual pasa junto a la ciudad por la parte del poniente, donde las naos llegan a diez pasos del muro della torre del Oro, que es junto al muelle, donde las naos cargan y descargan sus mercaderías" (*Libro de grandezas*, fol. li).

31. Montoto de Sedas, *Sevilla*, p. 36.

32. Morgado, *Historia*, p. 142: "A las grandes salas donde se bañan, salen sus cañas, que corren de agua caliente y también fría. Con la qual y cierto ungüento que se les da, refrescan y limpian sus cuerpos."

33. Fabié, *Viajes*, p. 382. Mercado said the following about the frauds and artifices of Gradas: "Es menester particular ingenio para entenderlos, y aun ayuda y favor de Dios para vista la ocasión no cometerlos y travarlos [trovarlos]" (*Summa de tratos y contratos* [Seville, 1587], p. A2).

34. Morgado, *Historia*, p. 167.

35. *Ibid.*

36. Francisco de Sigüenza, *Traslación de la imagen de Nuestra Señora de los Reyes* (Seville, 1579), quoted in Montoto de Sedas, *Sevilla*, p. 32.

37. Ariño, *Sucesos*, pp. 22–24.

38. Morgado, *Historia*, p. 170.

39. Montoto de Sedas, *Sevilla*, p. 18.

40. The park was called the Alameda de Hércules because of the large statue of Hercules which was placed at the entrance (Vélez de Guevara, *El diablo cojuelo*, p. 153).

41. Morgado, *Historia*, p. 173.

42. Montoto de Sedas, *Sevilla*, p. 18.

43. *Ordenanzas de Sevilla*, fol. lxxiii. Even cemeteries were not free from dumping, as can be seen from a petition sent to the municipal council by the clergy of the important and centrical parish of San Andrés. According to the priests, "the cemetery of the said church of San Andrés, in which more than a million persons are buried, has in its center, a large cross of much veneration. . . . Regardless of this fact, the inhabitants of the neighboring areas throw human excrement and all kinds of rubbish from their houses around this cross and in all parts of the said cemetery without any respect for the sanctity of the place" (AMS, *Papeles importantes*, III, quoted in Montoto de Sedas, *Sevilla*, p. 20).

44. Conditions such as these brought about the strange encounter between Espinel's Marcos de Obregón and a famous ruffian of Seville. As Espinel relates, "Sucedióme pasando por cal de Génova topar con uno destos valientes, encontrándome con él de suerte que por pasar yo por lo limpio le hice pasar por el lodo" (Vincente Espinel, *Vida de Marcos de Obregón*, ed. Samuel Gili Gaya [Madrid, 1940], II, 20).

45. Mercado, *Tratos y contratos*, p. A2.

46. Morgado, *Historia*, p. 166.

47. Mateo Alemán, *Guzmán de Alfarache*, Pt. II, Bk. III, chap. vii, p. 551.

48. Fabié, *Viajes*, p. 274. The name of the fruit is omitted in the original MS. Although Fabié believed that it might be a pineapple, it seems from the description to be more like a mango.

49. Peraza, "Historia," as quoted in Cervantes Saavedra, *Rinconete y Cortadillo* [1920 ed.], p. 372.

50. Morgado, *Historia*, p. 141. Foreign fabrics and exotic clothing were also in vogue in Seville. According to Peraza, "en Sevilla gozan en común de lo que en cada reino se aprecia particular; traen ropetas italianas, chamarras saoneses, capas lombardas con collares altos, ropetas inglesas, sayos sin pliegues de Hungría, ropetas cerradas que se visten por el ruedo, llamadas salta en barca, tomadas de las que se traen en el mar. Usan capeletes, que son sombreros chicos y hondos, chamarras angostas y largas hasta el suelo que es a vista de turco, calzas de muy gran primor enteras a la española, picadas a la flamenca y cortadas a la alemana" (Peraza, "Historia," as quoted in Cervantes Saavedra, *Rinconete y Cortadillo* [1920 ed.], p. 372).

51. Montoto de Sedas, *Sevilla*, p. 225.

52. Lope de Vega, *El amante agradecido*, Act I, quoted in *ibid.*

"Y con la caroza sal
con pajes que crujan seda

una tarde en la Alameda
y otra tarde en el Arenal."
53. Montoto de Sedas, *Sevilla*, p. 38. The list of convents, monasteries, churches, hospitals, schools, and other religious and charitable edifices erected in the city during the sixteenth century through the patronage of members of the Sevillian nobility is indeed too long to be mentioned here (see Montoto de Sedas, *Sevilla*, pp. 85–101, and Félix González de León, *Noticia artística histórica y curiosa de todos los edificios públicos, sagrados y profanos de* . . . *Sevilla, y de muchas casas particulares* . . . [2 vols.; Seville, 1844].

54. On March 19, 1522, some members of the Cathedral clergy sent the following petition to the municipal council: "Que todos los pobres que por necesidad se habían venido a esta ciudad de los lugares, causaban enfermedades muriéndose de ellos muchos habiendo por las calles más de 500 muertos y los pusieron en los hospitales, sustentándolo a costo del Cabildo y Arzobispo de la ciudad" (Bernardo Luis de Castro Palacios, "Diario de la Iglesia Catedral de Sevilla," unpub. MS, Biblioteca Municipal de Sevilla, quoted in Montoto de Sedas, *Sevilla*, p. 39).

"En Sevilla dicen que hay cofradía de ladrones con su prior y cónsules como mercaderes; hay depositario entre ellos, en cuya casa se recojen los hurtos, y arca de tres llaves, donde se echa lo que se hurta, y lo que se vende, y sacan de allí para el gasto y para cohechar las que pueden para su remedio" (Luis Zapata, *Miscelánea*, in *Memorial histórico español* [Madrid, 1859], XI, 49).

55. AMS, *Escribanía del Cabildo*, siglo XVI, No. 5.

56. Montoto de Sedas, *Sevilla*, p. 40.

57. Miguel de Cervantes Saavedra, *Coloquio de los perros* in *Novelas ejemplares*, ed. Francisco Rodríguez Marín, II (Madrid, 1957), 235.

58. Peraza, "Historia," as quoted in Cervantes Saavedra, *Rinconete y Cortadillo* [1920 ed.], p. 70.

59. Cervantes, *Rinconete y Cortadillo* [1952 ed.], p. 164; Castillo Solórzano, *La garduña de Sevilla*, p. 21.

60. At mid-century Gutierre de Cetina pictured his native city as follows:

"Aquí la emulación, la tiranía,
La envidia y la pasión hace y deshace
Cuanto ordena la falsa hipocresía. . . .
Aquí se gana crédito mintiendo;
Gánase la amistad lisonjeando
Y viénese a perder la verdad diciendo"

(Joaquín Hazañas y La Rúa, *Obras de Gutierre de Cetina* [Sevilla, 1895], II, 127–131).

61. Alemán, *Guzmán de Alfarache,* Pt. II, Bk. II, chap. vii, p. 477.
62. Cervantes Saavedra, *Rinconete y Cortadillo* [1920 ed.], p. 48. In the *Coloquio de los perros,* Berganza tells Cipión that all the butchers in the Matadero (Slaughterhouse) prided themselves on being bullies and ruffians, and "there was none of them who did not have his guardian in San Francisco Square and before it would lay propitiatory offerings in the form of loins and beef tongues" (Cervantes, *Coloquio de los perros,* p. 217).
63. Luque Fajardo, "Fiel desengaño contra la ociosidad," fol. 291v, quoted in *ibid.,* p. 49.
64. Alemán, *Guzmán de Alfarache,* Pt. II, Bk. II, chap. iii, p. 447.
65. *Ibid.,* Chap. vii, p. 475.
66. Morgado, *Historia,* p. 184.
67. Cervantes, *Rinconete y Cortadillo,* p. 175.
68. "Las varas que hay en Sevilla de Alguaciles de otros diferentes juzgados son tantas, que es la ciudad llena dellas" (Morgado, *Historia,* p. 184).
69. Alemán, *Guzmán de Alfarache,* Pt. II, Bk. II, chap. iii, p. 447.
70. Cervantes Saavedra, *Rinconete y Cortadillo* [1920 ed.], p. 59.
71. See Lope de Vega, *El Arenal de Sevilla,* Act III, scene iv, p. 1406.
72. Throughout the sixteenth century the Castillian Cortes complained about the sale of titles of nobility. In 1592, for example, the *procuradores* stated the following in their petition to the king: "Del venderse las hidalguías resultan muchos inconvenientes porque las compran de ordinario personas de poca calidad y ricas, y con ellas entran en oficios que requieren hidalguía, por el cual medio vienen muchas personas que no son convenientes a tener dichos oficios, y se acrecientan muchos hidalgos y exentos . . . y para que cesen esos inconvenientes y no se haga vendido lo que siempre fué premio de la virtud y remuneración de las hazañas y notables servicios que se hacen a los reyes . . . a V.M. suplicamos" (Montoto de Sedas, *Sevilla,* p. 232, 60).
73. There were thirty-six *veinticuatros* in Seville in the sixteenth century. To hold this position one had to be a denizen of the city, noble, and named to this honor by the king. The *veinticuatros* received an annual salary of 3,000 maravedís and had to reside in the city for at least four months a year. In reality, they governed the city.
Traditionally the office of *jurado* had been elective, two being selected by the denizens of each district. In 1552 they numbered fifty-six. Like the *veinticuatros,* they enjoyed exemption from royal and municipal taxes and had special legal privileges (Montoto de Sedas, *Sevilla,* pp. 61–63, 213).
74. AMS, *Actas capitulares,* siglo XVI, cabildo de 8 Apr. 1598. The

usual price of an aldermanship was 7,000 ducats. In the opinion of Mateo Alemán, "ninguno compra regimiento con otra intención que para granjería, ya sea pública o secreta; pocos arrojan tantos millares de ducados para hacer bien a los pobres, sino a sí mismos" (Alemán, *Guzmán de Alfarache*, Pt. I, Bk. I, chap. iii, p. 256).

75. F. Braudel, *La Méditerranée et le monde mediterranéen à l'èpoque de Philippe II* (Paris, 1949), p. 619.

76. C. Suárez de Figueroa, *El pasajero*, ed. F. Rodríguez Marín (Madrid, 1913), p. 201.

77. Joseph de Veitia Linaje, *Norte de la Contratación de las Indias occidentales* (new ed.; Buenos Aires, 1945), p. 161.

78. Castillo Solórzano, *La garduña de Sevilla*, p. 21: "Era Feliciano hijo de un hidalgo rico que habiendo tenido contratación en las Indias y sucedídole bien había aumentado mucha la hacienda."

"Es mi padre del solar
el más noble de Vizcaya
que a las Indias venga o vaya
¿qué honor le puede quitar?"

79. (Félix Lope de Vega Carpio, *El premio del bien hablar*, in *Obras de Lope de Vega Carpio*, ed. Emilio Cotarelo y Mori, XIII [Madrid, 1930], Act I, p. 376).

"Yo soy hija, don Juan, de un hombre indiano,
hidalgo montañés, muy bien nacido"

(*La esclava de su galán*, in *Obras de Lope de Vega Carpio*, ed. Emilio Cotarelo y Mori, XII [Madrid, 1930], Act I, p. 135).

80. Carande, *Carlos V*, p. 253.

81. Mercado, *Tratos y contratos*, p. A1.

82. Morgado, *Historia*, pp. 155, 156.

83. Fabié, *Viajes*, p. 269: "On the heights of this part of the city there is an olive-tree forest which extends for more than thirty leagues. The olive trees are exceedingly beautiful and bear such large olives that I confess that I have not seen their equal in any other part of the world."

84. Morgado, *Historia*, p. 156.

85. Seventy-two towns belonged to the district of Seville (Joaquín Guichot y Parody, *Historia del Excm. Ayuntamiento de la Ciudad de Sevilla* [Seville, 1896–1903], II, 142).

86. Miguel de Cervantes Saavedra, *El licenciado Vidriera*, in *Novelas ejemplares*, ed. Francisco Rodríguez Marín, II (Madrid, 1957), 25: "ofreció a Esquivias, a Alanís, Cazalla, Guadalcanal y la Membrilla."

87. See Carande, *Carlos V*, p. 250.

88. Fabié, *Viajes*, p. 268.

89. The best source for such an investigation is the notarial archive of

Seville, since the surviving papers of the *almojarifazgo* are far from complete (Carande, *Carlos V*, p. 254). Bennassar, using letters from the Ruiz agents in Seville, gives some additional information on this trade B. Bennassar, "Facteurs sévillans au XV⁰ siècle d'après des lettres marchandes, *Annales: Economies, sociétés, civilisations*, XII [1957], 60–107.

90. Carande, *Carlos V*, p. 225. See M. Bataillón, "Vendeja," *Hispanic Review*, XXVII (1959), 228–245.

91. Lope de Vega, *El Arenal de Sevilla*, Act I, scene i, p. 1382.

92. Mercado, *Tratos y contratos*, p. 85.

93. The following discussion is based upon chapters xv, xvi, xvii, xix, and xxi of the 1587 edition of Mercado's *Summa de tratos y contratos*. Quotations, unless otherwise indicated, are taken from pages 91–96, 107–109.

94. Mercado's analysis of the inflation was the same as that held by the *procuradores* of the Cortes during the sixteenth century (see Earl J. Hamilton, *American Treasure and the Price Revolution in Spain, 1501–1650* [Cambridge, Mass., 1934], pp. 284–285). Mercado uses the term *atravesar*, meaning "buying beforehand," that is, the purchase of large quantities of commodities so as to control the market or make a monopoly profit; today it would properly be considered similar to engrossing (Cervantes Saavedra, *Rinconete y Cortadillo* [1920 ed.], p. 52).

95. Even members of the *cabildo* were involved in regrating. On September 4, 1598, several councilmen wrote to Madrid saying that "there are in the *cabildo* persons who buy wheat so as to resell it" (*ibid.*, p. 53).

96. Mercado frequently uses the expression "los merchantes o regatones" to describe the American traders.

97. A. Goris, *Les colonies marchandes méridionales à Anvers de 1488 à 1567* (Louvain, Belgium, 1925), p. 111.

98. There were two fairs a year at Medina del Campo, one in May and the other in October. Fairs were also held at Ríoseco in September and Villalón in April but were not as popular as those at Medina (Carande, *Carlos V*, p. 218).

99. Goris, *Les colonies marchandes*, p. 116. The most important treatise on bookkeeping in the sixteenth century was that of Jan Christoffels Ympyn, which appeared in Antwerp in 1543 in three languages. It is actually a copy of the *Tractatus particularis de computis et scripturis* of Luca Pacioli (Venice, 1494), with examples taken from the business life of Antwerp. Eight forms of buying and selling are described in this work (*ibid.*, p. 122).

100. J. C. Ympyn, *A Notable and Very Excellent Work, Expressing*

and Declaring the Manner and Forms How to Keep a Book of Accounts . . . ('s-Gravenhage, 1934), chap. xvii. He points out the dangers inherent in bartering, quoting the Italian proverb "Chi barata, si imbratta [He who barters, cheats himself]." Ympyn lists three ways of bartering: to deliver ware and receive ware (*baratto semplice*), to deliver some ware and some money [*baratto composto*], and lastly, to deliver some ware, some ready money, and for the rest give time and receive like again (*baratto col tempo*).

101. "Otra quarta especie hay de barata y otras quatro mil aura, si se les antoja mercaderes y corredores" (Mercado, *Tratos y contratos*, p. 110).

102. *Ibid.*, p. 93v. In Medina and Seville, as well as Flanders, selling in bulk was used at times to fit out a fleet with mercery, "porque de la tienda, o casa de un mercero se surte casi un cargazón al menos tómanse juntos todos los géneros que suelen venir de las partes do trata. Como del que en Flandres, paños anascotes, tapicería, olandas, cobre, mercería o bujerías. Del que en Francia, ruanes, coletas y véndense de todo quinientos o mil libras a 1700. Unos con otros que parece imitar al despacho de cargazones" (*ibid.*, p. 95).

103. Gervasio de Artiñano y de Galdácomo, *Historia del comercio con las Indias durante el dominio de los Austrias* (Barcelona, 1917), p. 142. Three ports were designated for the reception of merchandise in America: Vera Cruz, Cartagena, and Nombre de Dios, the latter was supplemented by Portobello in 1584. From the port cities American merchants distributed goods throughout the mainland.

104. *Ibid.*, p. 145.

105. Haring, *Trade and Navigation*, p. 134.

CHAPTER III

1. After a short period of competition with the Jews—traditional moneylenders of the region—the Genoese succeeded in breaking their monopoly by the first decades of the fourteenth century. One of the prime factors in the success of the Genoese was their ability to mobilize large sums of money drawn from their widespread commercial network. By the mid-fourteenth century they were the principal creditors of the city (R. Carande, "Sevilla, fortaleza y mercado," *Anuario de historia del derecho español*, II [1925], 293).

2. A member of the Spínola family, Micer Gabriel, had several dealings with Ferdinand IV of Castile, and in 1309 the same monarch received an advance of 6,911 doblas from "Juan de Vivaldo, Consul of the Genoese and from others of his nation." In the fifteenth century the

Salvago family was particularly well known as moneylenders to the Sevillian aristocracy and the Castilian monarchs (H. Sancho de Sopranis, "Los genoveses en la región gaditano-xerience de 1400–1800," *Hispania, revista española de historia,* VIII [1948], p. 383; Carande, "Sevilla," pp. 316, 317).

3. The role of the Genoese in sixteenth-century international finance has been described by R. Ehrenberg, *Das Zeitalter der Fugger* (2 vols.; Jena, 1896), and F. Braudel, *Le méditerranée et le monde méditerranéen à l'époque de Philippe II* (Paris, 1949). Additional information can be found in R. Lopez, "Il predominio económico dei Genovesi nella monarchia spagnola," *Giornale stòrico e letterario della Liguria,* XII (1936), 65–74, and R. Carande, *La hacienda real de Castilla* (Madrid, 1949).

In 1573 the Venetian ambassador to Spain proclaimed that "the best merchants in the court are the Genoese. But they dedicate themselves little to real commerce that consists of sending merchandise from one country to another. On the contrary, the Genoese of the Spanish court, among whom we can find at least 100 principal great houses, devote themselves primarily to monetary transactions. They consider bills of exchange and monetary transactions as an honorable art of commerce and the trade of merchandise as an affair of shopkeepers" (Eugenio Albèri, *Relazione degli ambasciatori vèneti al Senato,* XIV (Florence, 1839–1863), 361).

4. In December 1526, A. de Vivaldo was in Seville engaged in commercial transactions (APS, 20 Dec. 1526, Oficio I, Libro I, Alonso de la Barrera, fol. 943v); in autumn of the same year he was at court (28 Nov. 1526, Libro II, fol. 808); a year later he was back again in Seville (10 Feb. 1527, Libro I, fol. 133).

5. APS, 17 Oct. 1551, Oficio XV, Libro II, Alonso de Cazalla, fol. 1710. Pedro Batista Spínola took charge of the business affairs of both Andrea Spínola and Hector Doria (16 Sept. 1551, fol. 1412).

6. A. Sayous, "Le rôle des Génois lors de premiers mouvements réguliers d'affaires entre l'Espagne et le Nouveau Monde (1505–1520)," *Comptes rendues des séances de l'Académie des Inscriptions et Belles-lettres* (July–Sept. 1932), p. 296.

Loans were much more important than partnership contracts, as indicated by their frequent appearance in the Sevillian Protocols for the early years of the century in contrast to the scarcity of the latter.

Mercado gave the following satirical description of these loans: "Quiso hazer para sí mención de un cambio que se usa en esta ciudad para Indias, porque es tan singular que no entra en la regla y canones communes de los otros y aún es tan disforme y tan feo, que parece un monstruo de cambios sin figura y apparencia entera dellos, una chimera con una parte de cambio otro de seguro, otro de usura, una mistura risible y horrible" (*Summa de tratos y contratos* [Seville, 1587], p. 220). These sixteenth-century sea loans resembled their medieval predecessors. For sea loans and other business contracts, see Robert Lopez and Irving Raymond, *Medieval Trade in the Mediterranean World* (New York, 1955).

7. In 1508 Rodrigo Bermejo, master of the ship *Santa Catalina*, obligated himself to pay Lucas Pinelo 12,000 maravedís for fifteen pieces of armor which he bought from Pinelo to sell in Santo Domingo (APS, 22 Sept. 1508, Oficio XV, Libro II, Bernal González Vallesillo, fol. segundo tercio del legajo).

8. Sayous, "Le rôle," p. 294. Shipmasters who borrowed from Genoese capitalists depended on the payment of the freight charges in order to repay the loan.

9. Sayous, "Les débuts de commerce de l'Espagne avec l'Amérique," *Revue historique*, CLXXIV (1934), 2ᵉ Fasc., 212. For a description of transactions payable in Seville, see APS, 3 Apr. 1506, Oficio IV, Libro I, Francisco Segura, fol. mitad del legajo; for a description of transactions payable in America, see APS, 3 Nov. 1512, Oficio VIII, Libro II, Bernal González Vallesillo, fol. tercer tercio del legajo.

10. On Genoese individualism see Yves Renouard, *Les hommes d'affaires italiens du moyen âge* (Paris, 1949), pp. 237–238, and Sayous, "Les débuts," p. 214. For the activities of Grimaldo and Centurión as public bankers in Seville see Chap. IV.

11. Martín Fernández de Navarrete, *Obras*, I (Madrid, 1955), No. 17, 302.

12. CDI, 2d ser., V, 68.

13. APS, 5 Oct. 1508, Oficio XV, Libro II, Bernal González Vallesillo, fol. segundo tercio del legajo.

14. "Porque de la tienda, o casa de un mercero se surte casi un cargazón al menos tómanse juntos todos los géneros que suelen venir de las partes do trata como del que en Flandes paños anascotes, tapicería, olandes, cobre, mercería o bujerías Del que en Francia, ruanes, coletas" (Mercado, *Tratos y contratos*, p. 95).

15. Georges Scelle, *La traité négrière aux Indes de Castille* (Paris, 1906), I, 122, 123. The first slaves introduced into America came from the Sevillian slave market. As early as the mid-fifteenth century, there were Negro slaves in Seville brought into the city by Portuguese slave traders and Andalusian shipowners, who were also engaged in the African slave trade during this period. Seville's Negro population grew so large that by the reign of Ferdinand and Isabella they had their own

district, chapel, ordinances, and special police. In 1474 the Catholic kings appointed a Negro named Juan de Valladolid, popularly called "El conde negro," judge and official leader of the city's Negro community, both slave and free. In Seville there still exists a street named after him, El Conde Negro (Salvador Brau, *La colonización de Puerto Rico* [San Juan, 1930], p. 87; Santiago Montoto de Sedas, *Las calles de Sevilla* [Seville, 1940], p. 152).

16. Clarence Haring, *The Spanish Empire in America* (New York, 1947), p. 219. According to Scelle (p. 126), the decree of 1510 marked the birth of the American slave trade, since Negroes were for the first time being sent to the New World for other than personal use and were bought with the object of resale. There was also some awareness by this time of the incapability of the Indians for severe physical labor as evidenced by the following statement in this decree: "Atendiendo a la flaqueza de los indios para el trabajo de las minas de la Española" (José Antonio Saco, *Historia de la esclavitud de la Raza Africana en el Nuevo Mundo y en especial en los países Américo-hispaños* [Havana, 1938], I, 104).

In 1512, for example, Ferdinand gave a license to Antonio Sedeño to take two slaves to Puerto Rico (L. Díaz Soler, *Historia de la esclavitud negra en Puerto Rico, 1493–1890* [Madrid, 1953], p. 16).

17. CDI, 2d ser., IX, 47: "Sy yo hiziere merced á alguna persona que pueda llevar a las dichas yslas yndias algunos esclavos pague por la carta al sello ciento y veynte maravedís por cada esclavo de los que asy le diere la dicha licencia."

The Catholic kings opposed the introduction of large numbers of Negroes into the New World for fear of slave uprisings, and a possible combination of Negroes and Indians against the Spaniards. This opinion is expressed in 1514 by King Ferdinand in a letter to the Bishop of La Concepción on Hispaniola denying the latter's request for an increase in the number of African slaves sent to the island (see Saco, *Historia de la esclavitud*, I, 127, 128). The first Negro uprising occurred on Hispaniola in 1522 when about forty fled to the hills and committed some murders. Ten years later fugitive slaves and rebellious Indians joined hands in an insurrection led by the Cacique Henríquez. Throughout the colonial period local slave rebellions continued to be a frequent occurrence, but there was always an insistent demand for more manpower and as such continuous importation (Haring, *The Spanish Empire*, p. 221).

18. APS, 12 Oct. 1513, Oficio XV, Libro II, Bernal González Vallesillo, fol. tercer tercio del legajo. To appreciate the profit that Jácome de Grimaldo made, it can be noted that even in 1518 when prices of slave licenses had reached a high point, the maximum cost was twelve

169

and a half ducats. For Nicolás Cataño see 10 June 1514, Oficio XV, Libro único, fol. primer tercio del legajo; and 12, 13 June 1514.

19. In 1515, for example, they purchased a license to export three slaves to Hispaniola from Sánchez Gómez de Córdoba, a courtier (APS, 30 Mar. 1515, Oficio XV, Libro II, Bernal González Vallesillo, fol. 460).

20. Antonio de Herrera, *Historia general de los hechos de los castellanos en las Islas y Tierra Firme de el Mar Oceano* (Buenos Aires, 1945), Dec. II, lib. ii, cap. 8, p. 345.

21. Scelle, *La traité négrière*, I, 130.

22. In a letter to the Emperor on Jan. 18, 1518, the Hieronymite Friars suggested that licenses be given to the inhabitants of Hispaniola, or to other persons, to bring Negroes there (CDI, 1st ser., XXXIV, 279–280).

As a result of the appeals of Las Casas, the Crown ordered a strict inquiry into the conditions of the Indians on Hispaniola, and at the same time asked the Casa de Contratación to determine the number of Negro slaves that would be necessary to relieve the labor shortage on the islands. It was decided that 4,000 would be sufficient, setting up a ratio of 1,000 for each island, e.g., Hispaniola, Cuba, Puerto Rico and Jamaica (Bartolomé de las Casas, *Historia de las Indias*, ed. Agustín Millares Carlo [Mexico City, 1951], III, chap. cii, pp. 176–177).

The Dominicans of Santo Domingo, not Las Casas, were the first to suggest the import of Negroes into the Indies to free the Indians from much of their hard labor (see Saco, *Historia de la esclavitud*, I, 144–145, and CDI, 1st ser., XI, 214).

23. The term license is used here in a generic sense to mean royal permission. In other words, Gouvenot received 4,000 slave licenses or a license for 4,000 slaves. This license was unique in that it allowed the slaves to be shipped directly from Africa to America. Previous licenses and those subsequently granted stipulated that the slaves had to be registered at the Casa de Contratación, which meant that the slave ships had to go to Seville before continuing their voyages to the New World. Eventually a system was worked out whereby ship captains reported to the officials of the Casa on their return to Seville, thereby permitting direct transport from Africa to America.

Laurent de Gouvenot, Baron of Montinay and Governor of Bresa was really a Burgundian. His name appears in contemporary Spanish documents as Garrevod, and he is often called the Governor of Bresa. (Elena F. S. De Studer, *La trata de Negros en el Río de la Plata durante el siglo XVIII* [Buenos Aires, 1958], p. 52; Scelle, *La traité négrière*, I, 141, 142).

24. The firm of Fernán Vázquez, Domingo and Tomás de Forne, and

Agustín de Vivaldo was based at the royal court. Fernán Vázquez, a Spaniard, was a councilman of the city of Toledo while Domingo and Tomás de Forne were Genoese bankers who left their native city in 1526 to take up residence at the Spanish royal court (Ehrenberg, *Das Zeitalter*, I, 340). Agustín de Vivaldo was a member of the Sevillian Genoese colony. See pp. 49, 130, 131.

25. The licenses that the government had given to Gouvenot were worth two ducats, and Gouvenot sold them to the Genoese at six ducats apiece. Scelle did not realize that Vázquez, Forne, and Vivaldo represented a partnership; therefore he referred to them as separate individuals (Scelle, *La traité négrière*, I, 152, 153).

26. Scelle (p. 152) suggested that the four businessmen actually sold their rights to Centurión and a Sevillian associate of his, Juan Fernández de Castro, who was charged with sending one quarter of the slaves to Cuba. On the contrary, Centurión and Castro were only agents for the Vázquez, Forne, and Vivaldo firm as evidenced by their official title "Procuradores y gobernadores de la licencia de Bresa." A further indication of Centurión's close relationship to the firm is brought out in the following: 'Como Gaspar Centurión mercader genovés, é otros sus compañeros enviaron los dichos esclavos" (CDI, 1st ser., II, 414). "Información de los servicios del adelantado Rodrigo de Bastidas, conquistador y pacificador de Santa Marta."

"É que á cabsa de la dicha merced por estar en poder de Gaspar Centurión, é por gozar del término de los ocho años, é por los vender á mayores precios, los traen poco á poco" (*ibid.*, p. 406). It is not then correct to assume, as did Saco (*La historia de la esclavitud*, pp. 179–180), that the Genoese failed to introduce a sufficient number of slaves into America because they lacked the means of obtaining them, due to Portuguese control over the trade.

27. APS, 1 Mar. 1514, Oficio I, Libro I, Mateo de la Cuadra, fol. 512v: "Melchor Centurión mercader ginovés residente de la cibdad de Seuilla."

28. "Que Gaspar Centurión . . . los envía, poco á poco á un hermano que tenía en esta isla, á cabsa de los vender muy bien." "Á Melchor Centurión, defunto que tenía cargo de pasar los dichos negros" (CDI, 1st ser., II, 414, 447).

29. CDI, I, 418.

30. Scelle, *La traité négrière*, I, 154, 155. It would have been impossible for Charles V, given the state of the royal treasury, to return the 25,000 ducats to the Genoese. See also Saco, *Historia de la esclavitud*, I, 179.

31. In 1528 the first *asiento*, or formal contract with an individual or

171

company for the exclusive right of furnishing Negroes to the colonies, was concluded with two German merchants connected with the Spanish court. They were obliged to ship 4,000 to America, to be sold at not more than 45 ducats apiece. They were to pay immediately into the royal treasury 20,000 ducats, in return for which Charles V promised to issue no more licenses for four years. Scarcity and the complaints of the colonists led to the abandonment of the monopoly after the expiration of the contract in 1532 (Scelle, *La traité négrière*, I, 169–177).

32. Irene Wright, "Documents—The Commencement of the Cane Sugar Industry in America, 1519–38," *American Historical Review*, XXI (1916), 770. The King to the Audiencia, Nov. 8, 1538, "E agora hernán vázquez e agostín de bibaldo e domingo de forne me han hecho relación que a ellos y a sus factores en su nombre se les deben en esa ysla muchos contías de mrs. de diez y doze y quinze años a esta parte, de lo procedido de ciertos esclabos que en dicha ysla se vendieron."

33. The following reference to payments in sugar can be found in Diego Columbus' will, dated May 2, 1523: "A los Ginobeses de la Contratación de los esclavos dos mil e quinientos arrobas de azucar por cinquenta negros que de ellos sean recibidos hasta la fecha desta" (Henri Harrisse, *Christophe Colomb son origine, sa vie, ses voyages, sa famille, et ses decendants* [Paris, 1884], p. 482). See Chap. VI, pp. 131–132, for a description of the activities of their factor on Hispaniola, Valián de Forne.

34. For Basiñana's participation in the Sebastian Cabot expedition see Chap. V, pp. 105, 195, n.17. Castro, a former royal chaplain and, at the time, Dean of the Chapter of the Church of La Concepción, Hispaniola, petitioned the king to allow him to import Negro slaves into the island to help relieve the severe labor shortage caused by the migration of Spanish settlers to the mainland. The royal license given to Castro included the following statement: "Por que vos adiades de tener compañia en lo susodicho con pero benito de basiniana ginobés" (Scelle, *La traité négrière*, I, 759).

35. APS, 3 Jan. 1527, Oficio I, Libro II, Alonso de la Barrera, fols. 71, 75; CPI, I, 206, No. 2951: "Esteban de Basiñana, genovés con licencia de residir en las Indias por diez años" (12 Sept. 1526).

36. Scelle, *La traité négrière*, I, 307. Scelle apparently read the documents incorrectly for he stated that they brought in 145 slaves on a license for 80, but on Sept. 15, 1530, the royal officials of Cuba reported to the king that "habrá cuatro años un Carreño [Carrega] y Esteban basiñana, ginovés, trujeron de Cabo Verde cuarenta negros con licencia; luego setenta y cinco con licencia para solos cuarenta" (CDI, 2d ser., VI, 2).

37. "Información hecha en Santiago de Cuba sobre haberse fugado de la cárcel Esteban Baseniano [Basiñana], genovés, á quien tenía preso por ciertos delitos" (CDI, 2d ser., I, 388, 27 May 1527).

38. In Guzman's later petition to Charles V he said "que el delito por el cometido fué de tal calidad que no podía gozar de las inmunidades de la dicha iglesia." "Petición del gobernador Gonzalo de Guzmán apelando ante Su Magestad de una provisión dada contra él por la Audiencia de Santo Domingo, por haber sacado de la iglesia á un criminal y otros actos" (ibid., I, 423, 13 Sept. 1527).

The description of this event comes from the Residencia of Gonzalo de Guzmán conducted by Licenciado Vadillo (CDI, 2d ser., IV, 220–221).

39. "Provisión dada por la Audiencia de Santo Domingo, ordenando á Juan Vázquez que haga pesquisa é información contra el teniente gobernador de la isla Fernandina, Gonzalo de Guzmán, por haber sacado de la iglesia a Esteban Baseniano [Basiñana]" (ibid., I, 422).

"Informacion hecha ante Sancho de Céspedes provisor de la isla Fernandina de como el teniente gobernador Gonzalo de Guzmán había cumplido la sentencia eclesiástica en que fué condenando por sacar de la iglesia a Esteban Baseniano [Basiñana]." And in Guzmán's own words, "Yo vine en obediencia de la madre Santa Iglesia, é fué absuelto é servido por el provisor de este obispado, por haber sacado el dicho preso" (ibid., 423–424).

40. In a letter of September 15, 1530, the judges describe the case and refer to their earlier communications to the King about it (ibid., VI, 20).

41. "É porque la justicia de Vuestra Magestad fuese tenida y ejecutada, yo fuí á la dicha iglesia y saqué al dicho malhechor della para hacer justicia" (ibid., I, 423).

42. The reprimand read: "Vos tened mucho cuidado de guardar la inmunidad de la iglesia é muy bien hecistes en someteros á su correción é cumplir la penitencia que vos dieron. . . . La dicha Audiencia está en nombre de nuestra persona Real y lo que allá se proveyere se ha de cumplir y ejecutar como si Nos lo proveyésemos y mandásemos, vos mando que vos así lo hagáis en todo y por todo" (ibid., p. 443). For the royal cedula, see ibid., IX, 285–286, 28 June 1527.

43. In their letter to the crown on September 15, 1530, the royal officials made this claim (CDI, 2d ser., VI, 20).

44. Dominican Republic, Archivo General, Boletín del Archivo General de la Nación, I (1938), Colección Lugo, Autos entre Partes, año de 1532, No. 3: "Pedro Benito de Baziniana [Basiñana], mercader genovés con Esteban Baziniana [Basiñana] vecino de Santo Domingo sobre las cuentas de la venta de sesenta negros esclavos."

45. Haring, The Spanish Empire, p. 219. The prices quoted represent

those established by the government in 1556. Complaints by merchants and royal officials against the policy of the price fixing led to its abandonment in 1561. In reality, the colonists were at the mercy of the merchants, who could set any price they wanted, especially in times of scarcity (Saco, *Historia de la esclavitud*, II, 42).

46. See pp. 76–77.

47. Scelle, *La traité négrière*, I, 225. In November 1536 they obtained a license for 500 slaves and in May 1537 for 66 slaves. APS, 5 Nov. 1544, Oficio XV, Libro II, Alonso de Cazalla, fol. 817v.

48. APS, 22 Sept. 1546, Oficio XV, Libro II, Alonso de Cazalla, fol. 751.

49. De Stuber, *La trata de Negros*, p. 48; Scelle, *La traité négrière*, I, 268–276, 769. This sum included 6,400 maravedís of interest at 5 per cent.

50. Scelle, *La traité négrière*, I, 770–772. Both Lomelín and Marín spent most of their time at court and were usually represented in Seville by members of the Cataño family (APS, 14 Nov. 1550, Oficio XV, Libro II, Juan Franco, fol. 562).

51. APS, 26 June 1551, Oficio XV, Libro I, Alonso de Cazalla, fol. 759.

52. For a description of these two mills see Fernando Sandoval, *La industria del azúcar en Nueva España* (Mexico City, 1951), chap. ii.

53. This contract was signed in Valladolid in May 1542 (*ibid.*, pp. 36, 42).

54. Sandoval incorrectly uses the name Fresco for Fiesco. Fiesco was present at the signing of the contracts (*ibid.*, p. 42).

55. *Ibid.*, pp. 42, 64.

56. We know very little about those financial difficulties. There is a document, however, in the Archivo de Protocols in which the Chief Officer of Justice in Seville, on the request of Cortes, ordered the "attachment of the property of Leonardo Lomelín, Genoese merchant, at present in Seville, to guarantee a debt proceeding from a sugar contract" (APS, 7 May 1547, Oficio XVI, Martín de Ávila, fol. cuaderno de 7 de Mayo).

For a description of Juan Bautista de Marín's activities see Woodrow Borah, *Early Colonial Trade and Navigation between Mexico and Peru* (Berkeley, 1954).

57. Sandoval, *La industria del azúcar*, p. 68.

58. APS, 29 Jan. 1550, Oficio XV, Libro I, Alonso de Cazalla, fol. 233.

59. Sandoval, *La industria del azúcar*, pp. 64, 65.

60. Negro slaves were used on both the mills and plantations in the

Antilles. In Mexico they were employed only in the mills while Indians worked the plantations (*ibid.*, p. 36).

61. APS, 17 Dec. 1522, Oficio IV, Libro IV, Manuel Segura, fol. 467v.

62. B. Bennassar, "Facteurs sévillans au xvᵉ siècle d'après des lettres marchandes," *Annales: Economies, sociétés, civilisations*, XII (1957), p. 63. The Jesuit historian Acosta pointed out the importance of sugar and the growing demand for it in 1587: "Es ésta del azúcar la principal granjería de aquellos islas [Antillas]; tanto se han dado los hombres al apetito de lo dulce" (José Acosta, *Historia natural y moral de las Indias*, ed. Edmundo O'Gorman [Mexico City, 1940], p. 197).

63. CDI, 2d ser., XIV, 109; XXIV, 153. Their partner in Santo Domingo was Antonio de Villasante. According to Pierre Pomet (*History of Drugs* [London, 1725], p. 53), the balsam of Santo Domingo, or new balsam as he called it, came from small red fruit that grew on a tree native to the island. *Cañafístola* or cassia fistula was highly solicited in Spain and elsewhere is sixteenth-century Europe as a purgative. Nevertheless, so much *cañafístola* had been produced on Hispaniola during the first three decades of the century that the market went to pieces. The growers therefore decided to ship it all to one consignee in Seville to be sold at a fixed price, and this was the origin of the Leardo-Basiñana monopoly (see Irene Wright, "History of Sugar," *Louisiana Planter and Sugar Manufacturer*, LIV [1915], 302).

64. Cochineal, a reddish purple dye had by this time taken the place of madder and orchil used in the European cloth industry during the Middle Ages (V. Vázquez de Prada, *Lettres marchandes d'Anvers* [Paris, 1960], I, 101).

65. Gregorio Martín "mercader estante en la isla de San Juan," general powers Rodrigo de Narváez, "maestre," specific powers (APS, 5 Apr., Oficio XV, Libro único, Bernal González Vallesillo, fol. primer tercio del legajo); Juan Rodríguez, "maestre," general powers (6 July, fol. segundo tercio del legajo); Miguel Díaz, "residente en la isla de San Juan" (12 Apr., Oficio IV, Libro I, Manuel Segura, folio falta, Indias 12). The Sevillian Protocols contain countless numbers of these grants of power.

66. Mercado, *Tratos y contratos*, p. 91. The commercial companies (*compañías*) used in the sixteenth-century trade between Spain and the New World have been described by Mercado, *Tratos y contratos*, chap. ix. The volumes of Sevillian Protocols contain innumerable contracts of *compañía* formed between Genoese residents of Seville, and between Genoese and Spaniards.

67. *Ibid.*, p. 91v. The transition from *compañero* to commission agent was foreseen in the partnership contract (*ibid.*, p. 52v; chap. x).

68. CDI, 2d ser., X, 445.

69. Mercado, *Tratos y contratos*, pp. 56–57. When return merchandise arrived in Seville, all those who had formed *compañías* with the shipper claimed, if not all the goods, at least part of their value.

70. APS, 26 Feb., Oficio XV, Libro único, Bernal González Vallesillo, fol. 157; 21 May, fol. 554; and 21 Oct., fol. 667.

71. He is always called Juan Rodríguez in the Sevillian Protocols although the Registers published by Chaunu list him as Juan Rodríguez Ginovés (I, 152, year 1525), and at times, Juan Ginovés (I, 160, year 1525). We can only speculate as to the origin of his name. It may be an hispanization of his original Genoese name just as Cristòforo Colombo became Cristóbal Colón. On the other hand, he might not have used his Genoese last name, and simply assumed the name of Rodríguez, a common Spanish name, especially for seamen in sixteenth-century Seville. The second supposition seems to have firmer basis, since we have another example of a Genoese shipmaster with the name of Rodríguez— Diego Rodríguez (APS, 27 Aug. 1524, Oficio V, Libro I, Francisco de Castellanos, fol. 533v). See also APS, 12 Apr. 1514, Oficio I, Libro I, Mateo de la Cuadra, fol. 397: "Juan Rodríguez, ginovés, vezino de Triana, maestre de la nao *Santa María de la Antigua*"; APS, 1 Sept. 1524, Oficio V, Libro I, Francisco de Castellanos, fol. 590v.

72. For example, a sea loan for 300 ducats from Bautista and Alejandro Cataño in 1507 (APS, 17 May 1507, Oficio IV, Libro II, Manuel Segura, fol. principio del legajo); and 21 Jan. 1507, Libro I, fol. Mitad del legajo: "40 toneladas de mercaderías, 13 asnos y dos yeguas . . . a la isla española" for Jácome de Riberol; and 9 Jan. 1512, Bernal González Vallesillo, fol. primer tercio del legajo, for freighting contract with Gaspar Centurión.

73. APS, 16 Feb. 1513, Oficio XV, Libro II, Bernal González Vallesillo, fol. 61v; and 6 July 1514, Libro único, fol. segundo tercio del legajo; and 12 Aug. 1517, Libro II, fol. 216; and 19 Aug., fol. 289.

74. The Sevillian Protocols abound in examples of this practice. During the whole century, the steady demand in the New World for European goods encouraged passengers, regardless of trade or profession, to carry merchandise to America to sell. Even the impoverished hero of Lope de Vega's *De cosario a cosario* managed to take "seis vestidos, un trencellín, dos cadenas" to the New World for sale (in *Obras de Lope de Vega*, ed. E. Cotarelo y Mori, XI [Madrid, 1929] Act. I, 636).

75. APS, 22 Sept. 1508, Oficio XV, Libro II, Bernal González Vallesillo, fol. segundo tercio del legajo.

76. For the summer 1517 trip he granted eight loans amounting to 65 ducats. In February 1517 he loaned Juan de Ribera, a resident of San Germán, Puerto Rico, 7,800 maravedís—the freight charges on the

merchandise that he was taking with him on his return trip (APS, 12 Feb. 1517, Oficio XV, Libro I, Bernal González Vallesillo, fol. 79).

77. APS, 1 Sept. 1524, Oficio V, Libro I, Francisco de Castellanos, fol. 590v; and 10 Jan. 1526, fol. 88.

78. H. and P. Chaunu, *Séville et l'Atlantique 1504 à 1650*, II (Paris, 1955), 198, year 1529.

79. In theory, the law prohibited the entrance of foreigners into the colonies, except for a short interval under Charles V, but just as in the case of the participation of foreign merchants in the transatlantic trade, special dispensations and royal permits were always available and especially to the Genoese as a reward for their loans to the crown (Haring, *The Spanish Empire*, p. 199).

80. "Queste testigo [Rafael Cataño] vino con el dicho Almirante á esta isla Española en el viaje que hizo quand truxo las diez é siete naos." He must have been in his early twenties at that time, for in the above document, dated 1514, he declared that he was "more than forty years old."

"Queste testigo [Rafael Cataño] . . . questaba en esta isla Española quando el dicho don Cristóbal Colón dezía que venía de la provincia de Paria [Third Voyage] porque él á la sazón era contador con el dicho Almirante" (CDI, 2d ser., VII, 378, 379).

81. CDI, 2d ser., V, 46, 29 Mar. 1503; and p. 68, 8 Jan. 1504; APS, 7 Feb. 1509, Oficio III, Libro único, Juan Ruiz de Porras, fol. segundo tercio del legajo; CDI, 1st ser., I, 130: "A Rafael Cataño, vecino de la ciudad de Santo Domingo, se le encomendó once naborías de las allegadas que él é Diego de Alvarado registraron"; APS, 2 May 1516, Oficio XV, Libro único, Bernal González Vallesillo, fol. 358; CPI, I, 148, No. 2103, 17 May 1516.

82. APS, 13 Aug. 1511, Oficio VI, 16 del cuaderno 2, 3v, Juan Núñez. In 1510 King Ferdinand granted Bernaldo de Grimaldo the special privilege of allowing his factor to reside permanently in the Indies while this permission was denied to all other foreigners. The Grimaldo were particularly favored by King Ferdinand because of their large loans to him on the occasion of his daughter Catherine's marriage to the Prince of Wales (Carande, *Carlos V*, p. 318).

The eight members were Ambrosio Spínola, Benito Doria, Alejandro Cataño, Batista Centurión, Juan Tomás de Monte, Esteban Centurión, and Domenegro de Castellón.

83. For both Tomás and Jácome de Castellón see Chap. VI.

84. APS, 10 Feb. 1508, Oficio XV, Libro I, Bernal González Vallesillo, fol. primer tercio del legajo; and 17 Feb.; 10 Mar., fol. mitad del legajo. Antonio Italián died in 1515, leaving a minor daughter in Seville under the guardianship of Valián Salvago (APS, 22 Feb. 1515,

Oficio VII, Libro I, Gómez Álvarez de Aguiler, fol. 21v, cuaderno 2).
85. APS, 13 Aug. 1511, Oficio VI, Juan Núñez, fol. 16 del cuaderno
2 y 18v del 3; APS, 21 Feb. 1508, Oficio I, Libro I, Bernal González
Vallesillo, fol. primer tercio del legajo; and 10 Mar.; APS, 5 June 1512,
Oficio IV, Libro II, Bernal González Vallesillo, fol. segundo tercio del
legajo; and 13 Aug. 1511.
86. According to Las Casas, "El piloto Roldán edificó una reglera de
casas para su morada y para alquilar en las cuatros calles. Luego, un
Hiéronimo Grimaldo, mercader y otros y cada día, fueron creciendo los
edificios [en Santo Domingo]" (Bartolomé de las Casas, *Historia*, II,
235); APS, 13 Aug. 1511, Oficio IV, Libro II, Bernal González
Vallesillo, fol. segundo tercio del legajo; and fol. 17 del cuaderno 2 y 20
del 3. In 1515 Jerónimo's financial manipulations caused a lawsuit
between his uncle and Diego Columbus, governor of the island of
Hispaniola. The elder Grimaldo began proceedings against the governor,
believing that the latter had not repaid a debt of 400,000 maravedís.
When Diego Columbus's account books were presented in Seville,
however, they showed an acknowledgment of repayment of the debt
signed by Jerónimo. The money had been appropriated by Jerónimo
(APS, 10 July, Oficio II, Libro III, Francisco Castellanos, fol. 50v);
APS, 26 July, Oficio XV, Libro II, Bernal González Vallesillo, fol. 591,
608; APS, 22 Sept., Oficio II, Libro III, Francisco Castellanos, fol. 251.
87. APS, 7 May 1516, Oficio I, Libro I, Mateo de la Cuadra, fol.
491v. In 1508 the royal favor that his uncle enjoyed enabled him to
receive an encomienda of forty or fifty Indians. "Por parte de Bernaldo de
Grimaldo vezino de la Ciudad de Sevilla me es fecha relación quel tiene
en esas Yndias por hasedor a Jerónimo de Grimaldo su sobrino; e me
suplicó le mandase darle XL o L Yndios en administración como se den a
los otros vezinos destas dichas Yndias" (Eduardo Ibarra y Rodríguez, ed.
*Documentos de asunto económico correspondientes al reinado de los
Reyes Católicos, 1475–1516* [Madrid, 1917], p. 58, Feb. 1508).
88. APS, 19 Feb. 1517, Oficio XV, Libro I, Bernal González
Vallesillo, fol. 129; APS, 1517, Oficio XVIII, Pedro Díaz de Alfaro, fol.
missing, registro 6. Part of the document is also missing.
89. APS, 30 Oct. 1490, Oficio XVIII, Libro III, fol. 1040; APS, 3
Mar., 1490 Oficio XV, Libro I, Bernal González Vallesillo, fol. primer
tercio del legajo.
90. A notary deed of 19 November 1510 mentions the "bricks, biscuit
and other merchandise" that Ambrosio sent to the Indies to be sold there
by Jerónimo de Grimaldo (APS, Oficio I, Libro I, Mateo de la Cuadra,
fol. 189; for Nicolás de Grimaldo, APS, 13 Mar. 1509, Oficio XV, Libro
I, Bernal González Valesillo, fol. primer tercio del legajo).

178

91. Francisco A. de Icaza, *Conquistadores y pobladores de Nueva España* (Madrid, 1923), No. 1342: "Xcriptóbal Despíndola . . . dize quest vezino del Sevilla hidalgo notorio, casado con Doña Francisca Cataño . . . que a deziocho años que se casó. . . . According to Garcilaso de la Vega, el Inca in *La Florida del Inca, historia del adelantado Hernando de Soto, gobernador y capitán general del reino de la Florida* . . . (Madrid, 1723), pp. 9, 22, Cristóbal Spínola was a captain of the guard who had sixty halberdiers under him. Garcilaso calls him "micer Espínola"; this is just one of the variations of the Spínola name. Another spelling often found in the documents is Espíndola.

92. Icaza, *Conquistadores*, No. 1342. The encomienda was a grant of authority over Indians, which carried the obligation to christianize them and to protect them, as well as the right to collect tribute (D. Worcester and W. Schaeffer, *The Growth and Culture of Latin America* [New York, 1956], p. xvi).

93. CPI, III, 223, No. 3031.

94. APS, 5 June 1512, Oficio XV, Libro II, Bernal González Vallesillo, fol. segundo tercio del legajo; and 15 June 1515, fol. 502: "Melchor Centurión, mercader genovés, residente de la ciudad de Sevilla en el nombre y boz de Esteban Centurión, su hermano, vecino de la ciudad de Granada"; APS, 20 Aug. 1525, Oficio I, Libro I, Alonso de la Barrera, fol. 259v; APS, 5 June 1512, Oficio XV, Libro II, Bernal González Vallesillo, fol. segundo tercio del legajo; and 7 Nov. 1511, fol. tercer tercio del legajo; APS, 20 Nov. 1527, Oficio V, Libro I, Francisco de Castellanos, fol. 440; APS, 25 July 1525, Oficio, Libro II, Alonso de la Barrera, fol. 3v.

95. A. Sayous, "La genèse du systeme capitaliste: La pratique des affaires et leur mentalité dans l'Espagne du XVIème siècle," *Annales d'histoire économique et sociale*, VIII (1936), 346.

96. After 1550 the Sevillian Protocols register scarcely any sea loans involving the Genoese. During the sixteenth century insurance premiums oscillated between 5 and 7 per cent. At times, due to war or the increased activity of pirates, they reached 30 per cent (R. Carande, *Carlos V y sus banqueros* [Madrid, 1943], p. 280).

97. See Chaunu, *Séville et l'Atlantique*, II, III. Grandees such as the Dukes of Arcos and Medina Sidonia and the Count of Ayamonte owned vessels. The lower nobility also owned vessels in the American trade, but were more active in the shipment of goods to the New World (see Pike, "Sevillian Nobility").

98. APS, 7 May 1517, Oficio XV, Libro I, Bernal González Vallesillo, fol. 484.

99. From beginning to end, passage to and from America was a

hazardous undertaking. Boats were unseaworthy, inadequately manned and equipped, and the West Indian hurricanes and pirates took a disastrous toll of the ships (C. Haring, *Trade and Navigation, between Spain and the Indies in the Time of the Hapsburgs* [Cambridge, 1918], pp. 293–294).

100. The laws requiring owners or masters of ships in the India navigation to be native Spaniards did not disqualify the Sevillian Genoese, who by this time were naturalized or represented the second generation, born in Seville.

101. Chaunu, *Séville et l'Atlantique,* III, IV.

102. Ehrenberg, *Das Zeitalter,* I, 346. In the first part of the century the outstanding crown bankers from the Sevillian colony were Agustín de Vivaldo, Jácome and Juan Francisco de Grimaldo, and Agustín Italián.

103. These receipts are preserved among the Protocols of the city.

104. Francisco de Laiglesia, *Estudios históricos, 1515–1555* (Madrid, 1918), II, Apps. IV, VI. The following statistics are drawn from these two reports.

105. *Ibid.,* App. VI.

106. Braudel, *La Méditerranée,* p. 785; Ehrenberg, *Das Zeitalter,* p. 347. The escudo was equal to 400 maravedís (R. Trevor Davies, *The Golden Century of Spain, 1501–1621* [London, 1954], p. 297).

107. APS, 14 Nov. 1550, Oficio XV, Libro I, Juan Franco, fol. 562.

108. Carande, *La hacienda,* p. 172. The term "asiento" (French, sixteenth-century "parti") means contract or agreement. In the financial language of the time, money transactions between the monarchs and businessmen were called *asientos,* which could involve the farm of a tax, the provision of the army, or the advance of money (Henri Lapeyre, *Simón Ruiz et les asientos de Philippe II* [Paris, 1953], pp. 12–13).

109. APS, 5 Nov. 1544, Oficio XV, Libro II, Alonso de Cazalla, fol. 815v; and 7 Oct. 1545, fol. 921.

110. Carrrande, *La hacienda,* p. 173.

111. Both Nicolás and Jerónimo Cataño were affiliated with the Sevillian bank of Domingo de Lizarrazas (APS, 26 Nov. 1545, Oficio XV, Libro II, Alonso de Cazalla, fol. 1359; and 20 Dec. 1528, fol. 1614v; and 6 Nov. 1549, Libro I, fol. 1076v; APS, 14 Jan. 1551, Oficio XV, Libro I, Juan Franco, fol. 875).

112. In particular to the Gelves family, descendants of Columbus. For example, in May 1551 the Countess of Gelves declared that, in the name of her son, Don Álvaro, she "had borrowed 259,615 maravedís that with interest amounted to 271,946 maravedís from Jerónimo Cataño" (APS, Oficio XV, Libro I, Alonso de Cazalla, fol. 349).

113. Carande, *Carlos V,* p. 155; Haring, *Trade and Navigation,* p.

109; Herbert Heaton, *Economic History of Europe* (New York, 1948), p. 165.

114. In the sixteenth century the nonfamily partnership of unlimited liability began to rank alongside the *commenda* form of partnership (James W. Thompson, *Economic and Social History of Europe in the Latter Middle Ages* [New York, 1931], p. 442); and most often the shares were equal (S. Clough and C. Cole, *Economic History of Europe* [3d ed.; New York, 1952], p. 75). In France this type of partnership came to be known as the "société en nom collectif" in contrast to the "société en commandite" used in the American trade, in which the partners were liable to lose only their investments (Arthur Robert Burns, "Partnerships," *Encyclopedia of the Social Sciences*, ed. E. R. A. Seligman, XII [1934], 3–6).

115. A. Goris, *Étude sur les colonies marchandes, méridionales (portugais, espagnols, italiens) à Anvers de 1488 à 1567* (Louvain, 1925), p. 1105.

116. Polo Centurión, Constantín Spínola, and Lucas Pinelo, for example (APS, 14 Dec. 1551, Oficio XV, Libro II, Alonso de Cazalla, fol. 201).

117. With the king, Galeazo de Negrón, Jacome Calvo, and Cristóbal Lercaro; with the regional nobility, Juan Antonio Spínola and Jerónimo and Pascual Cataño.

118. Luis Spínola's father was also a wealthy merchant and a denizen of the city (APS, 16 Aug. 1549, Oficio XV, Libro I, Alonso de Cazalla, fol. 416; and 19 Mar. 1549, fol. 587; APS, 21 June 1580, Oficio XVII, Libro II, Francisco de Vera, fol. falta (fin de legajo).

CHAPTER IV

1. The Ricorsa bill, or *recambium*, was originally intended to allow recourse on the drawer of the bill by the holder in case of default. In the sixteenth century the "Ricorsa bill in two acts" (between Seville and the Spanish fairs or Seville and Antwerp), was not only a credit instrument, but also contained a strongly speculative element, as no one could foresee the exchange rate at the time of re-exchange. Accordingly, there was a possibility of making a profit, not only on the interest, but on the difference in the exchange rate (Richard Ehrenburg, *Capital and Finance in the Age of the Renaissance*, trans. H. M. Lucas [New York, 1928], p. 244; R. Carande, *Carlos V y sus banqueros* [Madrid, 1943], p. 207).

Arbitrage in bills contained three elements: the wish to make money on the difference between the prices of bills in different places, speculation on their fluctuations, and the wish to obtain the highest possible interest. Sometimes one element was more prominent, sometimes another, but in most cases they were all inextricably mixed (Ehrenberg, *Capital and Finance*, p. 245). Mercado described arbitrage in Seville as follows: "Libran [*los cambiadores*] suma en parte donde no la tienen, y no la libraran sin conjetura andara allí más baja la plaza y avisan al otro que allí está la tome a cambio a Envers o Barcelona, do tienen ya ellos moneda para consumirla y gastarla" (T. de Mercado, *Summa de tratos y contratos* [Seville, 1587], p. 167, fol. 167).

Ramón Carande was the first to suggest that the Genoese played an important role in public banking in Seville. Although he did not give any examples of Genoese bankers (he failed to recognize that Franco and Pedro Juan Leardo were Genoese), he emphasized their participation as bondsmen of the several Sevillian banks.

There is no specific work devoted to a description of banking in Seville in the sixteenth century. Many economic historians, notably Ehrenberg, Sayous, and Lapeyre, have mentioned Sevillian banking in their more general works of the period, but none has gone into as much detail as has Ramón Carande. In his description of the Sevillian banks, Carande utilized documents from the Archivo de Protocolos, never before used in a study of this kind (*Carlos V*, chap. x).

2. The banks of deposit and transfer owe their origin to the extension of the functions of the moneychangers. By 1200 they had already expanded their activities beyond mere moneychanging and had begun to accept deposits on current account. The moneychangers in this way became private bankers (Raymond de Roover, "New Interpretations of the History of Banking," *Cahiers d'histoire mondiale* [Paris, 1954], II, 38, 57; A. P. Usher, *The Early History of Deposit Banking in Mediterranean Europe* [Cambridge, Mass., 1943], p. 238).

"Que devo dar e pagar a vos Domingo de Lizarrazas banquero público en esta ciudad de Sevilla 750,000 maravedís a cumplimiento de toda la cuenta de entrada y salida que tenía en dicho banco" (APS, 15 Jan. 1550, Oficio XV, Libro I, Alonso de Cazalla, fol. 131).

We do have some evidence that written orders of payment were also used. Lapeyre has found examples of them in the Ruiz Archives and we can assume that they were also utilized in Seville. The lack of private archives in Seville prevents us from obtaining any further information on this point (Henri Lapeyre, *Une famille de marchands: Les Ruiz* [Paris, 1959], p. 261).

3. Mercado, *Tratos y contratos*, p. 170.

4. Usher, *Deposit Banking*, p. 14. In 1553 a customer of the bank of Pedro Juan Leardo declared that he owed the bank more than 28,000,000 maravedís "de la cuenta corriente de debe y ha de haber mediante la cual yo libré y pagué muchas cuantías de maravedís" (APS,

1553, Alonso de Cazalla, as quoted in Carande, *Carlos V*, p. 367).
5. Hamilton, *American Treasure and the Price Revolution in Spain,
1501–1650* (Cambridge, Mass., 1934), pp. 27, 30; Hamilton assumed
that the silver merchants "formed banks in their homes and casually
engaged in buying treasure, the magnitude of their operations depending
on the extent of the funds entrusted to them." On the contrary, the silver
merchants were not bankers and did not need to be, since they "obtained
funds through their current accounts in the Sevillian banks" (Carande,
Carlos V, p. 209). In 1553, for example, a silver merchant who was a
customer of Lizarrazas stated that he owed the bank more than 7,000,000
maravedís "de la cuenta corriente de debe y ha de haber mediante la cual
yo libré y pagué muchas cuantías de maravedís" (APS, 1553, Alonso de
Cazalla, as quoted in Carande, *Carlos V*, p. 367).
    6. Carande, *Carlos V*, p. 206. The sureties for the Lizarrazas bank in
the 1540's amounted to 200,000 ducats. "Las fianças que dicho banco
tiene dadas son buenas y en cantidad de dozientos mill ducados" (AGI,
Indiferente General, Legajo 2000, fol. 92v). In 1519 the bank of Gaspar
Centurión presented a guarantee of 50,000 ducats (APS, 31 Oct. 1519,
Oficio XV, Legajo 2, Bernal González Vallesillo, fol. 383).
    7. At the Castilian fairs the bankers took a commission "por la pena
del cambio" (Henri Lapeyre, "La banque, les changes et le crédit au
XVI⁰ siècle," *Revue d'histoire moderne et contemporaine*, III [1956],
288).
    8. Mercado, *Tratos y contratos*, p. 170. In Mercado's own descriptive
language, "Que un banquero abarca en esta república un mundo y abraça
más que el Oceano aunque a las veces aprieta tan poco que da con él todo
al traste."
    9. Lapeyre, *Les Ruiz*, p. 263.
    10. In 1554 the city council received complaints that the bankers had
bought up stocks of sugar with the intention of cornering the market and
raising the price (AMS, *Papeles importantes*, siglo XVI, tomo 1, No.
71. "Raro es el banquero que no pase los límites de su trato dando a
cambio" (Mercado, *Tratos y contratos*, fol. 223).
    11. AMS, *Papeles importantes*, siglo XVI, tomo 1, Nos. 71, 72.
    12. B. Bennassar, "Facteurs sévillans au XV⁰ siècle d'après des lettres
marchandes," *Annales: Economies, sociétés, civilisations*, XII (1957), 63.
    13. Lapeyre, *Les Ruiz*, p. 267.
    14. Carande, *Carlos V*, p. 199.
    15. According to Guzmán de Alfarache, "la flota no venía, la ciudad
estaba muy apretada, cerradas las bolsas" (M. Alemán, *Guzmán de
Alfarache*, in A. Valbuena y Prat, *La novela picaresca española* [Madrid,
1956], Pt. I, Bk. III, chap. vi, p. 553. In 1536 the merchants of Seville

explained their position as follows: "Tomándonos los dichos nuestros caudales se atajan e impiden los tratos: nosotros no podemos cumplir con nuestros acreedores: falta el dinero en las ferias y en esta plaza tenemos necesidad de tomar a cambio" (Carande, *Carlos V*, pp. 156, 208).

An appreciation of the dangers involved in government attachment of private bullion in exchange for *juros* found expression in the protests of the Cortes. At Valladolid in 1555, for example, the deputies petitioned the king to desist from these confiscations since "de tomar el dinero en Sevilla a los mercaderes y pasajeros que vienen de las Indias, darles juro por ello, se recrecen muchos daños, así a aquellos a quien los toman, porque no pueden hacer sus tratos y negociaciones y poco a poco se iría disminuyendo la contratación, como a aquellos a quienes ellos daban, porque no pudiéndoles pagar, se vienen a alzar con sus haciendas" (C. Haring, *Trade and Navigation between Spain and the Indies in the Time of the Hapsburgs* [Cambridge, 1918], p. 173).

16. Genoese control over the Sevillian money market is brought out in the following statement by Gerónimo de Valladolid in 1563. According to the Ruiz agent in Seville, "there isn't any money to lend and it cannot be found at any price: this is due in large part to its monopolization by the Genoese; since they are not offering any money there are few lenders" (Bennassar, "Les facteurs sévillans," p. 66).

17. In his study of Genoa in the fifteenth century, Jacques Heers found that the "Genoese public banker was almost always a successful merchant who often remained a merchant" (J. Heers, *Gênes au XV* siècle [Paris, 1961], p. 92. Furthermore, those who operated banks of deposit and transfer also dealt in bills of exchange, both local and foreign. The opinion of Heers conflicts with the point of view expressed by both De Roover and Lapeyre. Both these historians divide the money dealers into two categories: the moneychanger-bankers (*changeurs-banquiers*), who were public bankers, and the merchant-bankers (*marchands-banquiers*), who engaged in all forms of the trade of goods and money, but did not practice public banking (Lapeyre, "La banque," p. 21; Raymond de Roover, *L'évolution de la lettre de change, XIV*-*XVIII* siècle [Paris, 1953], p. 134). The participation of the Genoese merchants of Seville in public banking supports the thesis of Heers. The Centurione, for example, controlled the largest bank in Genoa, played an important role in the trade with Spain, and were among the most important farmers of the Tolfa alum (Heers, *Gênes*, p. 92). An excellent example of a varied career in the trade of goods and money including public banking is that of the fifteenth-century Genoese merchant, Giovanni Piccamiglio (see Jacques Heers, *Le livre de comptes de Giovanni Piccamiglio, homme d'affaires Génois, 1456–1459* [Paris, 1959]).

18. Nothing could be more confusing than the term "banker" as used in this period. It was loosely applied to all those who engaged in the trade in money. In Seville merchants who dealt in bills of exchange, as well as moneychangers and others who practiced public banking, were all called bankers. Contemporary Spanish treatises on trade and finance usually mention three types of bankers: public bankers, those who accepted deposits; fair bankers, who were public bankers also, but who were closely connected with the operations of exchange; and court bankers, those whose principal activity was to lend money to the sovereigns (Sayous, "Les affaires," p. 347). As for the designation "merchant," in Seville it was used to describe all those who traded in goods, but it was also applied to those who dealt in bills of exchange and lent money to the nobility and royalty. We even find, in the case of Juan Francisco de Grimaldo and Gaspar Centurión, the following designation: "Juan Francisco de Grimaldo y Gaspar Centurión, mercaderes genoveses, banqueros públicos de Sevilla" (APS, 24 Aug. 1518, Oficio XV, Libro II, Bernal González Vallesillo, fol. 34). The term "banquero público" could be used only by bankers who had given the required securities and were therefore licensed by the city. All the banks described in this chapter fall into this category. See also APS, 31 Oct. 1519, Oficio XV, Legajo 3, Bernal González Vallesillo, fol. 383.

Since all who dealt in money were called bankers, Sayous concluded erroneously that there was no change of activity involved in this case ("Les débuts," p. 247). This was mere speculation on his part, since he did not have access to the documents that prove conclusively that the two Genoese businessmen had extended their activities to include public banking.

19. *Carlos V*, p. 206. Carande came to this conclusion on the basis of the important role that the Genoese played in Sevillian economic life, and their experience with the Bank of Saint George.

The fact that both Grimaldo and Centurión were foreigners did not prevent them from becoming public bankers in Seville, although the laws of Castile specifically prohibited foreigners or naturalized foreigners from being moneychangers or bankers (J. A. Rubio, "La fundación del banco de Amsterdam (1609) y la banca de Sevilla, *Moneda y crédito* [1948], p. 19). The Sevillian environment, permeated as it was with the spirit of materialism, reflected a most tolerant attitude toward foreigners during almost all the sixteenth century.

20. APS, 5 Nov. 1519, Oficio X, Legajo 2, Diego López, fol. 11: "Yo Francisco de Alcázar, veinticuatro y fiel ejecutor de Sevilla . . . otorgo y conozco que do e otorgo todo mi poder . . . a vos Juan Francisco de Grimaldo, banquero público de esta ciudad de Sevilla y a vos Juan

Bautista de Grimaldo mercader genovés estante en esta dicha ciudad de
Sevilla especialmente para que por mí e en mi nombre puedan demandar
e rrecabdar e rrescebir e aver e cobrar . . . a Adán de Bivaldo y a Tomás
de Forne y compañía, mercaderes genoveses estantes en la corte 10,900
ducados de oro que ha de pagar al dicho Juan Francisco de Alcázar por
una cédula de cambio para la feria de octubre de Medina del Campo."

21. In the second will of Diego Columbus, dated Santo Domingo,
May 2, 1523, the following item appears: "A Gaspar Centurión mill
ducados que salió a pagar por mí" (Harrisse, *Cristophe Colomb*, II,
500). In 1519 Diego Columbus sold the villa of Palma and the fortress
of Alpizar to Francisco del Alcázar for 11,700,000 maravedís. Alcázar
paid 7,500,000 maravedís immediately, 3,750,000 maravedís of which
Diego subsequently turned over to "Juan Francisco de Grimaldo, public
banker who had lent them to Ferdinand Columbus in the name of his
brother," in addition to 6,000 ducats that Diego owed him for a bill of
exchange (APS, 7 Nov. 1519, Oficio X, Libro II, Diego López, fol. 14,
cuaderno de novembre).

22. They began their dealings with the Spanish monarchs in March
1525, when they loaned 25,000 ducats to Charles V. Juan Bautista and
several other Italian and German merchants farmed the revenues of the
maestrazgos (military-religious orders) from 1528–1532 (see Ehrenberg,
Das Zeitalter, I, 330–334, and Carande, *La hacienda real*, p. 386).

23. APS, 24 Aug. 1518, Oficio XV, Legajo 2, Bernal González
Vallesillo, fol. 34: "Niculao de Grimaldo, mercader genovés estante en la
corte en nombre de don Hernando Colón . . . nombra procuradores
sustitutos a Juan Francisco de Grimaldo genovés, banquero público de
Sevilla y a Niculoso Cataño mercader genovés estante en esta dicha
ciudad"; APS, 17 Dec. 1519, Oficio VI, Legajo 2, Juan Núñez, fol. 21:
"Don Hernando Colón . . . por sí propio y en nombre de su hermano
otorgo e conozco que devo dar e pagar a vos Juan Francisco de Grimaldo
genovés banquero público de Sevilla y a vos Juan Bautista de Grimaldo
mercader genovés estante en la corte 900,000 maravedís."

24. APS, 30 Oct. 1953, Oficio XV, Legajo 1, Bernal González
Vallesillo, fol. 674: "Por comisyon de Juan Francisco de Grimaldo
difunto que dios aya"; APS, 7 June 1525, Oficio III, Libro I, Anton Ruiz
de Porras, fol. 27v, cuaderno 7.

25. APS, 8 May 1538, Oficio XV, Libro I, Alonso de Cazalla, fol.
1226: "Doña María de Toledo, Virreina de las Indias . . . otorgo e
conozco que devo dar e pagar a vos Cristóbal Francesquín y a vos Diego
Martínes banqueros públicos en esta cibdad de seuilla 700,000 maravedís"; and 4 Aug. 1542, Libro II, fol. 333: "Y los de vos rrecibí en el

banco de Cristóbal Francesquín e Diego Martínes banqueros públicos en esta cibdad." Cristóbal Francesquín [Francesche] was originally from Lucca and Diego Martínez was of Portuguese origin. In March 1538 they sent twenty-three toneladas of merchandise on the *San Martín* bound for Santiago, Cuba (2 Mar. 1538, Libro I, fol. 626). In September 1537 they delegated full powers to Luis Sánchez to take charge of their affaires in Nombre de Dios (27 Sept. 1537, Libro II, fol. 1066). Their insurance operations can be seen in 12 July 1536, fol. 198; see also G. Scelle, *La traité négrière aux Indes de Castille* (Paris, 1906), I, 768.

26. Carande found Iñíguez mentioned as a public banker in a document, dated 1536, of the notary Pedro de Castellanos. His name also appears on the official list of the banks operating in Seville in 1545 drawn up by the Casa de Contratación and on a similar list for the year 1553 (AGI, Contratación, Legajos 4677, 4339. "En los tres bancos que al presente hay en esta ciudad de Alonso y Pedro de Espinosa, de Juan Iñíguez y Octaviano de Negrón (Legajo 4399).

27. John W. Burgon, *The Life and Times of Sir Thomas Gresham* (London, 1839), I, 155. Gresham was in Seville to obtain money for Queen Mary Tudor. Previous to his arrival, his factor Edward Hogan had received 100,000 ducats, but the sudden removal of so vast an amount of treasure had disastrous consequences. Gresham described the situation in a letter to the Privy Council in November 1554: "For my part, I am not abell with my pen to set forthe unto you the great scarcity that is now through all Spayne"; and after noting the failure of the Iñíguez bank he added, "I fere I shall be the occasione they shuld play all banke-rowte [bankrupt]."

28. Leardo was not a denizen of Seville until 1525 (APS, 27 June 1525, Oficio III, Libro I, Antón Ruiz de Porras, fol. 7v cuaderno 8); APS, 26 July 1537, Oficio V, Legajo 4, Pedro de Castellanos, fol. 117v: "20 ducados de oro que de vos rrecibí en el banco de Franco Leardo y Baptista de Brinén banqueros públicos en esta ciudad de Seuilla." The name Brine also appears as Briven and Brinén. ". . . en el banco de Franco Leardo" (AGI, Contratación, Legajo 4677).

29. APS, 6 Sept. 1512, Oficio XV, Libro II, Bernal González Vallesillo, fol. tercer tercio del legajo; APS, 19 Apr. 1512, Oficio I, Libro II, Mateo de la Cuadra, fol. 546v, cuaderno 23 (liquidation of the company); APS, 8 Oct. 1523, Oficio V, Libro III, Francisco de Castellanos, fol. 144; APS, 12 Dec. 1525, Oficio I, Libro II, Alonso de la Barrera, fol. 931.

30. In his testament Ferdinand Columbus lists the following item: "Confieso que soy debdor a Franco Leardo ginovés banquero dozientas e

treynta e quatro mill e un maravedís" (J. Hernández Díaz and Antonio Muro Orejón, El testamento de don Hernando Colón [Seville, 1941], p. 140).

31. APS, Oficio V, Legajo 4, Pedro de Castellanos, fol. 182v, as quoted in Hernández Díaz, pp. 206–207.

32. Henry Harrisse, Don Fernando Colón, historiador de su padre (Seville, 1871), p. 158.

33. Harrisse believed that Pedro Juan Leardo was the son of Franco Leardo, but there is no evidence to support this contention—we do not know what their exact relationship was. It is interesting to note that members of the Leardo family were important bankers in Genoa in the fifteenth century. Cristòforo Leardo, for example, did a large business and even maintained a branch in Broussa, Turkey (Heers, Gênes, p. 91). See also APS, 5 Sept. 1542, Oficio XV, Libro III, Alonso de Cazalla, fol. 9; and 29 Jan. 1549, Libro I, fol. 227. Pedro Juan is not mentioned on the list of 1545.

34. Carande, Carlos V, p. 204.

35. Like the rest of the Sevillian nobility, Antonio Farfán invested in trade and did not consider it dishonorable. The creditor Hernando de Illescas had died and his heiress ceded her rights over the property to Franco Leardo and Pedro Benito de Basiñana, who in turn transferred their claim to Pedro Juan Leardo and Antonio Farfán (Hernández Díaz, El testamento, p. xxi, and APS, 29 Jan. 1549, Oficio XV, Libro I, Alonso de Cazalla, fol. 227); APS, 11 Feb. 1563, Oficio IX, Legajo 1, Mateo de Almonacid, fol. 1116, as quoted in Hernández Díaz, El testamento, p. 293; APS, 14 Mar. 1594, Oficio XV, Legajo 2, Juan de Tordesillas, fol. 262, as quoted in Hernández Díaz, El testamento, p. xxii. It was purchased for 1,863 ducats by the Mercedarian Order of Seville to be used as a colegio.

36. During the early years of the sixteenth century a large number of northern merchants—Guipuzcoans, Biscayans and Castilians—attracted by the opening of the trade with the New World, migrated to Seville. Within a short period of time these outsiders became wealthy in the American trade and were fully incorporated into Sevillian economic life. Domingo de Lizarrazas was a member of this group; he appears on the 1545 list (AGI, Contratación, Legajo 4677).

37. "Supimos que Jerónimo Cataño de Aulín y Juan Jácome Spínola con mañas y cautelas que tuvieron hizieron fiançar este banco" (ibid., Legajo 167). Lizarrazas had cooperated with Jerónimo Cataño in several commercial ventures (for example, APS, 1 Oct. 1543, Oficio XV, Libro II, Alonso de Cazalla, fol. 865v). "Jerónimo Cataño y compañía de

ginobeses . . . compañeros secretos del dicho Domingo de Lizarrazas"
(AGI, Contratación, Legajo 167).

38. AGI, Indiferente general, Legajo 2000, fol. 92; and Contratación,
Legajo 166: "Ya . . . tiene noticias de la quiebra del banco de Domingo
de Lizarrazas en cuyo poder esta sazón estavan de su magestad más de
cinquenta quentos que allí avían puesto los mercaderes que compraron el
oro y plata"; "Jerónimo Cataño y compañía de ginobeses que fueron causa
deste daño y quiebra"; "Ellos sacaron LXXX" quentos del dicho banco
quando supieron que las partidas de su magestad estavan en él."

39. AGI, Indiferente general, Legajo 2000, fol. 92v.

40. AGI, Contratación, Legajo 167.

41. References to the actions of the creditors in APS, 2 May, 16 June,
and 16 Sept. 1553, of the notary Alonso de Cazalla, as quoted in Carande, *Carlos V*, p. 364.

42. Lizarrazas was the owner of two galleons, the *Santa María* and
the *Santa Cruz* (APS, 5 Nov. 1544, Oficio XV, Libro II, Alonso de
Cazalla, fol. 404).

43. Carande, *Carlos V*, p. 203; APS, 30 July 1549, Oficio XV, Libro
II, Alonso de Cazalla, fol. 295v; APS, 14 Jan. 1551, Oficio XV, Libro I,
Juan Franco, fol. 875.

44. Carande believed that Morga operated this new bank alone (p.
203), but a document in AMS contains a declaration by "Pedro de
Morga banquero público y Gimeno de Bertendona acerca de la compañía
que tuvieron en dicho banco" (AMS, siglo XV, tomo 3, No. 34, 25 May
1565). J. Gentil Da Silva, *Marchandises et finances, lettres de Lisbonne*,
II (Paris, 1959), No. 140, p. 160, 22 Mar. 1576, Manuel Gomes to
Simón Ruiz: "Ay carta de Sevilla como los bancos de Spinoza y Morga an
faltado y lhebaron atrasi toda Sevilla y a muchos daquí. Parece que se
quiere acabar el mundo."

45. "En 8 de noviembre de 1571, 2,995 maravedís a Juan Martín por
230 cargas de arena que echó en la calle de Pedro de Morga." Morga
purchased the house in August 1567. We have the following description
from the deed of sale: "Casas con su patio, palacios e sobrados, e corral, e
cocina, e otras pertenencias que son en esta ciudad en la collación de
Santa Cruz" (AMS, Libro de caja de 1570–1574 as quoted in S.
Montoto de Sedas, *Las calles de Sevilla* [Sevilla, 1940], p. 420).

46. Carande, *Carlos V*, p. 100. The Espinosa were originally from
Ríoseco and were related by marriage to Fabio Nelli, the well-known
banker of Valladolid. During the sixteenth century several Espinosa
appear as moneychangers (*cambiadores*) at the fairs of Medina del
Campo (Carande, *Carlos V*, p. 199); grant of power by "Pedro de

Espinosa, mercader" to a shipmaster to sell the merchandise that he had
loaded on the latter's ship bound for Castilla de Oro (APS, 23 Apr.
1515, Oficio V, Libro III, Francisco Castellanos, fol. 63v; and 23 Sept.
1525, fol. 508v). Carande's first reference to Pedro as a banker comes
from a document (AGI, Contratación, Legajo 2439, No. 5) dated 1533.
See also APS, 28 Nov. 1525, Oficio I, Libro II, Alonso de la Barrera, fol.
872; APS, 27 Feb. 1538, Oficio XV, Libro I, Alonso de Cazalla, fol.
603v: "200 ducados . . . que los cobró por su libramento de Pedro e
Melchor de Espinosa banqueros públicos en esta cibdad de Seuilla."
Pedro had operated on his own as a banker for several years before
joining with Alonso (APS, 16 Mar. 1551, Oficio XV, Libro I, Juan
Franco, fol. 1204).

47. Alonso also sold linen goods and tapestries (APS, 21 Feb. 1538,
Oficio XV, Libro I, Alonso de Cazalla, fol. 535; APS, 16 Apr. 1548,
Oficio X, Libro III, Melchor de Portes, fol. 146; Carande, *Carlos V*, p.
200. Licentiate Gaspar de Espinosa came to Panama with Pedrarias in
1514 as alcalde mayor [governor of a district] and took part in the trial of
Balboa. He furnished the 20,000 pesos for the Pizarro expedition in
March 1526 through his agent Fernando de Luque (Bartolomé de las
Casas, *Historia*, III, 32, 85; C. L. G. Anderson, *Old Panama and Castilla
del Oro* [Washington, 1911], p. 138).

48. Carande, *Carlos V*, p. 200; APS, 28 May 1574, Oficio XXI, Libro
II, Juan Bernal de Heredia, fol. 410: "Juan y Pedro de Espinosa
banqueros públicos vecinos de Seuilla en la collación de la Magdalena"
accept a bill of exchange for 654,687 maravedís drawn on them by their
brother Juan Fernández de Espinosa, Royal Treasurer. His relatives'
claims amounted to more than two million ducats.

49. The second royal bankruptcy had such severe consequences for
the banks all over Spain that Philip II issued a decree placing their
organization on a firmer basis. Higher sureties were demanded and
bankers were forbidden to engage in the trade of goods or any other type
of business. This decree of August 5, 1578 applied particularly to the fair
bankers, but similar regulations were adopted by the Sevillian municipal
council (Cristóbal Espejo and Julián Paz, *Las antiguas ferias de Medina
del Campo* [Valladolid, 1908], pp. 272–276; AMS, siglo XVI, tomo 3,
No. 35, year 1581). See also Lapeyre, *Les Ruiz*, p. 266.

50. APS, 26 Jan. 1580, Oficio XIX, Libro I, Gaspar de León, fol. 654:
"Diego de Albuquerque vecino y jurado de Seuilla." The combination of
trading and office holding was common among the Sevillian nobility in
the sixteenth century. Lambías received a shipment of 1000 hides from
the Indies (APS, 30 Jan. 1577, Oficio XV, Libro I, Francisco Díaz, fol.
172).

51. AGS, Contratación general, Legajo 88. Asiento entre Diego de Albuquerque y Miguel Angel Lambías y Felipe II, 13–12–1583, as quoted in Lapeyre, *Les Ruiz*, p. 266.

52. Rubio, "La banca de Sevilla," p. 19.

53. Lapeyre, *Les Ruiz*, p. 267.

54. AGI, Contratación, Legajo 902, as quoted in Rubio, p. 19. The document containing Philip's grant to Vivaldo was discovered by Rubio in AGI. It appears that Vivaldo was also a bondsman of the bank.

55. We know very little about Mortedo and Serra. Vázquez de Prada has found members of the Serra family in Antwerp in 1598 and a reference to a Bautista Serra in Madrid in 1599 (V. Vázquez de Prada, *Lettres marchandes d'Anvers* [Paris, 1960], I, 193).

56. Ernst Schäfer, "Una quiebra ruidosa del siglo XVII," *Investigación y Progreso*, VII (1934), 309.

57. Rubio, "La banca de Sevilla," p. 19.

58. Throughout the century, the Castilian Cortes complained against the economic activities of foreigners, particularly the Genoese, in Spain. In 1528, for example, they claimed that the Genoese owned all the large businesses, and that they made loans at high interest. In 1542 they accused the Genoese of monopolizing the trade in grain, wool, silk, and many other items (Hamilton, *American Treasure*, pp. 284–286; Rafael Altamira y Crevea, *Historia de España y de la civilización española*, III [Barcelona, 1928], 480–481). Such writers as Mateo Alemán and Cervantes frequently satirized the Genoese and criticized their business transactions in Spain. Alemán, for example, in *Guzmán de Alfarache*, accused the Genoese of being devoid of conscience: "Los tratantes de Génova, que traen las conciencias en faltriqueras descosidas, de donde se les pierde, y ninguno la tiene" (Alemán, *Guzmán de Alfarache*, Pt. I, Bk. III, chap. v. p. 351). Quevedo's description of the Genoese merchant in his *Vida del buscón* is an excellent example of the anti-Genoese feelings expressed by the seventeenth-century writers: "Topamos con un ginovés —digo destos anticristos de las monedas de España—que subía al puerto, con un paje detrás, y él con su guardasol, muy á lo dineroso. Trabamos conversación con él, y todo lo llevaba a materia de maravedís, que es gente que naturalmente nació para bolsas" (Francisco de Quevedo, *Vida del Buscón* [Madrid, 1954], p. 100).

59. Baltasar Gracián, *El Criticón*, ed, M. Romera-Navarro (Philadelphia, 1939), II, 107. For a further discussion of anti-Genoese sentiment of the seventeenth-century Spanish writers, and the conflict of values between the Spaniards and the Genoese see R. Pike, "The Image of the Genoese in Golden Age Literature," *Hispania*, XLVI (1963), 705–714.

60. During the last quarter of the sixteenth century, public banks,

established and administered by municipal authorities, were set up in the most important European banking centers. In 1609 the city fathers of Amsterdam founded the bank of Amsterdam, the most famous of all of these banks (De Roover, "New Interpretations of the History of Banking," *Cahiers d'histoire mondiale,* II (1954), 57; Lapeyre, "La banque," p. 289).

CHAPTER V

1. Francisco de Riberol and the Florentine merchant Juanoto Berardi financed the conquest of the island of La Palma in the Canary group. In 1492 Alonso Fernández de Lugo formed a partnership (*compañía*) with the two merchants; the merchants contributed the funds and Lugo, his military skill to the conquest (Dominik Wölfel, "Alonso de Lugo y la compañía sociedad comercial para la conquista de la isla de La Palma," *Investigación y Progreso* [Madrid, 1934], pp. 246–247). Riberol also facilitated funds to Lugo for the conquest of Tenerife and can be considered one of the Adelantado's principal creditors. In return for his services to the conqueror, he received large grants of land in Tenerife and La Palma, the majority of which he gave over to the cultivation of sugar cane, which was the most important cash crop of the islands during this period. He also had interests in several sugar mills on Tenerife, and with his brother Cosme de Riberol of Cadiz carried on an active trade in sugar and slaves between the Canaries and Spain during the first years of the sixteenth century. For a description of the activities of the Riberols and other Genoese merchants in the Canary Islands, where their economic role was similar to the one they later assumed in the New World, see Manuela Marrero, "Los genoveses en la colonización de Tenerife (1496–1509)," *Revista de historia de la Facultad de filosofía y letras de la Laguna de Tenerife,* XVI (1950), 53–65; Luisa Fabrella, "La producción de azúcar en Tenerife," *ibid.* XVIII (1952), 456–459; and Charles Verlinden, "Gli Italiani nell'economia delle Canaria all'inizio della colonizzazione spagnola," *Economia e Storia,* VII (1960), 149–172.

2. Cèsare de Lollis, "Memorial to son Diego, 1502," *Scritti de Cristòforo Colombo* (Rome, 1892), II, No. 36, p. 170; A. Ballesteros *Cristóbal Colón y el descubrimiento de América* (Barcelona, 1945), I, 530–531.

3. Ballesteros, *Cristóbal Colón,* I, 524; CDI, 2d ser., XXXIX, 32–33, 113–115.

4. The funds for the Third Voyage were transferred in part through the members of the Centurión family in Seville. (S. E. Morison, *Admiral of the Ocean Sea a Life of Christopher Columbus* [Boston, 1942], p.

511). Gaspar Centurión, particularly, was an active creditor of Columbus. In his will drawn up on February 22, 1515, Diego Columbus, brother of the Admiral, mentioned 2,000 ducats that he had left in the hands of Gaspar Centurión and Juan Francisco Grimaldo. Of this sum, 500 ducats belonged to the merchants in return for their loans to him, while the rest was to be used to carry out the provisions of his will. Likewise, Columbus' son, Diego, acknowledged debts to Gaspar and Melchor Centurión in his will of May 2, 1523. (H. Harrisse, *Christophe Colomb: Son origine, sa vie, ses voyages, sa famille, et ses descendants* [Paris, 1885], II, 475–500). See Chap. IV for further information on the financial relations between the Genoese and members of the Columbus family.

5. Both the recruitment of men for the various expeditions and the contract between merchants and New World captains took place in Gradas. Oviedo refers to this custom as follows: "Señor capitán . . . cuando hiciéredes compañía para venir a las Indias y en especial en Sevilla porque allí acuden a las Gradas" (Gonzalo Fernández de Oviedo, *Historia general y natural de las Indias,* ed. Juan Pérez de Tudela Bueso in *Biblioteca de autores españoles,* CXVIII [Madrid, 1959], 400.

6. The labor of discovery, conquest, and settlement in Spanish America was from the time of Christopher Columbus pre-eminently the achievement of private enterprise. Very rarely did the king contribute to the cost of the undertaking (C. Haring, *The Spanish Empire in America* [New York, 1947], p. 22). The following lines from the 1501 contract (*capitulación*) of Alonso de Ojeda with the crown are typical of the royal attitude: "Item: que todo lo susodicho hagáis a vuestra costa e misión de los que con vos se juntasen, así en el armar e fornecer los navíos como lo de la gente e todas las otras cosas que hubiéredes de menester para el dicho viaje, e sus altezas no sean obligados a cosa alguna" (Amando Melón y Ruiz de Gordejuela, "Los primeros tiempos de la colonización Cuba y las Antillas—Magallanes y la primera vuelta al mundo," in A. Ballesteros y Beretta, *Historia de América y de los pueblos americanos,* VI [Barcelona, 1952], 17–18).

7. Martín Fernández de Navarrete, *Colección de los viajes y descubrimientos que hicieron por mar los españoles desde fines del siglo XV* (Madrid, 1825), II, No. 133, p. 244: "Asiento con Rodrigo de Bastidas, vecino de la ciudad de Sevilla para descubrir por el mar océano con dos navíos, año mil y quinientos."

8. APS,—1500, Oficio IV, Libro I, Francisco Segura, fol. el tercio final del legajo: This document was published in the *Catálogo de los fondos americanos del Archivo de Protocolos* (Seville, 1930), I, 445–451. The largest investment amounted to 50,000 maravedís and the smallest, 5,000 maravedís.

9. Fernández de Navarrete, *Colección*, III, 545; M. y Ruiz de Gordejuela, *Los primeros tiempos*, pp. 52–62.

10. Martín Fernández de Enciso, a former lawyer on Hispaniola, had been in charge of the struggling colony of Darien on the Isthmus of Panama until he was deposed and sent back to Spain by Balboa. At court Enciso told his story of Balboa's usurpation and the King sent out a new governor, Pedro Arias de Ávila, better known as Pedrarias, who sailed in 1514 with Enciso for Panama (M. Serrano y Sanz, "Preliminares del gobierno de Pedrarias Dávila en Castilla del Oro," in *Orígenes de la dominación española en América* [Madrid, 1918], XXV, cccxii–xxxxvii). See also APS, 13 Dec. 1513, Oficio XV, Libro II, Bernal González Vallesillo, fol. tercer tercio del legajo; and Pablo Álvarez Rubiano, *Pedrarias Dávila* (Madrid, 1944), App. V, p. 415: "Libro del Armada que llevó Pedrarias Dávila a Tierra Firme."

11. The King asked Pinzón to accompany the fleet, but at the last moment he fell ill and had to remain in Spain. While the exact date of his death is unknown and most historians including Melón y Ruiz de Gordejuela merely state that he died sometime before 1519, a document from the Archivo de Protocolos gives certain proof that he was dead by October 1514. On the fifth of that month his widow granted powers of attorney to Fernando de Jerez for all her affairs (APS, 14 Sept. 1513, Oficio XV, Libro II, Bernal González Vallesillo, fol. primer tercio del legajo; and Libro único, fol. Papel suelto; and 30 Jan. 1514, Libro único, fol. primer tercio del legajo; and 14 (?) 1514, Libro único. See also APS, 14 Oct. 1517, Oficio XV, Libro II, Bernal González Vallesillo, fol. 643; and 17 Mar. 1517, fol. 553; and 13 July 1535, as quoted in Enrique Otte, "Aspiraciones y actividades heterogéneas de Gonzalo Fernández de Oviedo, cronista," *Revista de Indias*, LXXI [1958], p. 46).

12. APS, 13 Jan, 1514, Oficio XV, Libro único, Bernal González Vallesillo, fol. primer tercio del legajo.

13. This royal decree, dated September 1513, was published by Serrano y Sanz (*Preliminares*, I, cccxxv), who incorrectly concluded that Vivaldo and Grimaldo actually accompanied the fleet to America. This misinterpretation has been repeated by many modern authors, including Charles L. C. Anderson (*Life and Letters of Vasco Núñez de Balboa* [New York, 1941], p. 234).

14. Alvarez Rubiano, *Pedrarias*, p. 519.

15. In 1516, for example, Juan Francisco de Grimaldo and Gaspar Centurión granted powers of attorney to Enciso to collect debts owed them in Panama (APS, 21 Oct. 1516, Oficio XV, Libro único, Bernal González Vallesillo, fol. 667). In a letter written in 1542 to the Viceroy of Mexico, Antonio de Mendoza, Oviedo called Leardo one of his best

friends. This letter is inserted in Oviedo, XX, 254. See also Otte, *Aspiraciones*, p. 46. In a more recent article ("Gonzalo Fernández de Oviedo y los genoveses," *Revista de Indias*, LXXXIX-XC [1962], 517) Otte also refers to the business dealings between Leardo and Oviedo.

16. APS, 27 Apr. 1513, Oficio XV, Libro I, Bernal González Vallesillo, fol. 412; APS, 7 Feb. 1509, Oficio III, Libro único, Juan Ruiz de Porras, fol. Segundo tercio del legajo; APS, 8 Oct. 1517, Oficio XV, Libro II, Bernal González Vallesillo, fol. 597; APS, 7 May 1547, Oficio XVI, Martín de Ávila, fol. cuaderno de 7 de mayo. See Chap. III for Genoese dealings with Cortes and his heir, Martin Cortes.

17. In the works of such Spanish chroniclers as Oviedo, Herrera, and Gómara, the sponsors of the Sebastian Cabot expedition of 1525 are always referred to as "the Sevillian merchants," leading historians to conclude that the Sevillian merchants conceived of this enterprise and sponsored it. There is, however, a document in the Archivo de Protocolos that establishes certain proof that the idea for this venture originated with the Genoese. On December 2, 1524, four months before he entered into his capitulation agreement with Charles V, Sebastian Cabot formed a partnership (*compañía*) with four members of the Genoese colony of Seville and with Robert Thorne, an English merchant who was one of his personal friends, for a commercial expedition to the Moluccas. All of the four Genoese—Franco Leardo, Leonardo Cataño, Pedro Benito de Basiñana, and Pedro Juan de Riberol—later became the largest investors in the actual expedition. According to Oviedo, the expedition was sponsored by "cobdiçiossos mercaderes, é aun de otras personas principales, engañados del olor de sus mismas cobdiçias y esperança, fundada en la sciencia é industria de Sebastián Gaboto" (Oviedo, *Historia*, CXVIII, 353).

18. Andrea Navagero described the expedition and its objective in one of his dispatches to the Council of Ten written from Toledo on September 21, 1525. According to the Venetian diplomat: "The captain of this fleet is one Sebastian Cabot, a Venetian, he is going to make new discoveries, and in Spain their hopes of these islands increase daily, and they think about them more and more and believe that they will at length obtain the spices likewise by that track and by a much shorter voyage than the one performed by the ship *Victoria*" (Great Britain, Public Records Office, *Calendar of State Papers and Manuscripts* [Venetian], III, ed. Rawdon Brown [London, 1869], 1115).

19. Antonio de Herrera, *Historia general de los castellanos en las Islas y Tierra Firme de el mar Océano* (Asunción, 1945), III, Bk. 4, chap. XX, p. 243. Peter Martyr also held the opinion that the islands Magellan passed by contained great wealth (Peter Martyr D'Anghera, *De Orbe*

Novo: The Eight Decades of Peter Martyr D'Anghera, trans. Francis MacNutt [New York, 1912], VII, Bk. 6, pp. 289–290.

20. "Las muestras que la Nao Victoria traxo de las Especias, i otras cosas de los Malucos, dió ánimo á muchos Hombres de Sevilla, para solicitar á Sebastian Gaboto, Piloto Maior de el Rei, á ofrecer de hacer aquel viaje, prometiendo de armarle para él" (Herrera, *Historia,* III, Bk. 10, chap. i, p. 55). The Council of the Indies approved of their plan and in September they gave Cabot permission to take charge of the expedition. Martyr mentions here that Cabot had told the Council of the Indies that he had found partners at Seville, and that they had proposed to furnish him with 10,000 ducats for the expenses of the fleet (Martyr, *De Orbe Novo,* VII, BK. 6, pp. 288, 289). See also Francesco Tarducci, *John and Sebastian Cabot,* trans. Henry Brownson (Detroit, 1893), p. 153.

21. Herrera, *Historia,* III, Bk. 9, chap. i, p. 55.

22. *Ibid.* Cathay corresponds to the northern part of China; Ophir and Tarshish are places of wealth mentioned in the Bible. Cipango (Japan) was an island "abounding with gold, pearls and gems," as Pablo Toscanelli wrote to Fernam Martins (Fernando Martínez) of Lisbon. Marco Polo had said that Cipango was to be found 1,500 miles from Cathay (Fernando Colombo, *Le historie della vita e dei fatti di Cristòforo Colombo,* ed. Rinaldo Caddeo [Milan, 1930], I, chap. viii.

23. José Toribio Medina, *El Veneciano Sebastián Caboto al servicio de España* (Santiago de Chile, 1908), I, 60.

24. Robert Thorne was a member of the small English merchant colony in Seville and a personal friend of Cabot. He was the only non-Genoese merchant who took part in the original agreement between Cabot and the Genoese in Debember 1524. In 1527 he wrote the letters that make up *The Book of Robert Thorne,* a propagandist work of geographical information that circulated in manuscript for many years until the work was printed in *Hakluyts Divers Voyages,* published in 1528 (Boies Penrose, *Travel and Discovery in the Renaissance, 1420–1620* [Cambridge, Mass., 1952], p. 170).

25. The largest non-Genoese investment—401,250 maravedís—was made by Miguel de Rifos. The rest ranged between 25,000 and 100,000 maravedís. Peter Martyr and Dr. Beltrán of the Council of the Indies were among the nonmerchant investors, contributing 37,500 and 75,000 maravedís respectively. Francisco de Santa Cruz invested 127,461 maravedís, but his important role as the spokesman of the sponsors led Medina (I, 71), to conclude that he must have made a larger contribution, and that the notary had mistakenly written "un ciento [one hundred]" for "un cuento [one million]," so that his investment was

really 1,027,461 maravedís. Medina's conclusions seem unacceptable, since Santa Cruz's 127,461 maravedís represented the largest sum invested by any Sevillian merchant in the enterprise. Only the contributions of the foreign merchants—the Florentines and the Germans—fell within the 100,000 to 250,000 range, while the Genoese went much beyond this. Again Santa Cruz's selection as one of the spokesmen of the investors was a reflection of his prominent place in the Sevillian business community and precisely because his investment was larger than those of the other native merchants. See Medina, *Sebastián Caboto*, II, 70–73, for a list of the investments of all the sponsors. Martyr states that the Genoese originally promised Cabot 10,000 ducats to be divided into supplies for two years, wages for 150 men, and merchandise to trade with the islanders (Martyr, *De Orbe Novo*, VII, Bk. 6, p. 288).

26. We know something about Gaspar Cazaña's life from the statements that he made at the time of Cabot's trial. Born in Genoa in 1497, he came to Seville at an early age and became acquainted with Franco Leardo and Pedro Benito de Basiñana. He claimed to have known them for ten years and apparently also worked for them during this time. By 1525 he must have accumulated some money since he was able to invest 37,500 maravedís in the expedition. During the voyage he stayed at the side of Brine, but did not openly associate with the anti-Cabot group. After Brine's death Cazaña tried unsuccessfully to get Cabot to turn over his compatriot's property to him, and once in Seville, he testified against Cabot in the Brine suit (Medina, *Sebastián Caboto*, I, 234; and II, 71, 73).

27. Tarducci, *John and Sebastian Cabot*, p. 154. "Los Diputados de los Armadores, por diferencias, que con el General havían tenido, quisieron que fuese Martín Méndez, i no Miguel de Rufis, á quien pretendía llevar en este cargo, Sebastián Gaboto" (Herrera, *Historia*, III, Bk. 9, chap. i, p. 56).

28. All of these complaints against Cabot were summarized in a letter which the sponsors sent to the Council of the Indies (see Medina, *Sebastián Caboto*, I, 73; Tarducci, *John and Sebastian Cabot*, p. 155).

29. Salvago took with him a memorial, directed to Charles V and the Council of the Indies, in which the sponsors reiterated their complaints against Cabot's wife and her influence over him. The description of Salvago's mission comes from the testimony of Diego Gutiérrez at Cabot's trial. "El dicho bachiller dijo que había ido á hablar sobre ello á Su Majestad el Emperador, nuestro señor é que le había hablado dos veces, que le había hallado de buena voluntad para hacer lo que sobre este caso le iba a suplicar." The Council of the Indies told the sponsors on October 16, 1525, that the removal of Cabot and his substitution by another

captain would cause a scandal. "La armada está tan adelante que no se podría hacer ninguna mudanza sin mucho daño é perjuicio della; y asimismo en dar acompañado al dicho Sebastián Caboto se seguiría escándalo é diferencia." Then hoping to quiet Cabot in the humiliation to which he was being subjected by the enforced acceptance of Méndez, they wrote him: "Su Majestad os tiene por su capitán general desa armada, y que no ha de haber otra persona que se entremeta en cosa tocante al dicho oficio" (Medina, *Sebastián Caboto*, I, 72–77; II, 530–531).

30. *Ibid.*, I, 93–97; II, 366.

31. None of the chroniclers give the exact date of the fleet's departure from Seville. According to Medina, it must have left that city before March 11, 1526. After spending almost three weeks in San Lucar, it left on April 3, 1526 (*ibid.*, I, 101, 103).

32. The testimony of Casmiro de Nuremberg, (*ibid.*, II, 222).

33. *Ibid.*, I, 91; Tarducci, *John and Sebastian Cabot*, pp. 161–162.

34. Medina, *Sebastián Caboto*, I, 109.

35. Alonso de Santa Cruz was the son of merchant Francisco de Santa Cruz, who with Franco Leardo served as the spokesman of the investors. He contributed 20,000 maravedís to the expedition and went along as an inspector for the merchants on the *Santa María del Espinar*. He was associated with Brine, Rojas, and Méndez, and his home in La Palma served as their meeting place. It is not clear why Cabot never moved against him, perhaps because of his youth—he was in his early twenties —or fear of his father. It was one thing to attack Brine and the Genoese, but Cabot did not want to become involved with the native Sevillian merchants. Alonso de Santa Cruz eventually returned home with Cabot (*ibid.*, I, 297–298).

While the fleet was at La Palma, Méndez and his friends wrote letters to the Council of the Indies and the King describing the voyage to the Canaries, and apparently reported unfavorably on the conduct of Cabot toward Méndez. Before the ships departed, Cabot allowed Rifos to remain on shore an extra day for the purpose of obtaining these letters. Rifos found them in the possession of a Genoese merchant from whom he seized them, and brought them on board to Cabot (*ibid.*, I, 110–113). Even Tarducci, who is obviously an apologist for Cabot, admits the possibility that these visits were related to Santa Cruz's illness (Tarducci, *John and Sebastian Cabot*, p. 167).

36. Medina, *Sebastián Caboto*, I, 122–126. Tarducci, on the other hand, believes that Rojas lied so as to appear before the members of the Council of the Indies as a victim of his loyalty to the Emperor's orders (Tarducci, *John and Sebastian Cabot*, p. 172).

37. Testimony of Casmiro de Nuremberg, Medina, *Sebastián Caboto*, II, 222: "Que el dicho capitán Francisco de Rojas le había respondido que no debía de dejar el viaje é derrota [sic] por su Majestad mandado, é de otra manera, que aunque trajesen grandísimos tesoros, les cortarían las cabezas, é dando ejemplo de otros capitanes que no habían cumplido lo que sus príncipes les mandaban. . . . Y que dende en adelante vi proceder contra el dicho Francisco de Rojas . . . é que de allí vi llevar preso al dicho Francisco de Rojas á la nao del capitán Caro." Tarducci makes Méndez and Rojas—he does not mention Brine—leaders of an anti-Cabot group who were about to mutiny against their commander when he imprisoned them, but the only evidence for this comes from Cabot's own statements (Tarducci, *John and Sebastian Cabot*, pp. 174–176).

38. Medina, *Sebastián Caboto*, I, 133.

39. *Ibid.*, I, 229.

40. "Más parte es el dicho Octaviano para hacer bien é mal, que no el Capitán General, por questá en mano deste Octaviano está el todo; é más os hago saber que desque seamos vueltos de nuestro viaje al puesto donde aportaremos, quél es el que puede hacer mercedes, porque toda la hacienda ha de ir en manos deste, é lo ha de hacer como él quisiere" (*ibid.*, II, 323). After his return to Seville, Cabot, in his declaration before the royal officials, claimed that Rojas and Méndez wanted to seize the *Trinidad* and escape with it (*ibid.*, II, 521).

41. Cabot later maintained that he could not have continued the voyage to the Moluccas because "he had lost his flagship which was two thirds of the expedition." Witnesses in the suit between Cabot and Catherine Vázquez testified that with the wreck of the flagship the expedition lost heavily in provisions and ammunition (Tarducci, *John and Sebastian Cabot*, p. 179; Medina, *Sebastián Caboto*, I, 305).

42. Medina, *Sebastián Caboto*, I, 148; II, 352. According to the witness Antonio Ponce, "a few days after Brine's death, Cabot ordered his possessions sold at a public auction and purchased them himself" (*ibid.*, I, 229).

43. Medina, *Sebastián Caboto*, I, 140–141. After the return of the ship *Victoria*, the government equipped a fleet of seven ships under the command of García de Loaysa to bring aid to the men who had been left in the Moluccas and to secure Spanish possession of them. The expedition left Spain in July 1525 (Penrose, *Travel and Discovery*, p. 162). The Juan Díaz de Solís expedition was the first that Spain sent out to find an all-water route around South America to the Pacific. It left Spain late in 1515 with instructions to enter the South Sea and sail northward along the Pacific coast to the Isthmus. In February 1516 De

Solís arrived at the estuary of the Plata, which appeared to offer the hoped-for passage to the East. Here De Solís was slain by hostile Indians, after which event the rest of the expedition sailed back to Spain (*ibid.*, p. 121; José Toribio Medina, *Juan Díaz de Solís* [Santiago de Chile, 1897], I, chap. viii).

44. All the ten witnesses produced by Cabot mentioned the persistency of the two survivors, Enrique Montes and Melchor Ramírez, to win over Cabot and the rest of the expedition. Montes, for example, told them that never were men so fortunate as those of the fleet, for it was said there was enough silver and gold at the Río de Solís to make them all rich (Tarducci, *John and Sebastian Cabot,* pp. 183, 184; Medina, *Sebastián Caboto,* I, 140).

45. It seems that Rojas was the only one of the officers to oppose Cabot publicly (Medina, *Sebastián Caboto,* I, 143–144). On his return to Seville, Cabot told the royal officials that Rojas and Méndez "planned his assassination" (*ibid.,* I, 160). Late at his trial he declared: "Que . . . Rojas, Méndez é Rodas e otros con ellos acordaron de matar al dicho capitán Sebastián Caboto é alzar con la armada" (*ibid.,* II, 521). According to Alonso de Santa Cruz, "luego á hora vido, que el dicho Miguel Rifos mandó en la dicha armada como teniente de capitán general" (*ibid.,* II, 305). This lost survivor of the Solís expedition was Francisco del Puerto, who, in Cabot's words, "confirmed the reports of the wealth of the region" (*ibid.,* I, 160).

46. Penrose, *Travel and Discovery,* p. 122.

47. Medina, *Sebastián Caboto,* I, 160.

48. An expedition under the command of Diego García left Spain several months after Cabot's departure, with the objective of exploring the river discovered by Juan Díaz de Solís. It was financed by Fernando de Andrade, Count of Villalba, who was at the time chief justice of Seville, and Cristóbal de Haro, merchant of Burgos and factor of the House of Trade of La Coruña. Haro had also contributed to the Magellan and Loaysa voyages (see José T. Medina, *Los viajes de Diego García de Moguer* [Santiago de Chile, 1908]). Roger Barlow was another member of that small group of English merchants living in Seville, and a personal friend of Cabot's. He contributed 206,250 maravedís to the expedition, and went along as supercargo. In 1541 he translated Martín Fernández de Enciso's *Suma de Geographia* into English, a work which circulated in manuscript form in much the same manner as the collected letters of his friend Robert Thorne (Penrose, *Travel and Discovery,* p. 170). See also Medina, *Sebastián Caboto,* I, 179, 182.

49. Charles V sent Barlow to Seville to convince the sponsors, and they later delegated him to inform the Emperor of their decision. The

Council of the Indies forced the merchants to meet by threatening to take action against them (*ibid.*, I, 187–189).

50. Letter of Dr. Simão Affonso to the King of Portugal, August 2, 1530, quoted in F. Adolpho de Varnhagen, *História geral do Brazil* (Madrid, 1854), I, 439.

51. Medina, *Sebastián Caboto*, I, 309.

52. *Ibid.*, I, 304.

53. Méndez and Rodas died as a result of quarrels with Rojas and the other Spaniards on the Island of Patos. Actually they were drowned as they tried to escape from the island in a small boat (*ibid.*, II, 378). Catherine Vázquez's accusations against Cabot are published in *ibid.*, II, 360–475, and the Rojas case can be found in II, 487–549. Cabot's defense is in II, 318–360.

54. *Ibid.*, I, 229. The Brine suit can be found in *ibid.*, II, 545–558.

55. *Ibid.*, I, 314.

56. Royal cedula of October 12, 1530, as quoted in *ibid.*, II, 82. As no prospective buyer presented himself, Charles V then ordered the ships sold at a public auction.

57. "Porque las dichas naos eran de los dichos sus partes é se compraron de sus propios dineros, é los maravedís por que se habían vendido pertenecen á los susodichos" (*ibid.*, II, 83).

58. *Ibid.*, I, 316.

59. The documents relating to this case are in *ibid.*, II, 570–596.

60. *Ibid.*, I, 311–313, and chap. xv.

61. Medina, *Sebastián Caboto*, I, 399. Documents from the Archivo de Protocolos published by Medina indicate that from at least 1546 Cabot was busily arranging his personal affairs in Seville; they leave little doubt that he was planning to leave the country. His activities during these years consisted of carrying out the provisions of his wife's will (she had died in September 1547), drawing up his own last will and testament, and finally renting the houses that he owned in the city (*ibid.*, I, 527–549). Tarducci, *John and Sebastian Cabot*, 263: In January 1549 Edward VI of England granted Cabot a life pension and made it retroactive to September 29, 1548, which was most probably the day of his arrival in England.

62. A large number of native and foreign merchants, including the Welsers, contributed to the Pedro de Mendoza expedition of 1535, but it does not seem likely that the Genoese invested in this enterprise, since the memory of the Cabot fiasco was still too fresh in their minds. Members of the Cataño family had close dealings with Welser agents in Seville, but we have no evidence that they invested in the Welser expedition of 1531 even though Nicolás Cataño appeared as a witness at

the Casa de Contratación for Ambrose Alfinger (Ehinger) and four other Germans, all members of his party, before their departure for America (CPI, I, Nos. 2860–2864, pp. 200–201). At the same time, June 15, 1526, Nicolás Cataño and his partner Jácome Rico had business relations with García de Lerma, who in 1528 had been named Governor of Santa Marta (Colombia), and it is probable that they lent Lerma funds to outfit himself for the voyage. In any case, on January 2, 1527, Lerma authorized them to receive everything that would arrive in Seville for him from New Spain (APS, 2 Jan. 1527, Oficio I, Libro I, Alonso de la Barrera, fol. 67v).

63. The legend of El Dorado (the Gilded Man), who lived in the golden city of Manoa on the shores of the fabled lake of Parima, drew treasure-seekers to America for almost a century. In the beginning, when the legend first reached the ears of the Spaniards around 1530, El Dorado was located in the neighborhood of Bogotá, Columbia, but as time passed it was moved to the Amazon Basin and finally into the Venezuela-Guiana borderland. In essence the legend had some historical basis and referred to a religious rite practiced by an Indian tribe near the sacred lake of Guatavita near Bogotá. In this rite their chief smeared his body with turpentine and then rolled in gold dust. Thus gilded and resplendent, he entered a canoe filled with gold, emeralds, and other precious things, which, after having reached the center of the lake, he deposited as offerings; he then jumped in himself to bathe (Joaquín Acosta, *Compendio histórico del descubrimiento y colonizatión de la Nueva Granada* [Paris, 1848], pp. 199–206). In 1539 Gonzalo Pizarro and his followers set out from Quito in search of the Gilded Man. After incredible hardships they succeeded in crossing the Andes and arrived at the Coco River. There they built a brigantine, and Francisco de Orellana was sent off in her with fifty men to find the junction of the Coco and the Napo where the Indians reported a land well supplied with provisions and rich in gold. The current of the river was strong, and the further Orellana proceeded, the more difficult it was to return to Pizarro's expedition. Finally, on August 26, 1541, after a voyage of eight months, he reached the open sea; after a perilous voyage along the coast he arrived at the island of Cubagua. Thus the Amazon River had been traversed for the first time (Penrose, *Travel and Discovery*, p. 115).

64. The Council of the Indies was at first skeptical of Orellana's account, since they suspected that the river that he described was within the jurisdiction of Portugal. Finally they decided that, even though it might be in Portuguese territory, this had never been clearly ascertained, and under these circumstances it would be advantageous for the Spanish King to send out an expedition to that region, at least before the Portuguese did (Gaspar de Carvajal, *The Discovery of the Amazon,*

introd. José Toribio Medina, trans. Bertram T. Lee, ed. H. C. Heaton [New York, 1934], p. 323).

65. *Ibid.*, p. 128. At this time the future Philip II was ruling Spain in the absence of his father.

66. *Ibid.*, pp. 129–130. He was also given the title of Adelantado and command of the two fortresses he might build, subject to approval by royal officials.

67. *Ibid.*, p. 130.

68. These letters, seven in number, written from August to November 1544, can be found in *ibid.*, pp. 340–352. We also have five letters written by Orellana to the King during the months from May to November that give additional details concerning the preparations for the expedition from the Adelantado's point of view. They have also been published in *ibid.*, pp. 335–340.

69. *Ibid.*, p. 336.

70. *Ibid.*, p. 338, letter of June 28, 1544.

71. *Ibid.*, p. 132.

72. *Ibid.*, p. 135.

73. *Ibid.*, pp. 134–135.

74. *Ibid.*, p. 348, letter of October 6, 1544.

75. The notary deeds published by J. Hernández Díaz, *El testamento de don Hernando Colón* (Seville, 1941), show that Monte managed Ferdinand Columbus' business affairs at least from 1533 on. At Columbus' death, Monte was named one of the executors of his will (*ibid.*, p. 22). On November 7, 1533, for example, the Sevillian merchant Juan Fernández de Utrera granted Monte powers of attorney to represent him at court in a suit before the Council of the Indies (APS, 7 Nov. 1533, Oficio I, Alonso de la Barrera, leg. 2, fol. 973, as quoted in *ibid.*, p. 96).

76. In his letter of September 28, 1544, Torres describes the situation as follows: "I firmly suspect that there cannot fail to be, a person or persons who are working [to bring it about] that this enterprise be not carried out and are obstructing it with all their skill and with all their might, saying bad things about it and exaggerating the dangers and belittling either it or the persons who are going on it, because in the afternoon we will have some agreement all mapped out with some merchants, and by the next morning we find them with their minds changed. We find people willing to give trust [sufficiently to enable us] to get from them the things which we need, and shortly after we perceive that someone has caused us to lose our credit and they are not willing for anything in the world to aid us without being paid cash, or to wait even an hour; yet formerly they waited days and were paid."

The attitude of the Genoese is described by Torres in his letter of

September 28: "The Genoese proposed a contract designed to facilitate the raising of funds for getting the expedition started, and what with article this and article that and conditions and reservations and clauses on advice of counsel to guarantee their security, they keep adding on, they never stop, although we beg them and urge them [to consider] what in all justice and conscience ought to and can be done. They are ready to sign the terms which they have fixed" (Carvajal, *The Discovery*, pp. 345–347).

77. Orellana made the following revealing remarks in his letter to the King written on October 22: "Certain Genoese merchants through the intercession and kind friendship and negotiating of Vicencio de Monte, Your Majesty's revenue collector, have come to my aid with two thousand five hundred ducats toward the expediting of my affairs, which persons have offered a larger sum, in case it be needed" (*ibid.*, p. 339).

78. *Ibid.*, p. 348.

79. *Ibid.*, p. 349: He added furthermore that, "since this [copy of the agreements] has been in my hands, they have made changes and modifications as they have seen fit, and [have] inserted unreasonable clauses in them . . . but I hold my tongue . . . not to frighten away the Genoese."

80. He also noted that he could not give any clear account of the expedition for "I do not understand either Orellana or the affairs of this fleet, nor do I believe that he understands them himself" (*ibid.*, p. 137).

81. Since the loan conditions as set down in the official documents preserved in the Archivo de Indies did not go into effect, we can obtain a more accurate description of the actual agreements between Orellana the Genoese from the notary deeds of the Archivo de Protocolos. I found several documents relating to the Genoese participation in the Orellana expedition during one of my investigations in that Archive in the summer of 1963. See also Carvajal, *The Discovery*, pp. 137, 143, APS, 16 Mar. 1545, Oficio I, Libro I, Alonso de la Barrera, fol. 367; and fol. 368; and fol. 489; and fol. 490.

82. *Ibid.*, p. 351, letter of November 20, 1544.

83. *Ibid.*, p. 351.

84. Letter written by the royal officials in Seville to the King on April 4, 1545 in *ibid.*, p. 353.

85. *Ibid.*, p. 354.

86. *Ibid.*, p. 358: "In connection with what you [Friar Torres] say to the effect that the said Adelantado Orellana has made Vicencio de Monte, the revenue collector for the said province, his lieutenant-general and [that] to a brother of the said Monte he has given the office of chief constable, I am sending word to the said Adelantado ordering him not to

give the said positions to the above mentioned [individuals] or to any foreigner whatsoever [that is to say, to any persons] other than natives of these realms."

87. "Porque sencastillaron [sic] todos en los navíos, e aquellos dos noches salían en tierra a saltear vacas e vecerros e carneros e gallinas, e erían los pastores" (from a letter of Friar Torres written on May 20, 1545, several days after the expedition had left. This letter as well as one dated May 19, 1545, are published in CDI, 1st ser., III, 282–290).

88. "El lunes syguiente quedó el Alguacil major de Sant Lucar a meter sobre la dicha armada un ombre por sentencia desterrado destos Reynos como le vieron con la vara de xustycia en la barca alzan las velas e sálense del puerto" (*ibid.*, p. 288). The official report of the inspection of the fleet can be found in *ibid.*, pp. 268–281.

89. *Ibid.*, pp. 283, 289.

90. "E la popa de la nave major donde va el Adelantado va llena de mugeres, e ya ponían guardias que pasagero no pasase a la popa e andavan en questión porque así lo supimos cuando estaban surtos fuera de la barra de los pilotos que les sacaron fuera de la barra" (*ibid.*, p. 290). The description of the journey is taken from the report of Francisco de Guzmán, a member of the party, and published in *ibid.*, pp. 358–361 (see also pp. 147, 362–374).

91. "We came upon four or five Indian cabins where we stopped to build a brigantine, and we struck a country [so poor] that there was little food to be had [in it]." They had to tear apart one of the ships in order to use its nails and planking to build the brigantine (*ibid.*, p. 359).

92. There are several versions of this episode. The one given in the text has been accepted by Medina and is based on testimony given by several survivors of the expedition in a "Judicial Inquiry" conducted in Lima, Peru, in December 1558, relating to the services rendered by Diego Muñoz Tenero in the expedition of Francisco de Orellana to New Andalucia. In contrast, another survivor, Francisco de Guzmán, claimed that although Orellana did return to the camp after twenty-seven days or so, he set out again on his search, telling the men on the island to follow him after they had completed their boat (*ibid.*, pp. 360–374).

93. *Ibid.*, p. 151. This is Medina's estimate.

CHAPTER VI

1. Juan Bautista de Marín is a good example of a Genoese investor. In his position as accountant general of the Cortés estate, he invested in silver mining in the Zacatecas area and put to use the shipyard and ships originally built by Hernando Cortés at Tehuantepec by employing them in the intercolonial trade. His activities have been described by W. Borah

(*Early Colonial Trade and Navigation between Mexico and Peru* [Berkeley, 1954], chap. iv). Genoese merchants had been importing sugar from the Levant into western Europe at least from the thirteenth century and were well acquainted with the methods of its cultivation in Sicily, Cyprus, and the Algarve (southern part of Portugal). The earliest record of the cultivation of sugar in the Algarve clearly points to Genoese enterprise. In 1404 King John I gave lands in that region to "João da Palma, Genoese, to plant sugar." It is interesting to note that this concession annulled a previous one granted to a "Micer João, also a foreigner and probably a Genoese" (J. Lúcio de Azevedo, *Épocas de Portugal económico* [Lisbon, 1929], p. 226).

2. The first sugar produced on the island of Madeira came from the villa of Tristão Vaz Teixiera, *Capitão mor* of Machico, whose son-in-law was a "Micer João, Genoese," and by the end of the fifteenth century the Genoese were the owners of some of the largest mills on the island (*ibid.*, pp. 226–227). It should also be remembered that Columbus spent his honeymoon on Maderia buying sugar for the Centurione of Lisbon, who were active in the sugar trade between Madeira and Portugal (see Virginia Rau, "The Settlement of Madeira and the Sugar Cane Plantations," *Afdeling Agrarische Geschiedenis Bijdragen*, II (1964), and M. L. Fabrella, "La producción de azúcar en Tenerife," *Revista de historia* [La Laguna de Tenerife], XVIII [1952], 455–475.

3. See Chap. V, note 1. The Riberols maintained Jácome de Cazaña as their factor in Tenerife. In return for large loans to Adelantado Lugo the Sevillian Genoese Tomás Justinián received lands in Güímar and La Orotava on Tenerife, which he turned over to the cultivation of sugar cane. The contract for the construction of his mill in Taoro is dated February 8, 1506. He was at once a planter, millowner, merchant (Guanche slaves, wheat, sugar, and European goods), and moneylender.

Other Genoese merchants and mill owners on Tenerife included the wealthy and powerful Cristóbal de Ponte; Mateo Viña, one of the conquerors of the island; Bautista Ascanio; and several members of the Sopranis family (Marrero, "Los genoveses," pp. 57–64; Fabrella, "Azúcar en Tenerife," pp. 456, 459).

4. Mervyn Ratekin, "The Early Sugar Industry in Española," *The Hispanic American Historical Review*, XXXIV (1954), 6, 7. The minimum cost of constructing a good mill rarely fell below 15,000 ducats, a sum far beyond the means of most settlers (small land owners) at the time. The best description of the numerous sugar mills on Hispaniola during the first half of the sixteenth century can be found in G. Fernández de Oviedo, *Historia general y natural de las Indias*, ed. J. P. de Tudela Bueso in ("Biblioteca de Autores Españoles," CXVII; Madrid, 1959), chap. VIII.

5. Esteban Justinián collected a sea loan for Oberto de Sopranis (APS, 5 Sept. 1525, Oficio V, Libro III, Francisco de Castellanos, fol. 329). He sold merchandise for Agustín de Vivaldo (APS, 16 Nov. 1526, Oficio I, Libro II, Alonso de la Barrera, fol. 738). For his other business activities see APS, 19 Mar. 1536, Oficio I, Libro I, Alonso de la Barrera, fol. 322; 19 Dec. 1526, Libro II, fol. 940; and 16 Nov. 1526. Justinian founded his own company; Dominican Republic, *Boletín*, I [1938], 345, autos entre partes, año de 1528, No. 4: "Esteban Justiniano y compañía"; año de 1530, No. 1: "Esteban Justinián, vecino de Santo Domingo, con Pedro Sarmiento de la propia vecindad, sobre pago de una estancia y negros que le vendió"; No. 4: "Los herederos de Melchor Centurión, difunto con Esteban Justiniano y compañía." See APS, 16 Sept. 1549, Oficio XV, Libro II, Alonso de Cazalla, fol. 703; and APS, 19 Mar. 1536, Oficio I, Libro I, Alonso de la Barrera, fol. 322.

6. Oviedo, *Historia*, p. 108, 109; Dominican Republic, *Boletín*, I (1938), 359, autos entre partes, año de 1535, No. 2: "Los herederos de Esteban Justiniano, vecino que fue de la ciudad de Santo Domingo, con los herederos del Licenciado Pedro Vázquez de Mella de la misma vecindad sobre pago de 1 D ps; E. Rodríguez Demorizi, *Relaciones históricas de Santo Domingo* II (Ciudad Trujillo, 1945), 105: "Vecinos de Santo Domingo en 1586 hábiles para armas. . . . Juan Bautista Justinián y Tomás de Justinián."

7. I. Wright, "History of Sugar," *Louisiana Planter and Sugar Manufacturer*, LV (1915), 190: On October 8, 1536, Domingo de Forne and Co., owners of an *ingenio* in Hispaniola, were authorized to convey there from Spain up to 8,000 ducats in silver and copper to pay off employees. See also Oviedo, *Historia*, CXVII, 109; APS, 10 Jan. 1551, Oficio XV, Libro I, Juan Franco, fol. 849; Dominican Republic, *Boletín*, I (1938), 359, autos entre Partes, año de 1536, No. 4: "Valián de Torne [Forne] y Cía de mercaderes."

8. *Ibid.*, año de 1539, No. 1: "Valián de Torre [Forne] y Cía de mercaderes genoveses con la ciudad de Santo Domingo, sobre tasación en la venta de esclavos." See also pp. 356, 359, años de 1531 y 1536.

9. APS, 16 Sept. 1549, Oficio XV, Libro II, Alonso de Cazalla, fol. 703; 18 Sept. 1549, fol. 716; and 1 Feb. 1550, Libro I, fol. 257v; Dominican Republic, *Boletín*, I (1938), 359, año de 1536: "Valián de Torre [Forne] vecino de la ciudad de Santo Domingo"; and p. 364, autos fiscales, año de 1546: "Con Valián de Torne [Forne] genovés, vecino de Santo Domingo sobre las cuentas de la avería que estuvo a su cargo desde 1542 a 1544 para los gastos de la guerra e indios alzados."

10. Ratekin, "Sugar Industry," pp. 14, 15. My description is based on Ratekin's account of a typical mill, drawn from the inventories of two mills in the 1540's.

11. See Oviedo, *Historia,* CXVII, 109, for a description of Castellón's mill. The origin, personality, and character of Jácome de Castellón have long puzzled historians of the Spanish conquest, although most of them have incorrectly assumed that he was Spanish. The following comments from Ricardo Majo Framís, *Navegantes y conquistadores españoles del siglo XVI* (Madrid, 1946), pp. 810–811, are typical: "Jácome Castellón . . . He aquí un nombre oscuro . . . ¿Era de humilde condición y llevado a la capitanía por obra de su ingenio y de su corazón ancho? ¿Era, contrariamente, un cultivado hidalgo? . . . Hay muy precarias noticias en las historias a propósito de este hombre. Hubiera conquistado la Nueva España si a ella va; otro Perú, si el Perú hubiera incidido." The notarial deeds of the Archivo de Protocolos give certain proof that Jácome de Castellón was of Genoese origin and by profession a merchant.

12. Bernardo de Castellón, father of Jácome, represents a fifteenth-century assimilated Genoese. He was a denizen of Toledo and married to a native of that city, Inés Suárez (CPI, I, 40, No. 552). The family name is a hispanized form of the original Italian, Castello or di Castro. The Castello or di Castro belonged to the ancient aristocracy of Genoa, tracing their descent from the feudal families "Visconti" (Antonio Cappellini, *Dizionario biográfico di Genovesi illustri e notàbili* [Genoa, 1932], p. 32). See also APS, 11 May 1510, Oficio IV, Libro II, Manuel Segura, fol. 1460v: "Jácome de Castellón, vecino de Toledo, residente en la ciudad de Seuilla"; CPI, I, 6, No. 75; APS, 7 Nov. 1511, Oficio XV, Libro II, Bernal González Vallesillo, fol. tercer tercio del legajo; and 29 Mar. 1512, Libro I; CPI, I, 40, No. 552 and p. 44, No. 604: "Jácome de Castellón, mercader genovés, hijo de Bernardo de Castellón y Inés Suárez, vecinos de Toledo, que presentó carta de naturaleza." He took with him two Spanish employees Alonso de Salvanes of Toledo and Andrés de Villacorta of Olmedo. Villacorta later accompanied Castellón to Cumaná and served from 1528 on as resident warden of the fortress of Cumaná for Castellón (Enrique Otte, ed., *Cedularios de la monarquía española relativos a la isla de Cubagua* [1523–1534] [Caracas, 1961], I, xxxiii).

13. Among the merchants who employed Castellón as a commission agent were Andrea Palavicino, Francisco Riberol and Benito de Pumar (APS, 16 Sept. 1512, Oficio I, Libro I, Mateo de la Cuadra, fol. 433v.; APS, 8 Jan. 1513, Oficio IV, Libro I, Manuel Segura, fol. carece, registro, I; APS, 28 July 1523, Oficio IV, Libro II, Manuel Segura, fol. 1663.

14. Oviedo, *Historia,* CXVII, 79; C. Haring, *The Spanish Empire in America* (New York, 1947), pp. 256–257; APS, 8 Jan. 1513, Oficio IV, Libro I, Manuel Segura, fol. carece, registro I.

15. Oviedo, *Historia*, CXVII, 109. Las Casas tried to colonize this area with Spanish farmers organized into villages of forty families each. An allotment of Indians was given to each village (instead of to an individual as in the encomienda system) and the land was worked in common under the supervision of the Friars (Lewis Hanke, *Bartolomé de las Casas: An Interpretation of His Life and Writings* [The Hague, 1951], pp. 22–23).

16. Marie Helmer, "Cubagua, L'Île des Perles," *Annales: Économies, societés, civilisations*, XVIII (1962), 752. Both the Ocampo and Castellón expeditions have been described by Enrique Otte, "La expedición de Gonzalo de Ocampo a Cumaná en 1521 en las cuentas de Tesorería de Santo Domingo," *Revista de Indias*, LXIII (1956), 51–82.

17. Enrique Otte claims that one of the reasons for Audiencia's choosing Castellón was the fact that Castellón had accompanied the expedition that took the Dominican Pedro de Córdoba and his fellow priests to Cumaná in 1515 and knew the coastal area well. Otte does not, however, give any source for this statement. According to Otte, the Audiencia promised Castellón to build the fortress of Cumaná and to name Castellón warden [alcaide] as one of the conditions determining the Audienca's participation in the venture (*ibid.*, xxv).

18. Direct trade between Seville and Cubagua was illegal, but the ships came anyway—seventeen of them in seven years (Helmer, "Cubagua," p. 755).

19. Francisco López de Gómara, *Historia general de las Indias* (Madrid, 1932), p. 186.

20. CDI, 1st ser., XXXVII, 433: "E esto asentado por los Oydores e Oficiales con el dicho Xácome [de Castellón], se le mandó estubiese cargo de fascer los dichos rescates." In addition to the Bishop, an interpreter and notary also had to be present at such transactions. The notary, through the interpreter, was required to ask each prisoner whether or not he had been captured as a result of war. If he answered negatively, he was freed, if not, he was declared a slave "in good faith" and branded with the king's iron. This procedure was considered to be equivalent to the "requerimiento" or "requirement" that conquistadors were called upon to have read to the Indians before their territory could be taken or hostilities against them started (Helmer, p. 754).

21. The upkeep of the fortress amounted to 900 pesos a year (Otte, *La expedición*," p. 71).

22. CDI, 1st. ser., XXXVII, 434; CDI, 1st. ser., I, 548–549. The following additional unfavorable comments on Astudillo are included in the report: "Fue [Astudillo] a estos reinos poco menos que desterrado, y tuvo maña para venir de veedor de las fundaciones, veedor de la Audiencia y regidor, tres oficios, que con uno solo estaría cualquier vecino

honrado. Él está procesado por varios delitos y sentenciado a desdecirse públicamente o ser traído a la vergüenza y cosas todas que hacen un hombre infame."

23. "Colección de documentos inéditos para la historia de Ibero-América," *Nobilario hispano-americano del siglo XVI*, II (Madrid, 1928), 829.

24. The town of New Cadiz was at its height between 1530 and 1535, at which time it contained one thousand inhabitants (Helmer, "Cubagua," p. 756).

25. Otte, *Cedularios*, I, xxvii; APS, 2 May 1536, Oficio I, Libro I, Alonso de la Barrera, Sin folio, único cuaderno; and 19 Mar., fol. 322; and 19 May 1536.

26. On September 26, 1519, Tomás de Castellón appeared as a witness in the *residencia* of Sancho Velázquez, chief justice of Puerto Rico, at which time he declared that he was thirty years of age (Vicente Murga Sanz, *Historia documental de Puerto Rico* [Santander, 1957], II, 294); APS, 9 May 1509, Oficio XV, Libro I, Bernal González Vallesillo, fol. segundo tercio del legajo; and 24 Apr. 1509, fol. segundo tercio del legajo: "Tomás de Castellón, mercader genovés otorga haber recibido de Bautista Cataño, mercader genovés, 45 varas de paño de Londres para venderlas en la isla española"; APS, 9 Mar. 1509, Oficio I, Libro I, Mateo de la Cuadra, fol. 296.

27. APS, 8 Jan. 1513, Oficio IV, Libro I, Manuel Segura, fol. carece registro 1; Aurelio Tío, *Nuevas fuentes para la historia de Puerto Rico* (San Germán, 1961), p. 230. According to Las Casas, "Las granjerías de entonces no eran otras sino de criar puercos y hacer labranza del pan caçabí y las otras raíces comestibles, que son los ajes y batatas" (*Historia de las Indias*, ed. Agustín Millares Carlo [Mexico, 1951], II, chap. vi, pp. 225–226).

28. Tío, *Nuevas fuentes*, p. 141. This expedition, led by Juan Enríquez, eventually founded the town of Daguao. See also Serrano y Sanz, *Preliminares*, p. DXLVII, doc. xxiii. Oviedo, *Historia*, also mentions this mill in II, 108.

29. Vicente Murga Sanz, ed. *Biblioteca histórica de Puerto Rico*, I (Rio Piedras, 1960), p. 256. Al Emperador. Baltasar de Castro, Miguel de Castellanos, Puerto Rico, 15 July 1529: "Tomás Castellón tuvo arrendado el almojarifazgo desde 1524 por tres años. Murió en 1527." See also p. 241, 27 Mar. 1527; p. 258: "Auto de ejecución de los bienes de Doña Teodora de Castellón, mujer del tesorero de San Juan, Blas de Villasante, hecho por el licenciado de la Gama"; and Wright, "History of Sugar," p. 11; Murga Sanz, *Biblioteca histórica*, p. 527.

30. The dissension among the members of the *cabildo* has been described by Brau, *La colonización*, chap. xv.

31. *Ibid.*, p. 350.

32. *Ibid.*, p. 352: In the *residencia* of Sancho Velázquez, Pedro Moreno had accused Villasante of having illicit relations with both mother and daughter, but, according to Moreno, the treasurer had been acquitted because of his friendship with Velázquez: "Y se sabe que en esta ciudad ante Pedro Moreno fue denunciado de Villasante que se había echado con madre e hija y quel dicho Pedro Moreno lo prendió, y después de preso lo remitió al dicho Licenciado [Velázquez], pero que no sabe lo que se hizo sobre ello, mas de le ver andar suelto por ahí" (Murga Sanz, *Historia*, II, 152).

33. Brau, *La colonización*, pp. 352, 353. The descendants of heretics were ineligible for public office (Murga Sanz, *Biblioteca histórica*, pp. 256, 264).

34. Al emperador. Licenciado de la Gama, 15 June 1529. "Tomé la residencia al tesorero Villasante en la cárcel de la Inquisición do lo metió el Obispo a pocos días que llegué . . . ha cuatro meses le dió al Obispo por cárcel" (*ibid.*, p. 256).

35. *Ibid.*, p. 264.

36. Martín Ventura served as treasurer from March 14 to June 8 (*ibid.*).

37. *Ibid.*, p. 265. "Al tesorero Blas de Villasante mandándole ir a Castilla en el primer navío y presentarse al Consejo."

38. Brau, *La colonización*, p. 355.

39. Wright, "History of Sugar," LIV (1915), 206.

40. In a letter to Licentiate Espinosa, one of the judges of the Audiencia, Villasante described the attack on the mill by French corsairs in 1528 (Tío, *Nuevas fuentes*, p. 205).

41. Wright, "History of Sugar," LIV (1915), 206; *Boletín*, Dominican Republic, I (1938), 357; APS, 10 June 1551, Oficio XV, Libro I, Alonso de Cazalla, fol. 655v. See also APS, 25 Sept. 1550, Oficio XV, Libro II, Juan Franco, fol. 277v.

42. Wright, "History of Sugar," p. 206. In 1595 Drake destroyed whatever was left of the estate (Tío, *Nuevas fuentes*, p. 199).

43. In Quevedo's satirical poem, *Poderoso caballero es don dinero* he states:

> "Nace en Indias honrado
> donde el mundo le acompaña;
> viene a morir en España,
> y es en Génova enterrado"

(F. de Quevedo Villegas, *Obras completas*, ed. L. Astrana Marín [Madrid, 1952], p. 82).

Bibliography

PRIMARY SOURCES

Manuscripts

Archivo de Protocolos, Seville. Siglo XVI. Escribanos: Gonzalo
Álvarez de Aguilar, años 1515, 1518.
Martín de Ávila, año 1547.
Alonso de la Barrera, años 1525–1527, 1533, 1536.
Francisco de Castellanos, años 1515, 1523–1527.
Pedro de Castellanos, años 1537, 1539.
Alonso de Cazalla, años 1528, 1536–1538, 1540, 1542–1546, 1548–
1551.
Mateo de la Cuadra, años 1509–1510, 1512, 1514, 1515.
Francisco Díaz, año 1577.
Pedro Díaz de Alfaro, año 1517.
Juan Franco, años 1550–1551.
Bernal González Vallesillo, años 1507–1509, 1511–1519, 1523.
Juan Bernal de Heredia, año 1574.
Gaspar de León, año 1580.
Diego López, año 1519.
Juan Núñez, años 1511, 1519.
Melchor de Portes, año 1548.
Antón Ruiz de Porras, año 1525.
Juan Ruiz de Porras, año 1509.
Francisco Segura, años 1500, 1506.
Manuel Segura, años 1507, 1510, 1513–1514, 1522–1523.
Francisco de Vera, año 1580.
Archivo general de Indias, Seville. Sección: Contratación, legajos
166, 166v, 167, 167v, 2439, 4339, 4677; Indifferente general,
legajo 2000.

Archivo Histórico Nacional, Madrid. Sección: Inquisición, legajos 4519, 4683, 4731.

Archivo Municipal, Seville. Sección Tercera, Escribanía del Cabildo. 20 vols.

Biblioteca Nacional, Madrid. Sección de Manuscritos. Sevilla, 6754-s-110. "Representación de un vecino de Sevilla a fines del siglo XVI en favor de los comerciantes extranjeros que había en dicha ciudad."

Published Documents and Contemporary Writings

Acosta, José. *Historia natural y moral de las Indias*. Ed. by Edmundo O'Gorman. Mexico City: Fondo de Cultura Económica, 1940.

Albèri, Eugenio. *Relazione degli ambasciatori vèneti al senato*. Vol. XIV. Florence: Società Editrice Fiorentina, 1855.

Alcázar, Baltasar del. *Poesías*. Ed. Francisco Rodríguez Marín. Madrid: Real Academia Española, 1910.

Alemán, Mateo. "Guzmán de Alfarache," in Angel Valbuena Prat, *La novela picaresca española*. Madrid: Aguilar, 1956.

Alighieri, Dante. *The Divine Comedy*. New York: The Modern Library, 1950.

Argote de Molina, Gonzalo. *Nobleza del Andaluzia*. Seville: Fernando Díaz, 1588.

Ariño, Francisco de. *Sucesos de Sevilla de 1592 a 1604*. Seville: Impr. de Tarasco y Lassa, 1873.

Bandello, Matteo. *Tutte le òpere di Matteo Bandello*. Ed. by Francisco Flora. Vols. I, II. Milan: Mondadori, 1952.

Braun, Georg. *Civitates orbis terrarum*. Vols. I, IV, V. 1576–1618.

Carvajal, Gaspar de. *The Discovery of the Amazon*. Ed. by H. C. Heaton, trans. by B. T. Lee. With an introduction by José Toribio Medina. New York: American Geographical Society, 1934.

Castillo Solórzano, Alonso de. *La garduña de Sevilla y anzuelo de las bolsas*. Madrid: Clásicos Castellanos, 1942.

Cervantes Saavedra, Miguel de. *Coloquio de los perros*. (*Las Novelas ejemplares*, ed. by Francisco Rodríguez Marín, Vol. II.) Madrid: Clásicos Castellanos, 1957.

———. *La gitanilla*. (*Las novelas ejemplares*, ed. by Francisco Rodríguez Marín, Vol. I.) Madrid: Clásicos Castellanos, 1952.

———. *El Licenciado Vidriera.* (*Las novelas ejemplares,* ed. by Francisco Rodrígues Marín, Vol. II.) Madrid: Clásicos Castellanos, 1957.

———. *Rinconete y Cortadillo.* Ed. by Francisco Rodríguez Marín. Madrid: Revista de Archivos, Bibliotecas y Museos, 1920.

Chaunu, Huguette and Pierre. *Séville et l'Atlantique, 1504 à 1650.* Paris: S.E.V.P.E.N., 1955–1960. Vols. I–IV, VIII.

Colección de documentos inéditos, relativos al descubrimiento, conquista y organización de las antiguas posesiones españolas de América y Oceania. 42 vols. Madrid: 1864–1884. Especl. Vols. I, II, XXXIV, XXXVII, XXXIX, XL.

Colección de documentos inéditos, relativos al descubrimiento, conquista y organización de las antiguas posesiones españolas de ultramar. 25 vols. Madrid: Sucesores de Rivadeneyra, 1885–1932. Espec. Vols. I, IV, VI, VII, IX, X, XIV, XXIV.

Colombo, Fernando. *Le historie della vita e dei fatti di Cristòforo Colombo.* Ed. by Rinaldo Caddeo. Vol. I. Milan: Edizione "Alpes," 1930.

Colón, Cristóbal. *Los cuatro viajes del almirante y su testamento.* Ed. by Ignacio Anzoategui. Buenos Aires: Espasa-Calpe, 1958.

Doehaerd, Renée. *Les relations commerciales entre Gênes, la Belgique, et l'outremont d'après les archives notariles génoises aux XII*e *et XIV*e *siècles.* ("Études d'histoire économique et sociale," Vols. II–IV.) Brussels: Palais des académies, 1941.

——— and Charles Kerremans. *Les relations commerciales entre Gênes la Belgique, et l'outremont d'après les archives notariales génoises, 1400–1440.* ("Études d'histoire économique et sociale," Vol. V.) Brussels: Palais des académies, 1952.

Dominican Republic, Archivo General. "Colección Lugo," *Boletín del Archivo General de la Nación,* I (1938), 346–364.

Espinel, Vincente. *Vida de Marcos de Obregón.* Ed. by Samuel Gili Gaya. 2 vols. Madrid: Clásicos Castellanos, 1940.

Fabié y Escudero, José María, ed. and trans. *Viajes por España de Jorge de Einghen, del barón de Rosmithal de Blatna, de Francisco Guicciardini y de Andrés Navajero.* Madrid: F. Fe, 1879.

Fernández de Navarrete, Martín. *Collección de los viajes y descubrimientos que hicieron por mar los españoles desde fines del siglo XV.* Vol. II. Madrid: Imprenta Real, 1825.

Fernández de Oviedo, Gonzalo. *Historia general y natural de las Indias.* Ed. by Juan Pérez de Tudela Bueso. ("Biblioteca de

Autores Españoles," Vols. CXVII–CXXI.) Madrid: Ediciones Atlas, 1959.

Fernández de Ribera, Rodrigo. *El mesón del mundo.* Ed. by Edward Nagy. New York: Las Americas, 1963.

Garcilaso de la Vega, el Inca. *La Florida del Inca, Historia del adelantado Hernando de Soto, gobernador y capitán general del reino de la Florida y de otros heroicos caballeros españoles é indios.* Madrid: N. Rodríguez Franco, 1723.

Gentil Da Silva, José. *Marchandises et finances, Lettres de Lisbonne* (1563–1578). Vol. II. Paris: S.E.V.P.E.N., 1959.

Gracián, Baltasar. *El Criticón.* Ed. by M. Romera-Navarro. Vol. U. Philadelphia: University of Pennsylvania Press, 1939.

Great Britain, Public Records Office. *Calendar of State Papers and Manuscripts Relating to English Affaires Existing in the Archives and Collections of Venice and in the Libraries of Northern Italy.* Ed. by Rawdon Brown. Vol. III. London: H. M. Stationery Office, 1869.

Hazañas y La Rúa, Joaquín. *Obras de Gutierre de Cetina.* Vol. II. Seville: Impr. de F. de P. Días, 1895.

Hernández Díaz, J., and A. Muro Orejón. *El testamento de don Hernando Colón.* Seville: La Gavidia, 1941.

Herrera, Antonio de. *Historia general de los castellanos en las Islas y Tierra Firme de el mar Océano.* Asunción: Editorial Guarania, 1945. Vols. II, IV, V.

Ibarra y Rodríguez, Eduardo, ed. *Documentos de asunto económico correspondientes al reinado de los Reyes Católicos, 1475–1516.* Madrid: Academia Universitaria Católica, 1917.

Icaza, Francisco A. de. *Conquistadores y pobladores de Nueva España.* Madrid: Impr. de El Adelantado de Segovia, 1923.

——. *Tragedias y comedias de Juan de la Cueva.* ("Sociedad de bibliófilos españoles," Vol. XL.) Madrid: "Imprenta ibérica," E. Maestre 1917.

Las Casas, Bartolomé de. *Historia de las Indias.* Ed. by Agustín Millares Carlo. 3 vols. Mexico City: Fondo de Cultura Económica, 1951.

Lollis, Cèsare de. *Scritti di Cristòforo Colombo.* Vol. II. Rome: Ministero della Pùbblica Istruzione, 1892.

Lope de Vega Carpio, Félix. *El arenal de Sevilla.* (Obras escogidas, ed. by Federico Carlos Sáinz de Robles, Vol. I.) Madrid: Aguilar, 1952.

———. *De cosario a cosario*. (*Obras de Lope de Vega*, ed. by Emilio Cotarelo y Mori, Vol. XII.) Madrid: Real Academia Española, 1929.

———. *La esclava de su galán*. (*Obras de Lope de Vega*, ed. by Emilio Cotarelo y Mori, Vol. XII.) Madrid: Real Academia Espaola, 1930.

———. *El premio de bien hablar*. (*Obras de Lope de Vega*, ed. by Emilio Cotarelo y Mori, Vol. XIII.) Madrid: Real Academia Española, 1930.

———. *La prueba de los amigos*. (*Obras escogidas*, ed. by Federico Carlos Sáinz de Robles, Vol. I.) Madrid: Aguilar, 1952.

Lopez, Robert, and Irving Raymond. *Medieval Trade in the Mediterranean World*. New York: Columbia University Press, 1955.

López de Gómara, Francisco. *Historia general de las Indias*. Madrid: Espasa-Calpe, 1932.

Martyr D'Anghera, Peter. *De Orbe Novo: The Eight Decades of Peter Martyr D'Anghera*. Trans. by Francis MacNutt. New York: G. P. Putnam's Sons, 1912.

Medina, Pedro de. *Libro de grandezas y cosas memorables de España*. Seville: Doménico d'Robertis, 1548.

Mercado, Fray Tomás de. *Summa de tratos y contratos*. Seville: Fernando Días, 1587.

Mexía, Pedro. *Diálogos o Coloquios de Pedro Mexía*. Ed. by Margaret L. Mulroney. Iowa City, Iowa: The University, 1930.

Montoto de Sedas, S. *Nobilario hispano-americano del siglo XVI*. ("Colección de documentos inéditos para la historia de Ibero-América," Vol. II.) Madrid: Compañía ibero-americana de publicaciones, 1927.

Morgado, Alonso de. *Historia de Sevilla*. Sevilla: A. Pescioni y I. de León, 1587 (J. M. Ariza, 1887).

Murga Sanz, Vicente, ed. *Biblioteca histórica de Puerto Rico*. Vol. I. Río Piedras: Ediciones de la Universidad de Puerto Rico, 1960.

Ordenanzas de Sevilla. Seville: I. Varela, 1527.

Otte, Enrique, ed. *Cedularios de la Monarquía española relativos a la isla de Cubagua* (1523–1550). Vol. I. Caracas: La Fundación John Bolton y la Fundación Eugenio Mendoza, 1961.

Pacheco, Francisco. *Libro de descripción de verdaderos retratos, de ilustres y memorables varones.* Seville, 1599.

Quevedo Villegas, Francisco de. *Obras completas (Obras en Verso).* Ed. by Luis Astrana Marín. Madrid: Aguilar, 1952.

——. *Vida del Buscón.* Madrid: Clásicos Castellanos, 1954.

Ruiz de Alarcón, Juan. *El semejante a sí mismo. (Obras completas,* ed. by Agustín Millares Carlo, Vol. I.) Mexico: Fondo de Cultura Económica, 1957.

Seville, Archivo de Protocolos. *Catálogo de los fondos americanos del Archivo de Protocolos de Sevilla.* ("Colección de documentos inéditos para la historia de Hispano-América," Vols. X, XI, XIV.) Madrid–Buenas Aires: Compañía ibero-americana de publicaciones, 1930–1932.

Seville, Archivo de Protocolos. *Catálogo de los fondos americanos del Archivo de Protocolos de Sevilla.* Vol. IV. Madrid: Tipografía de archivos, 1935.

Seville, Archivo de Protocolos. *Catálogo de los fondos americanos del Archivo de Protocolos de Sevilla.* Vol. V. Seville: La Gavidia, 1937.

Spain, Archivo general de Indias, Seville. *Catálogo de pasajeros a Indias durante los siglos XVI, XVII y XVIII.* 3 vols. Seville: La Gavidia, 1940–1946.

Suárez de Figueroa, Cristóbal. *El pasagero.* Ed. by Francisco Rodríguez Marín. Madrid: Renacimiento, 1913.

Torre y del Cerro, José de la. *Beatriz Enríquez de Harana y Cristóbal Colón.* Madrid: Compañía ibero-americana de publicaciones, 1933.

Vázquez de Prada, Valentín. *Lettres marchandes d'Anvers.* 3 vols. Paris: S.E.V.P.E.N., 1960.

Veitia Linaje, Joseph de. *Norte de la Contratación de las Indias occidentales.* Seville: I. F. de Blas, 1672.

Vélez de Guevara, Luis. *El diablo cojuelo.* Ed. by Francisco Rodríguez Marín. Madrid: Clásicos Castellanos, 1951.

Villalón, Cristóbal de. *Viaje a Turquía.* ("Nueva Biblioteca de Autores Españoles," Vol. II.) Madrid: Bailly-Balliere, 1905.

Wright, Irene. "History of Sugar," *Louisiana Planter and Sugar*

Manufacturer, LIV (1915), 11, 125–126, 206–207, 270, 302, 366–367; LV (1915), 190.

Ympyn, Christoffels. *A Notable and Very Excellent Work, Expressing and Declaring the Manner and Forms How to Keep a Book of Accounts.* . . . 's-Gravenhage: Nijhoff, 1934.

Zapata, Luis. *Miscelánea.* ("Memorial Histórico Español," Vol. XI.) Madrid: La Real Academia de Historia, 1859

SECONDARY WORKS

Books

Acosta, Joaquín. *Compendio histórico del descubrimiento y colonización de la Nueva Granada.* Paris: Imp. de Beau, 1848.

Altamira y Crevea, Rafael. *Historia de España y de la civilización española.* 4th ed. Vol. III. Barcelona: Sucesores de J. Gili, s.s., E.L.E., 1928.

Álvarez Rubiano, Pablo. *Pedrarias Dávila.* Madrid: Consejo Superior de Investigaciones Científicos, Instituto Gonzalo Fernández de Oviedo, 1944.

Anderson, C. L. G. *Old Panama and Castilla del Oro.* Washington: Washington Press of the Sudwarth Company, 1911.

Artiñano y de Galdácomo, Gervasio. *Historia del comercio con las Indias durante el dominio de los Austrias.* Barcelona: Talleres de Oliva de Vilanova, 1917.

Azevedo, J. Lúcio. *Epocas de Portugal económico.* Lisbon: Teixeira, 1929.

Ballesteros y Beretta, Antonio. *Cristóbal Colón y el descubrimiento de América.* 2 vols. Barcelona–Buenos Aires: Salvat Editores, S. A., 1945.

——. *Sevilla en el siglo XIII.* Madrid: Pérez Torres, 1913.

Borah, Woodrow. *Early Colonial Trade and Navigation between Mexico and Peru.* Berkeley: University of California, 1954.

Brau, Salvador. *La colonización de Puerto Rico.* San Juan: Tipografía "Heraldo Español," 1930.

Braudel, Fernand. *La Méditerranée et le monde méditerranéen à l'époque de Philippe II.* Paris: Colin, 1949.

Burckhardt, Jacob. *The Civilization of the Renaissance in Italy.* New York: Harper, 1958.

BIBLIOGRAPHY

Burgon, John. *The Life and Times of Sir Thomas Gresham.* Vol. I. London: R. Jennings, 1839.

Cappellini, Antonio. *Dizionario biogràfico di Genovesi illustri e notàbili.* Sancasciano Val de Pesa (Florence) Stab. tip. Fratelli Stianti, 1932.

Carande, Ramón. *Carlos V y sus banqueros.* Madrid: Revista de Occidente, 1943.

——. *La hacienda real de Castilla.* Madrid: Sociedad de Estudios y Publicaciones, 1949.

Cassoni, Filipo. *Annali della repùbblica di Gènova del sècolo dècimo sesto.* Vol. III. Genoa: Stamperia Casamara, 1799–1800.

Clough, Shepard and Charles. *Economic History of Europe.* 3d ed. New York: D. C. Heath and Company, 1952.

Dahlgren, E. W. *Les relations commerciales et maritimes entre la France et les côtes de l'océan Pacifique (commencement du XVIII' siècle).* Paris: H. Champion, 1909.

Davies, R. Trevor. *The Golden Century of Spain, 1501–1621.* London: Macmillan Company, 1954.

De Roover, Raymond. *L'évolution de la lettre de change (XIV'–XVIII' siècles).* Paris: S.E.V.P.E.N., 1953.

De Stuber, Elena F. S. *La trata de Negros en el Río de la Plata durante el siglo XVIII.* Buenos Aires: Universidad de Buenos Aires, 1958.

Díaz Soler, Luis. *Historia de la esclavitud negra en Puerto Rico (1493–1890).* Madrid: Revista de Occidente, 1953.

Ehrenberg, Richard. *Capital and Finance in the Age of the Renaissance.* Trans. by H. M. Lucas. New York: Harcourt, Brace, 1928.

——. *Das Zeitalter der Fugger.* Vol. I. Jena: G. Fisher, 1896.

Espejo, Cristóbal, and Julián Paz. *Las antiguas ferias de Medina del Campo.* Valladolid: Imp. La Nueva Pincia, 1908.

Fernández de Navarrete, Martín. *Obras.* ("Biblioteca de Autores Españoles," Vols. LXXV–LXXVII.) Madrid: Ediciones Atlas, 154–155.

García Valdecasas, Alfonso. *El Hidalgo y el honor.* 2d ed. Madrid: Revista de Occidente, 1958.

Girard, Albert. *La rivalité commerciale et maritime entre Séville et Cadix jusqu'à la fin du XVIII' siècle.* Paris: Boccard, 1932.

González, Julio. *Repartimento de Sevilla*. 2 vols. Madrid: Consejo Superior de Investigaciones Científicas, 1951.

González de León, Félix. *Noticia artística histórica y curiosa de todas los edificios públicos, sagrados y profanos . . . de Sevilla, y de muchas casas particulares. . . .* 2 vols. Seville: José Hidalgo y Compañía, 1844.

Goris, Jan Albert. *Etude sur les colonies marchandes méridionales (portugais, espagnols, italiens) à Anvers de 1488 à 1567*. Louvain: Librairie Universitaire Uystpruyst, 1925.

Guichot y Parody, Joaquín. *Historia del Excm. Ayuntamiento de la Cuidad de Sevilla*. Vol. II. Seville: Tip. de la Región, 1896.

Hamilton, Earl J. *American Treasure and the Price Revolution in Spain, 1501–1650*. Cambridge, Mass.: Harvard University Press, 1934.

Hanke, Lewis. *Bartolomé de las Casas: An Interpretation of His Life and Writings*. The Hague: Martinus Nijhoff, 1951.

Haring, Clarence. *The Spanish Empire in America*. New York: Oxford University Press, 1947.

———. *Trade and Navigation between Spain and the Indies in the Time of the Hapsburgs*. Cambridge, Mass.: Harvard University Press, 1918.

Harrisse, Henry. *Christophe Colomb; son origine, sa vie, ses voyages, sa famille, et ses descendants*. 2 vols. Paris: E. Leroux, 1884–1885.

———. *Don Fernando Colón, historiador de su padre*. Seville: Sociedad de Bibliófios Andaluces, 1871.

Heaton, Herbert. *Economic History of Europe*. New York: Harper, 1948.

Heers, Jacques. *Gênes au XVe siècle*. Paris: S.E.V.P.E.N., 1961.

———. *Le livre de comptes de Giovanni Piccamiglio, homme d'affaires génois (1456–1459)*. Paris: S.E.V.P.E.N., 1959.

Heyd, Wilhelm von. *Histoire du commerce du Levant au Moyen Âge*. Trans. by F. Raynaud. Leipzig: O. Harrassowitz, 1923.

Laiglesiea, Francisco de. *Estudios históricos, 1515–1555*. Vol. II. Madrid: Imprenta Clásica Española, 1918.

Lapeyre, Henri. *Une famille de marchands, Les Ruiz: Contribution à l'étude du commerce entre la France et l'Espagne au temps de Philippe II*. Paris: S.E.V.P.E.N., 1955.

——. *Simón Ruiz et les asientos de Philippe II*. Paris: S.E.V.P.E.N., 1953.

Lopez, Robert. "Hard Times and Investment in Culture," *The Renaissance: A Symposium, Feb. 8–10, 1952*. New York: Metropolitan Museum of Art, 1953.

——. *Storia delle colonie genovesi nel Mediterràneo*. Bologna: N. Zanichelli, 1938.

Majo Framís, Ricardo. *Navigantes y conquistadores españoles del siglo XVI*. Madrid: Aguilar, 1946.

Manfroni, Camillo. *Gènova*. Rome: Edizione Tiber, 1929.

Matute y Gaviría, Justino. *Hijos de Sevilla señalados en santidad, letras, armas, artes o dignidad*. Vol. I. Seville: En la oficina de "El Orden," 1886.

Medina, José Toribio. *Juan Díaz de Solís*. 2 vols. Santiago, Chile: Impr. en casa del autor, 1897.

——. *El Veneciano Sebastián Caboto al servicio de España*. 2 vols. Santiago, Chile: Imprenta y Encuadernación Universitaria, 1908.

——. *Los viajes de Diego García de Moguer*. Santiago, Chile: Impr. Elzeviriana, 1908.

Melón y Ruiz de Gordejuela, Amando. *Los primeros tiempos de la colonización Cuba y las Antillas—Magallanes y la primera vuelta al mundo*. ("Ballesteros y Beretta, A. Historia de América y de los pueblos americanos," Vol. VI.) Barcelona: Salvat Editores, 1952.

Menéndez Pelayo, Marcelino. *Historia de los heterodoxos*. 2d ed. Vol. V. Madrid: V. Suárez, 1928.

Menéndez Pidal, Ramón. *Los españoles en la historia*. Madrid: Espasa-Calpe, 1959.

Montoto de Sedas, Santiago. *Las calles de Sevilla*. Seville: Imprenta Hispania, 1940.

——. *Sevilla en el imperio, siglo XVI*. Seville: Nueva Librería Vda. de C. García, 1938.

Moreno de Guerra y Alonso, Juan. *Guía de la grandeza; historia genealógica y heráldica de todas las casas que gozan de esta dignidad nobiliaria*. Madrid: Impr. parroquial, 1924.

Morison, Samuel E. *Admiral of the Ocean Sea, a Life of Christopher Columbus*. 2 vols. Boston: Little, Brown and Company, 1942.

Murga Sanz, Vicente. *Historia documental de Puerto Rico*. Río Piedras, P.R.: Editorial Plus ultra, 1956. Vols. II, III.

Ortiz de Zúñiga, Diego. *Anales eclesiásticos y seculares de la muy noble y leal ciudad de Sevilla, metrópole de la Andalucía.* Madrid: Imprenta real, 1796. Vols. III, IV.

Pandiani, Emilio. *Vita privata genovese nel Rinacimento.* ("Atti della Società ligure di storia patria," Vol. XLVII.) Genoa: Società ligure di storia patria, 1915.

Penrose, Boies. *Travel and Discovery in the Renaissance, 1420–1620.* Cambridge, Mass.: Harvard University Press, 1952.

Pérez de Guzmán y Boza, J. *Discursos leídos ante la Real Academia Sevillana el 26 de abril de 1892.* Seville: Impr. de E. Rasco, 1892.

Renouard, Yvres. *Les hommes d'affaires italiens au moyen âge.* Paris: Colin, 1949.

Rodríguez Demorizi, E. *Relaciones históricas de Santo Domingo.* Vol. II. Ciudad Trujillo: Editora Montalvo, 1945.

Ruddock, Alwyn. *Italian Merchants and Shipping in Southampton, 1270–1600.* Southampton: University College, 1951.

Saco, José Antonio. *Historia de la esclavitud de la Raza Africana en el Nuevo Mundo y en especial en los países Américo-hispanos.* Havana: Cultural S. A., 1938. Vols. I, II.

Sáinz de Robles, Federico Carlos. *Historia y antología de la poesía española del siglo XII al XX.* Madrid: Aguilar, 1955.

Sandoval, Fernando. *La industria del azúcar en Nueva España.* Mexico: Universidad nacional autónoma de México, 1951.

Scelle, Georges. *La traité négrière aux Indes de Castille.* 2 vols. Paris: L. Larose and L. Tenin, 1906.

Schäfer, Ernst. *El consejo real y supremo de las Indias.* 2 vols. Seville: M. Carmona, 1935.

Serrano y Sanz, Manuel. *Preliminares del gobierno de Pedrarias Dávila en Castilla del Oro* in *Orígines de la dominación española en América.* ("Nueva Biblioteca de Autores Españoles," Vol. XXV.) Madrid: Bailly-Balliere, 1918.

Tarducci, Francesco. *John and Sebastian Cabot.* Trans. by Henry Brownson. Detroit: H. F. Brownson, 1893.

Thompson, James. *Economic and Social History of Europe in the Latter Middle Ages.* New York: The Century Company, 1931.

Tío, Aurelio. *Nuevas fuentes para la historia de Puerto Rico.* San Germán, Puerto Rico: Universidad Interamericana, 1961.

Usher, A. P. *The Early History of Deposit Banking in Mediterranean Europe.* Cambridge, Mass.: Harvard University Press, 1943.

Varnhagen, F. Adolpho de. *História general do Brazil antes da sua separação e independencia de Portugal*. Vol. I. Rio de Janeiro: E. and H. Laemmert, 1877.

Vicens Vives, Jaime. *Historia social y económica de España y América*. Vols. II, III. Barcelona: Editorial Teide, 1957.

——. *Manuel de historia económica*. Barcelona: Editorial Teide, 1959.

Vitale, Vito. *Breviario della storia di Gènova*. Vol. I. Genoa: Società Ligure di Storia Patria, 1955.

Worcester, D. and W. Schaeffer. *The Growth and Culture of Latin America*. New York: Oxford University Press, 1956.

Articles

Bennassar, B. "Facteurs sévillans au XVe siècle d'après des lettres marchandes," *Annales: Économies, sociétés, civilisations*, XII (1957), 60–70.

Burns, Arthur Robert. "Partnerships," *Encyclopedia of the Social Sciences*, ed. by E. R. A. Seligman, XII (1934), 3–6.

Carande, Ramón. "Sevilla, fortaleza y mercado," *Anuario de historia de derecho español*, II (1925), 233–401.

Carlé, M. del Carmen. "Mercaderes en Castilla (1252–1512)," *Cuadernos de historia de España*, XXI–XXII (1954), 146–328.

De Roover, Raymond. "New Interpretations of the History of Banking," *Cahiers d'histoire mondiale*, II (1954), 38–76.

Fabrella, María Luisa. "La producción de azúcar en Tenerife," *Revista de historia* (La Laguna de Tenerife), XVIII (1952), 455–475.

Helmer, Marie. "Cubagua, L'Île des Perles," *Annales: Économies, sociétés, civilisations*, XVIII (1962), 751–760.

Lapeyre, Henri. "La banque, les changes et le crédit au XVIe siècle," *Revue d'histoire moderne et contemporaine*, III (1956), 284–297.

——. "Le commerce des laines en Espagne sous Philippe II," *Bulletin de la Société d'histoire moderne*, Mar.–May 1955, pp. 5–8.

Lopez, Robert. "Le marchand génois," *Annales: Économies, sociétés, civilisations*, XIII (1958), 501–515.

——. "Market Expansion: The Case of Genoa," *Journal of Economic History*, XXIV (1964), 445–464.

——. "Aux origines du capitalism génois," *Annales d'histoire économique et sociale,* IX (1937), 429–449.

——. "Il predominio econòmico dei Genovesi nella monarchia spagnola," *Gironale stòrico e letterario della Liguria,* XII (1936), 65–74.

Marrero, Manuela. "Los genoveses en la colonización de Tenerife (1496–1509," *Revista de historia* (La Laguna de Tenerife), XVI (1950), 53–65.

Otte, Enrique. "Aspiraciones y actividades heterogéneas de Gonzalo Fernández de Oviedo, cronista," *Revista de Indias,* LXXI (1958), 9–61.

——. "La expedición de Gonzalo de Ocampo a Cumaná en 1521 en las cuentas de Tesorería de Santo Domingo," *Revista de Indias,* LXIII (1956), 51–82.

——. "Gonzalo Fernández de Oviedo y los Genoveses," *Revista de Indias,* LXXXIX–XC (1962), 515–519.

Pike, Ruth. "The Image of the Genoese in Golden Age Literature," *Hispania,* XLVI (1963), 705–714.

——. "The Sevillian Nobility and Trade with the New World in the Sixteenth Century," *Business History Review,* XXXIX (1965), 439–465.

Ratekin, Mervyn. "The Early Sugar Industry in Española," *Hispanic American Historical Review,* XXXIV (1954), 1–19.

Rubio, J. A. "La fundación del banco de Amsterdam (1609) y la banca de Sevilla," *Moneda y crédito,* XXIV (1948), 3–31.

Sayous, André. "Les débuts de commerce de l'Espagne avec l'Amérique," *Revue historique,* CLXXIV (1934), pp. 185–215.

——. "La genèse du systeme capitaliste: La pratique des affaires et leur mentalité dans l'Espagne du XVI^ᵉᵐᵉ siècle," *Annales d'histoire économique et sociale,* VIII (1936), 334–353.

——. "Le rôle des Génois lors de premiers mouvements réguliers d'affaires entre l'Espagne et le Nouveau Monde (1505–1520)," *Comptes rendues des séances de l'Académie des Inscriptions et Belles-lettres,* July–Sept. 1932, pp. 287–299.

Schäfer, E. "Una quiebra ruidosa del siglo XVII," *Investigación y Progreso,* VIII (1934), 309–312.

Sopranis, Hipólito Sancho de. "Los genoveses en la región gaditano-xerience de 1400–1800," *Hispania, revista española de historia,* VIII (1948), 355–402.

Verlinden, Charles. "Gli Italiani nell'economia delle Canaria all'inizio della colonizzazione spagnola," *Economia e Storia*, VII (1960), 149–172.

——. "The Rise of Spanish Trade in the Middle Ages," *Economic History Review*, X (1940), 44–59.

Wölfel, Dominik. "Alonso de Lugo y la compañía sociedad comercial para la conquista de la isla de La Palma," *Investigación y Progreso*, VIII (1934), 246–248.

Wright, Irene. "Documents—The Commencement of the Cane Sugar Industry in America, 1519–1538," *American Historical Review*, XXI (1916), 755–780.

Index

Adorno family, 2
Africa, 61, 64, 76, 80, 170 n.23
Aguado, Juan, 56
Agüero, Hierónimo de, 130
Alameda, 28, 31, 33, 160 n.40
Alameda fountain, 28
Alba, Duke of, 79
Alburquerque, Diego de, 96, 98, 190 n.50
Alcaicería, 29
Alcalá, Duke of, 40
Alcalá de Guadaira (near Seville), 39
Alcántara, order of, 79
Alcázar, 24
Alcázar, Baltasar de, 151 n.35
Alcázar, Francisco de, 185–186 n.20
Aldermen, 37, 97, 163 n.74; see also *Veinticuatros*
Alemán, Mateo (quoted), 21, 32, 35–37 *passim*, 191 n.58
Aljarafe, 6, 39, 42, 143 n.3
Almojarifazgo, 38, 94, 139
Alumada, Pedro de, 66
Amazon River, 117, 118, 122, 125
American trade, *see* Transatlantic trade
Añasco Bay (Puerto Rico), 139
Andrade, Fernando de, Count of Villalba, 200 n.48
Annuities, 16, 87, 119; see also *Juros*
Anti-Genoese sentiments, 8; expressed by Golden Age writers, 97, 191 n.58; expressed by Castilian Cortes, 191 n.58; *see also* Genoese merchants
Antilles, 67
Antwerp: trade with Seville, 17, 42, 68; fluctuations on market, 17, 87; Genoese in, 49

Apipé, Rapids of, 112
Aranda, Luis de, 53
Arbitrage, 84; defined, 181 n.1
Arcos, Duke of, 179 n.97
Arenal, 23, 31, 33
Arenal Gate, 26, 159 n.22
Argote de Molina (quoted), 4, 5
Ariño, Francisco de (quoted), 30, 158 n.14
Ascanio, Bautista, 206 n.3
Asiento, 80; defined, 180 n.108
Asiento of Negroes, 171–172 n.31
Astudillo, Gaspar de, 136, 209 n.22
Asylum, right of, 61
Audiencia: of Gradas, 24, 30; of Santo Domingo, 62, 134, 136, 209 n.17
Avería, 132, 152 n.43
Ávila, Pedro Arías de (Pedrarias), 101, 102, 190 n.47, 194 n.10

Baguanamay, María, 140
Balsam, 68, 175 n.63
Bandello, Matteo (quoted), 11
Bankers: participation in trade, 86; profits of, 86; commission charges, 86, 183 n.7; trade in bills of exchange, 86, 183 n.10; failures, 87, 187 n.27; types of, 185 n.18
Banking, 84–99, 182 n.1
Bankruptcy, royal, 144, 190 n.49
Banks of deposit and transfer: and book transfers, 84, 182 n.2; current account, 84–85, 183 n.4; use of overdrafts, 85, 183 n.5; sureties required, 85, 183 n.6, 190 n.49; origin of, 182 n.2; royal regulations for, 190 n.49
Banquero público, 86; defined, 185 n.18; *see also* Bankers

227

Flour, 55

Forne, Domingo de, 171 n.24; *see also* Vázquez, Forne, and Vivaldo, firm of

Forne, Esteban: imports American sugar, 67

Forne, Nicolás: invests in Cabot voyage (1526), 105

Forne, Tomás de, 171 n.24; *see also* Vázquez, Forne, and Vivaldo, firm of

Forne, Valián de: as a commission agent in Santo Domingo, 72, 73, 131; part owner of sugar mill, 131; business dealings with Esteban Justinián, 131; accompanies María Justinián to Santo Domingo, 131; invests in urban real estate and cattle lands, 131; becomes denizen of Santo Domingo, 132; farms the *avería*, 132

Forne family, 2

Foreign merchants: in the colonies, 102, 177 n.79; as public bankers, 185 n.19; popular feeling against, 191 n.58

France, 30, 97

Francesquín, Cristóbal, 89, 186–187 n.25

Freight charges, 71, 168 n.8

Frucises, Juan Francisco de: invests in Cabot voyage (1526), 105

Fustian, 42

Gallego, Fernando, 53

Gama, Licenciate Antonio de la, 141

Garay, Francisco de, 56–57

García, Diego, 112, 200 n.48

Gelves, Countess of, 180 n.112

Genoa: conflict between noble factions in, 1–2, 147 n.8, 147 n.11; *vilas* in, 12; geographic location of, 12–13, 153 n.51; role in First Crusade, 153 n.51; and in fall of Latin Empire of Constantinople (1261), 154 n.56; public banking in, 184 n.17

Genoese merchants: number in Seville in the Middle Ages, 1, 145 n.3, 146 n.4; number in Seville in the sixteenth century, 2, 146 n.6; in other Andalusian cities, 2, 146

Genoese merchants (*cont.*)
n.6, 147 n.9; noble houses, 2, 147 n.8; *popolari*, 2, 147 n.11; intermarriage with nobility, 3; commercial mobility in Middle Ages, 3, 147 n.12; hispanization, 3, 8, 149 n.21; naturalization and assimilation, 3, 5, 7, 8, 151 n.38; control over city government, 7–8; popular feelings against, 8, 97; religious views, 8–9, 14–15, 154 n.57, 155 n.64; importers of foreign goods into Seville, 9; capitalistic role in the transatlantic trade, 9, 48, 77; shipment of slaves to America, 9, 60, 63, 64, 67, 128; as royal creditors, 9, 48–49, 77–79, 83, 166 n.2; role in establishing the Casa de Contratación in Seville, 10, 151 n.42; and preserving Seville monopoly, 10–11; town houses of, 11, 16; characteristics of, 11–15, 153 n.50, 153 n.52, 153 n.53, 155 n.66; business practices of, 13, 15, 153 n.54, 154 n.61; investments in real estate, 16, 155 n.71; and in annuities, 16–17; in trade of Sevillian agricultural products, 17; as importers of American sugar, 17, 67; and other American agricultural and forest products, 17, 68; as importers of Mexican cochineal, 17, 68; in grain trade, 17–18; as engrossers, 18, 42; as public bankers, 19, 87–88, 185 n.17, 185 n.19; sea loans of, 49–50, 51, 75, 179 n.96; sales credits of, 50; shipments of goods to America, 51, 55; purchase and sale of slave licenses, 56, 60; as owners of slave vessels, 64, 76; relations with factors in America, 68–69, 72; Genoese factors in America, 71–72, 128; owners of transatlantic vessels, 76, 77; insurance transactions of, 76, 179 n.96; loans to Sevillian nobility, 80; companies at mid-century, 80–81; in trade of bills of exchange, 84, 166 n.3; as bondsmen of Sevillian bankers, 85, 92, 95; loans to explorers and conquerors, 99–100, 101–103; as sponsors of

INDEX

Las Cabezas de San Juan (near Seville), 41

Las Casas, Bartolomé de, 57, 134, 135, 170 n.22, 209 n.15

Las Cuevas, monastery of, 24

Leardo, Cristòforo, 188 n.33

Leardo, Franco: imports American sugar, 67; as a public banker, 90, 182 n.1; grants sea loans and sends goods to America, 90; as slave trader, 90; loans to Columbus family, 90; serves as spokesman of sponsors of Cabot voyage, 90, 104–105; as a public banker, 90, 182 n.1; invests in Cabot voyage, 90, 104, 105, 195 n.17; relations with Ferdinand Columbus, 91, 187 n.30, 188 n.35; business dealings with Oviedo, 102–103; relationship to Pedro Juan Leardo, 188 n.33

Leardo, Pedro Juan: relations with Sevillian nobility, 91; as a public banker, 91, 182 n.1, 182 n.4; Duke of Veragua's lawsuit against, 91, 188 n.35; relationship to Franco Leardo, 188 n.33

Leardo family, 188 n.33

Leather, 42

León, Cristóbal, 54

Lercaro, Carlos Jufre: resides at court, 49, 82; see also Spínola, Centurión, and Lercaro, firm of

Lercaro, Cristóbal: resides at court, 49; as a royal creditor, 79; buys shares in Orellana expedition, 122; see also Negrón, Calvo, and Lercaro, firm of

Lerma, García de, 202 n.62

Liability, unlimited, 81, 181 n.14

Linen, 42, 45

Lisbon, 10, 122

Lizarazo, Miguel de, 141

Lizarrazas, Domingo, 6, 92–93, 180 n.111, 183 n.6, 188 n.36, 188 n.37, 189 n.42

Loaysa, García de, 111, 199 n.43

Lomelín, Andrea: buys shares in Orellana expedition (1545), 122

Lomelín, Francisco: buys shares in Orellana expedition (1545), 122

Lomelín, Leonardo, see Marín and Lomelín, firm of

Lomellini family, 129

Lopez, Robert (quoted), 15

López de Gómara, Francisco (quoted), 135

Losa, Andrés de la (quoted), 34

Lutheranism, 14–15

Macarena, parish of, 25

Madeira, 99, 129, 206 n.2

Magellan, Ferdinand, 103, 108, 195 n.19

Magellan, Strait of, 104

Magellan, voyage of, 103

Maize, 135

Malaga: Genoese in, 2, 146 n.7

Maldonado, Cristóbal de, 119

Manrique, Jorge, 155 n.66

Mansa, Alfonso, Bishop of San Juan, 140–142

Maravedís, value of, 147 n.14

Mares, 47

Margaret, Duchess of Parma, regent of the Netherlands (quoted), 87

Margarita Island, 126

Marín, Angel, see Spínola, Cataño, and Marín, firm of

Marín, Juan Bautista de: as a commission agent in Mexico, 65; as account general of Cortes estate, 66, 205 n.1

Marín, Tomás de, see Marín and Lomelín, firm of

Marín and Lomelín, firm of: sugar and slave transactions with Cortés, 65–66, 174 n.56; relations with Cataño family, 65, 174 n.50

Martínez, Diego, 89, 186–187 n.25

Martínez, Juan, 53

Martyr D'Anghera, Peter, 195 n.19, 196 n.25

Mary Tudor, Queen of England, 187 n.27

Mayorazgos, 6

Meatmarket Gate, 26, 159 n.22

Medina, José Toribio (quoted), 197 n.25, 198 n.31, 205 n.92

Medina, Pedro de, cosmographer (quoted), 28

Medina, Pedro de, merchant, 54

INDEX

Medina del Campo, 96, 140; *see also* Fairs

Medina Sidonia, Duke of, 179 n.97

Medina Sidonia, palace of, 21, 158 n.6

Medrano, Catherine de, 107, 108, 201 n.61

Medrano, Francisco, 5

Melón y Ruiz de Cordejuela, Amando (quoted), 194 n.11

Méndez, Diego, 54

Méndez, Hernán, 114

Méndez, Martín, 106–111 *passim*, 113, 114, 198 n.35, 199 nn.37–40, 201 n.53

Mendoza, Pedro de, 201 n.62

Mercado, Padre Tomás de (quoted), 6, 39, 42–47 *passim*, 69, 84–86 *passim*

Mercedarians, 188 n.35

Mercery, 42, 43, 45

Merchant-banker, functions of, 184 n.17

Merchants, Sevillian: desire for nobility, 6; country estates of, 6, 16; intermarriage with nobles, 6, 149 n.21; ennoblement of, 6–7, 37, 149 n.21, 163 n.72; role in preserving Seville monopoly, 10–11; embellishment of town houses, 12, 26–27; investments in urban real estate, 16; investments in annuities, 16; use of coaches as sign of prestige, 33; charitable donations of, 33; sale and purchase of municipal offices by, 37–38; profits of, 47; wealth of, 150 n.32; complaints against confiscation of American treasure, 183 n.15; financial participation in Cabot voyage (1525), 196 n.25

Mexía, Francisco, 97

Mexia, Pedro (quoted), 26

Mexico (New Spain), 64–68 *passim*, 72, 75, 80

Mexico City, 43, 80

Millowners, 131, 132; *see also* Sugar industry

Mint, 24, 31, 85, 92

Moluccas, 103, 104, 108–111 *passim*, 114, 116, 195 n.17, 199 n.41

Moneychanger-banker: functions of, 184 n.17; *see also* Bankers

Moneychangers, 182 n.2, 189 n.46; *see also* Moneychanger-banker

Montalbán, Gaspar de, 53

Montalbán, Lope de, 53

Monte, Juan Tomás de: employs Jerónimo de Grimaldo, 177 n.82

Monte, Vicencio: appointed revenue collector of Orellana expedition (1545), 118; secret dealings with Orellana, 120, 122, 124; and with Genoese, 120–121, 122, 204 n.77; relations with Ferdinand Columbus, 120, 203 n.75

Monte de Malbaratillo, 31

Montes, Enrique, 111, 200 n.44

Moradas, 40

Moreno, Pedro, 211 n.32

Morga, Pedro de, 86, 93–94, 189 nn.44–45

Morgado, Alonso de: quoted, 21, 22, 26–31 *passim*, 40; background of, 157 n.5

Mortedo, Jácome: purchases Espinosa bank, 96–97; background of, 191 n.55; *see also* Mortedo, Castellanos, and Co., bank of

Mortedo, Castellanos, and Co., bank of, 96–97; *see also* Mortedo, Jácome

Moslems, 26, 40, 143

Muscovado, 65

Naborías, 71

Naples, 124

Navajero, Andrea (quoted), 24, 29, 33, 40, 41, 195 n.18

Negrón, Ambrosio, 5

Negrón, Camilo de, 5

Negrón, Licenciate Carlos de: education, 4; government posts, 4; marries into Sevillian nobility, 4; owner of slave vessels, 4, 64, 76; children of, 4–5, 149 n.22

Negrón, Galeazo de, *see* Negrón, Calvo, and Lercaro, firm of

Negrón, Jerónimo de, 5

Negrón, Juan Batista de: as a commission agent in Mexico, 73

Negrón, Julio, 4, 149 n.22

INDEX

Spínola, Luis (*cont.*)
deposits funds in bank of Lizarrazas, 92; background of, 181
n.18; *see also* Spínola, Centurión,
and Lercaro, firm of
Spínola, Nicolás: becomes denizen
of Seville, 74; grants sea loans and
sales credit, 74
Spínola, Pedro Batista: as a royal
creditor, 78; *see also* Spínola and
Doria, firm of
Spínola, Tolomeo: as a commission
agent in Mexico, 66, 73; under-
takes trip to Seville, 72
Spínola, Tomás: as a royal creditor,
78
Spínola and Cataño, firm of: business
transactions of, 81, 181 n.117; role
in the bank of Lizarrazas, 92, 188
n.37
Spínola and Doria, firm of, 81, 167
n.5
Spínola, Cataño, and Marín, firm of,
81
Spínola, Centurión, and Lercaro, firm
of: business transactions of, 81, 82
Spínola family, 2
Spun gold, 42
Stock raising on Hispaniola, 133
Suárez, Cristóbal, 52, 53
Suárez, Inés, 208 n.12
Suárez de Figueroa, Cristóbal
(quoted), 38
Suárez del Pozo, Catalina, 142
Sugar, popularity of, 175 n.63
Sugar industry: on Hispaniola, 59,
60, 67, 128–129; in Puerto Rico,
60, 67, 128, 139; and Mexico, 65,
66; in the Canaries, 129; on Ma-
deira, 129
Sugar mill: description of, 132; *see
also* Sugar industry

Tapestries, 42
Tarducci, Francesco (quoted), 198–
199 nn.35–37
Tarifa, Marquis of, 24, 159 n.18
Tarshish, 104, 196 n.22
Tenerife (Canary Islands), 192 n.1,
206 n.3
Thorne, Robert, 105, 195 n.17, 196
n.24, 200 n.48

Tierra Firme, 45, 102
Tirso de Molina, 97
Tlaltenango sugar mill, 65
Toledo, 43, 133
Torre, María de la, 3
Torre Espinosa, Pedro de la, 96
Torres, Friar Pablo de, 118–124 *pas-
sim*, 203 n.68, 203 n.76, 204
n.79, 204 n.80
Trade: incompatibility with nobility,
38–39; prejudice against, 149
n.21, 150 n.27
Transatlantic trade: kinds of cargoes
shipped, 9, 17, 55, 66, 67, 166
n.102, 168 n.14; mechanics of,
42–47, 165 n.99, 166 n.103; gov-
ernment regulations, 47; cycles in,
155 n.69; hazards of, 179–180
n.99
Trapiche, 130, 139
Triana bridge, 22
Triana Gate, 28, 159 n.22
Triana quarter, 40, 69, 158 n.9
Trinidad, 65, 71, 80, 105, 109, 114,
199 n.40
Tuxtla sugar mill, 65, 67

Ulloa, Francisco de, 121
Usodimare family, 2, 147 n.9

Valladolid, 117, 142, 189 n.46
Valladolid, Juan de, 169 n.15
Valles, Cristóbal, 53
Vaz, Pedro, 101
Vázquez, Bautista, 28
Vázquez, Catherine, 108, 114, 199
n.41
Vázquez, Fernán, 170–171 n.24; *see
also* Vázquez, Forne, and Vivaldo,
firm of
Vázquez de Mella, Pedro, 129
Vázquez, Forne, and Vivaldo, firm
of, 170 n.24; create scarcity to
maintain high prices, 58, 59; obtain monopoly of slave trade, 58–
59; exchange of slaves for sugar,
60, 130, 131; owners of a sugar
mill on Hispaniola, 130–131, 207
n.7
Veedor, 105
Vega, Lope de (quoted), 21, 23, 37,
39, 40, 41, 150 n.28, 176 n.74

242